EDUCATORS' GUIDE TO SCHOOL MENTAL HEALTH

Also Available

Interventions for Reading Problems, Second Edition: Designing and Evaluating Effective Strategies
Edward J. Daly III, Sabina Neugebauer, Sandra M. Chafouleas, and Christopher H. Skinner

School-Based Behavioral Assessment, Second Edition: Informing Prevention and Intervention
Sandra M. Chafouleas, Austin H. Johnson, T. Chris Riley-Tillman, and Emily A. Iovino

Educators' Guide to SCHOOL MENTAL HEALTH

Jessica B. Koslouski
Kristabel Stark
Sandra M. Chafouleas

THE GUILFORD PRESS
New York London

A Division of Guilford Publications, Inc.
www.guilford.com

Printed in the United States of America

This book is printed on acid-free paper.

For product and safety concerns within the EU, please contact *GPSR@taylorandfrancis.com,* Taylor & Francis Verlag GmbH, Kaufingerstraße 24, 80331 München, Germany.

Last digit is print number: 9 8 7 6 5 4 3 2 1

This publication is intended to provide helpful and informative material. It is not intended to diagnose, treat, cure, or prevent any health problem or condition, nor is it intended to replace the advice of a health professional. No action should be taken based solely on the contents of this book. Always consult your physician or qualified health care professional on any matters regarding your health and before adopting any suggestions in this book or drawing inferences from it.

The authors and publisher specifically disclaim all responsibility for any liability, loss, or risk, personal or otherwise, which is incurred as a consequence, directly or indirectly, from the use or application of any contents of this book.

Any and all product names referenced within this book are the trademarks of their respective owners. Always read all information provided by the manufacturers' product labels before using their products. The authors and publisher are not responsible for claims made by manufacturers.

Library of Congress Cataloging-in-Publication Data is available from the publisher.

ISBN 978-1-4625-6419-4 (paperback)
ISBN 978-1-4625-6420-0 (cloth)

To all of the students, families, and educators
working day in and day out
to support one another and build a better future together—
please know that your efforts are seen and make a difference.

About the Authors

Jessica B. Koslouski, PhD, is Assistant Research Professor in the Neag School of Education and Codirector of the Collaboratory on School and Child Health at the University of Connecticut. Dr. Koslouski has specialty training in child and adolescent social, emotional, and behavioral development. She is particularly interested in how contextual assets and barriers affect student and educator well-being and success. Her scholarship focuses on supporting educators in using evidence-based practices, improving school-based assessment tools, and increasing access to evidence-based mental health interventions. Dr. Koslouski partners with schools to create effective, feasible, and contextually relevant solutions to persistent challenges. Prior to a career in academia, she worked in public schools as an elementary special education teacher.

Kristabel Stark, PhD, is Assistant Professor at the University of Vermont College of Education and Social Services, where she teaches courses in undergraduate and graduate teacher preparation programs. Dr. Stark's scholarly interests include teachers' emotional experiences and mental health, special education workforce issues, and the development and training of new special educators. Her current research is informed by her prior experiences as a special educator in Chicago and her partnerships with schools in the greater Boston and Washington, DC, areas.

Sandra M. Chafouleas, PhD, is Distinguished Professor in the Neag School of Education and Codirector of the Collaboratory on School and Child Health at the University of Connecticut. Dr. Chafouleas is a licensed psychologist with specialty training in school psychology and expertise in education settings and child development. Her scholarly focus includes social, emotional, and behavioral promotion and risk; evaluating responsiveness to supports critical to learning, health, and well-being; and understanding influences on use of particular strategies. Dr. Chafouleas regularly serves as a national presenter and invited speaker and has received awards including an American Psychological Association Presidential Citation.

Preface

Welcome to the *Educators' Guide to School Mental Health*! We are honored and humbled that you have chosen this book. To begin, we would like to provide a brief overview of who we are and why we wrote this book. We recognize that there is an urgent need to support student and educator mental health. There are many steps educators can take to promote mental health in their settings, and we know that an accessible and practical resource is needed to guide those steps. We hope that this book can be that resource.

We come to this work as educators ourselves. We each have worked in K–12 settings and are now researchers who partner with schools to improve student and educator mental health. Jess previously worked as an elementary general and special educator, Kristabel as a special education teacher at the elementary and middle school levels, and Sandy as a school psychologist and administrator for K–12 districts. Collectively, we have worked in rural, suburban, and urban school districts with hundreds of students and educators.

We have now each transitioned to university classrooms, training the next generation of teachers and school psychologists. We also work directly with schools to improve social, emotional, and behavioral outcomes for students and educators. We conduct research with schools to improve evidence-based measurement and intervention. We draw deeply on our experience as educators when developing new tools or interventions with schools, knowing that complicated or cumbersome recommendations are unlikely to be used. Jess's current research focuses on mental health and whole-child promotion, prevention, and response efforts in schools.

Kristabel's current research focuses primarily on the special education teacher workforce, exploring special educators' identity, emotional experiences, and professional learning and development. Sandy's current research addresses school mental health assessment and intervention, focusing on practices that support students' and educators' social, emotional, and behavioral well-being.

Collectively, our experiences as both practitioners and researchers provide us with many different lenses from which to explore and address the complex role of educators in school mental health. As described in Chapter 1, the current generation of K–12 students is facing a serious mental health crisis—as are many of their educators. The United States increasingly depends on school leaders and educators to address mental health needs *within* the school building, and the field of school mental health is rapidly evolving. The mental health challenges facing school communities continue to change, as do feasible, evidence-based solutions to address these challenges.

Throughout our careers we have witnessed educators going to great lengths to support student mental health and doing so with powerful results. Although not trained or licensed to deliver clinical mental health services, there is much that educators can do to support mental health within their schools without crossing professional boundaries. Supporting mental health is not only about responding to symptoms of distress but also about promoting well-being. Through small, everyday interactions with students, colleagues, and families, educators can promote mental health and well-being, as well as prevent and respond to mental health concerns.

Our goal in writing this book is to bring attention to the important roles of educators within school mental health, and to help readers reflect on their own roles, ultimately providing educators with a resource for sustainable ways to engage in this work. In Chapter 1, we offer an overview of school mental health and the terminology used throughout this book. Then, we present 12 practical chapters, each summarizing a different facet of school mental health. We hope that this book allows educators to recognize the importance of both individual classroom interventions and schoolwide systems in supporting mental health and reminds readers that they are not alone in the crucial work of supporting mental health in their setting.

We introduce ourselves and our intentions to welcome you into an ongoing conversation with us—and with the scholars and practitioners who contributed to the studies that we reference within this book. In writing this book, we reviewed hundreds of peer-reviewed studies covering many different aspects of school mental health. In the chapters that follow, we did our best to include and present as much of this research as we could in an accessible and practical way. Even so, we acknowledge that we are able to capture only a small portion of the collective wisdom and years of scholarship regarding school mental health. Our collective understanding of school mental health will continue to evolve. As such, we encourage readers to continue learning and to follow the work of the scholars presented in our reference list.

We write this book for both current and future generations of educators. To those of you reading this as you prepare to enter the classroom for the first time—welcome to this beautiful, messy, spectacular profession! To those of you who are already in the classroom—we are inspired by, and grateful for, your commitment to ongoing growth and development as an educator. Whatever career stage you join us from, we hope that this book helps you to recognize the skills and strengths you already have to promote mental health in your community. We also hope that each chapter generates ideas for ways that you might implement small (or large) changes to your practice. We encourage you to read this book in your own way—read the chapters in order, or after reading Chapter 1, jump around to the chapters that are most interesting to you. Throughout the book, we've embedded "stop and reflect" opportunities to encourage you to take a moment to apply the text to your own setting. In addition, we include reflection questions in the appendix to guide your integration of learning into practice. We invite you to take a few minutes to review that now.

Thank you for joining us on this journey to learn more about school mental health!

Note to the Reader

The vignettes included in this book are fictional. Any resemblance to actual students, educators, or family caregivers is purely coincidental.

Acknowledgments

Thank you to our families, friends, colleagues, mentors, and the editorial team at The Guilford Press for encouraging us to bring this book to life. None of this would have been possible without you.

Contents

CHAPTER 1

What Is School Mental Health?

KEY IDEAS

1. *School mental health* refers to supports and interventions to enhance social, emotional, and behavioral well-being in schools.
2. Promotion, prevention, and response efforts can improve student and educator mental health.
3. Educators play an important role in providing school mental health supports and referring students to more specialized interventions.

The National Center for School Mental Health (NCSMH, n.d.) defines *school mental health* as supports and interventions to enhance social, emotional, and behavioral well-being in schools. These supports can range from schoolwide efforts to individualized treatment provided by a specialized clinician. Some supports are intended to promote mental health or prevent mental health concerns and may be provided to all students or staff as universal intervention. Others are more intensive supports and are intended to treat or respond to existing concerns. Therefore, school mental health supports can be thought of as on a continuum, from those intended to promote mental health, followed by those intended to prevent concerns from developing or intensifying, and finally, those intended to respond to existing concerns. School mental health involves all school community members, not just students (National Academies of Sciences, Engineering, and Medicine, 2019a). As authors, we take the stance that the mental health and well-being of all school community members can and should be actively promoted as a primary strategy, and we will share evidence that these promotion and prevention efforts can reduce mental health concerns.

In this chapter, we will first define key terms used in this book. Then, we will describe the current need for mental health supports in schools as well as the roles of various school mental health providers. We will then explain the organization of this book and our rationale for organizing the chapters into sections on promotion, prevention, and response. Finally, we will introduce "goodness-of-fit" as a framework for prioritizing next steps in implementing what you learn from this book into your own practice.

To begin, we invite readers to peruse Figure 1.1, which lists and defines some key terms that appear throughout this book. These terms will prove important for understanding our discussion of student and educator mental health. The World Health Organization (WHO, 2022) defines *mental health* as "a state of well-being that enables us to cope with the stresses of life, realize our abilities, learn well and work well, and contribute to our community." WHO further clarifies that mental health exists on a continuum, is more than the absence of mental health concerns, and is

School mental health: Supports and interventions to enhance social, emotional, and behavioral well-being in schools (NCSMH, n.d.).

Mental health: "A state of well-being that enables us to cope with the stresses of life, realize our abilities, learn well and work well, and contribute to our community" (WHO, 2022). Mental health exists on a continuum, is more than the absence of mental health concerns, and is likely to fluctuate over time.

Well-being: "Well-being is a complex combination of a person's physical, mental, emotional and social health factors" (Victoria Department of Health, 2022).

Social: How a person *interacts* (Chafouleas, 2020).

Emotional: How a person *feels* (Chafouleas, 2020).

Behavioral: How a person *acts* (Chafouleas, 2020).

Promotion: Efforts to develop skills that promote mental health and well-being, such as self-regulation, self-efficacy, goal setting, and positive relationships (National Academies of Sciences, Engineering, and Medicine, 2019a).

Prevention: Efforts to prevent mental health concerns from emerging, intensifying, or going unnoticed (adapted from National Academies of Sciences, Engineering, and Medicine, 2019a).

Response: Efforts implemented with individuals who are demonstrating mental health challenges or have been diagnosed with a mental health disorder (adapted from National Academies of Sciences, Engineering, and Medicine's [2019a] definition of *treatment* to reflect the nonclinical role of educators).

FIGURE 1.1. Key definitions.

likely to fluctuate over time. Although we primarily focus on mental health throughout this book, we sometimes use the term *well-being* when sharing broader implications. We particularly appreciate the Victoria Department of Public Health's (2022) definition of well-being as "a complex combination of a person's physical, mental, emotional and social health factors" (p. 1).

Next, we frequently use the terms *social*, *emotional*, and *behavioral development* or *well-being*. By *social*, we mean how a person interacts with others (Chafouleas, 2020). By *emotional*, we mean how a person feels (Chafouleas, 2020). By *behavioral*, we mean how a person acts (Chafouleas, 2020). We also refer to supports and services that can be provided to students and educators. Generally, we conceptualize *services* as documented interventions and *supports* as more general actions taken to facilitate positive outcomes. We tend to refer to negative mental health symptoms as *mental health concerns* to capture the range of impairment that can occur (e.g., experiencing some symptoms that are distressing but do not qualify for an official mental health diagnosis; symptoms that cause substantial impairment and qualify for an official diagnosis). When using the term *mental health disorder*, we are referring to conditions that meet criteria for a medical diagnosis. We use the term *educators* to refer to teachers, paraprofessionals, related service providers, and any other staff members regularly interacting with students in schools. When discussing specific research studies, we use terms (e.g., *teachers*, *administrators*) employed by study authors to accurately reflect their findings or conclusions. We refer to those with specific mental health training and credentials (e.g., school social workers, school psychologists, school counselors) as *school mental health professionals* or *licensed clinicians*. We use the terms *caregivers* and *family caregivers* to refer to the people who are responsible for taking care of a child. These might be parents, grandparents, aunts, uncles, older siblings, or foster care providers.

As we describe in greater detail at the end of this chapter, this book is divided into three sections: promotion, prevention, and response. When discussing *promotion*, we are referring to efforts to develop skills that promote mental health and well-being, such as self-regulation, self-efficacy, goal setting, and positive relationships (National Academies of Sciences, Engineering, and Medicine, 2019a). When discussing *prevention*, we mean efforts to prevent mental health concerns from emerging, intensifying, or going unnoticed (adapted from the National Academies of Sciences, Engineering, and Medicine, 2019a). Last, when discussing response, we mean efforts implemented with individuals who are demonstrating mental health challenges or have been diagnosed with a mental health disorder. We have adapted this definition from the National Academies of Sciences, Engineering, and Medicine's (2019a) definition of *treatment* to account for educators' nonclinical role (e.g., not providing treatment) in responding to mental health.

At times, we refer to Tier 1, 2, or 3 interventions. By *Tier 1*, we mean interventions or curriculum provided to all students in a classroom, grade level, or school. By *Tier 2*, we mean targeted interventions provided in response to identified concerns (e.g., social skills groups). Finally, by *Tier 3*, we mean intensive 1:1 or small-group interventions provided to those requiring the most support (e.g., behavior support plans).

This book is for preservice and inservice K–12 educators. Although much of the content could apply in schools around the world, we focus on implementation in the United States context because that is where we can offer the most experience and expertise. We draw upon international peer reviewed literature, but when providing statistics or examples of specific policies and practices, we focus on those from the United States.

Schools range in their provision of mental health supports to students and educators. The National Center on School Mental Health suggests seven components to a *comprehensive* school mental health system. These seven components are summarized in Table 1.1. Although not all schools have the resources to enable a comprehensive school mental health system, they may engage in some or many of these practices. For example, schools may offer some universal and targeted mental health supports (e.g., universal social and emotional learning [SEL], skills groups for students exhibiting a need for targeted instruction). They may have a process for educators to refer students about whom they are concerned, or screen for specific mental health concerns (e.g., anxiety, depression). A comprehensive school mental health system requires many parties—school administrators, school mental health professionals, teachers, related service providers, and community leaders, for example—and no one educator can feasibly develop a comprehensive school mental health system on their own.

We encourage growing capacity in schools to develop comprehensive school mental health systems but also understand that a key component to enabling such a system is strengthening the knowledge and skills of personnel within the school. In this book, we focus on what individual educators can do within their spheres of influence. We aim to build educators' knowledge, skills, and self-efficacy related to mental health with full recognition that they are not trained school mental health providers. As we will do often in this book, we invite readers to stop and reflect for a moment.

STOP AND REFLECT

1. Looking at Table 1.1, what elements of a comprehensive school mental health system are present in your setting?
2. How could you become more involved with these processes in your setting?

TABLE 1.1. Components of a Comprehensive School Mental Health System (NCSMH, 2023)

Component	Example structures or practices
Teaming	• Assembling a multidisciplinary school mental health team • Involving students and families in school mental health planning and improvement • Using data to determine the mental health services and supports needed by students • Providing referrals to school and community-based mental health services
Needs assessment/ resource mapping	• Conducting a needs assessment of student mental health strengths and needs • Mapping existing school and community mental health services and supports • Seeking out additional services to match unmet student needs
Screening	• Planning and conducting mental health screening • Determining who will be screened (e.g., which grade levels) and on what schedule (e.g., annually) • Deciding the areas in which to screen (e.g., anxiety, depression, suicidality, substance use, trauma, strengths)
Mental health promotion services and supports	• Assessing and working to improve school climate • Assessing and working to improve educator well-being • Engaging strategies to build healthy relationships and school community • Increasing students' social and emotional skills • Providing professional learning in Tier 1 services and supports
Early intervention and treatment services and supports	• Providing evidence-informed early intervention and treatment services and supports to students identified through screening or referral • Ensuring resource capacity to provide early intervention and treatment services and supports • Providing professional learning in early intervention and treatment services and supports • Monitoring student progress across tiers • Implementing a crisis response plan
Funding and sustainability	• Using multiple funding sources to provide a continuum of mental health services and supports • Enacting strategies to retain staff • Maximizing opportunities for professional learning • Maximizing reimbursement opportunities for eligible services
Impact	• Documenting the number of students accessing school mental health services • Measuring impact of school mental health services on student academic, social, emotional, and behavioral outcomes • Sharing outcomes with key groups (e.g., youth, families, school and community partners)

Current Need for Mental Health Supports in Schools

The need for school mental health supports is urgent. In 2023, more than 50% of U.S. girls and nearly 66% of lesbian, gay, bisexual, and questioning (LGBQ+) students reported symptoms of depression in the past year (Centers for Disease Control and Prevention [CDC], 2024a; Verlenden et al., 2024). One in five high school students reported seriously considering suicide (with rates twice as high for LGBTQ+ students), and nearly 10% of high school students reported attempting suicide in the past year (again with rates twice as high for LGBQ+ students; CDC, 2024a; Verlenden et al., 2024).

In addition to these clear indicators of distress, many students reported not feeling safe or supported at school. In 2023, between 40–50% of students of color reported being treated poorly or unfairly at school because of their race or ethnicity (McKinnon et al., 2024). Nearly one in five high school students reported being bullied at school in the past 12 months, and one in twelve high school students reported being in a physical fight on school grounds in the past year (CDC, 2024a). One in eight students reported missing at least one day of school in past month because they did not feel safe there or en route (CDC, 2024a).

Educators are also experiencing poor mental health in schools. Across three national surveys conducted between 2023 and 2025, 59–77% of teachers reported that their work was often or always stressful, in comparison with 33% of working adults in the United States (Doan et al., 2024; Lin et al., 2024; Steiner et al., 2025). Approximately one in five teachers reported having difficulty coping with job-related stress, and one in five experienced symptoms of depression (Steiner et al., 2025). One in four teachers reported fearing for their physical safety at school, most commonly attributing this fear to student behavior or the threat of active shooters (Doan et al., 2023). In summary, there is substantial room for improvement in the mental health of educators and students as well as the conditions in which they are teaching and learning.

A Vision for School Mental Health

Recent decades have brought increased attention to school mental health. This has been, in part, because of the strong connection between mental health and learning. Another compelling consideration has been that many students with mental health concerns never receive clinical care (Bitsko et al., 2022; Duong et al., 2021). Schools may be an opportune site in which to increase access to mental health care because they serve the vast majority of U.S. youth.

Since the early 1900s, professionals in education, psychology, and public health have been engaged in efforts to understand and address the role of mental health in school-aged youth (Flaherty & Osher, 2002). Federal laws such as the Community Mental Health Act of 1963 and the Individuals with Disabilities Act (first introduced as the Education of Handicapped Children Act 1975, and amended and reauthorized in 1990, 1994, and 2004) have catalyzed interaction between mental health professionals and educators (Weist et al., 2017). In the 1990s and early 2000s, the federal government invested in national centers focused on school mental health (Weist et al., 2017). These centers provided training on mental health and helped school districts to hire additional school mental health professionals. Today, there are many academic journals, conferences, and national networks directly focused on school mental health. Despite this progress, the most recent data from the National Center for Education Statistics (NCES; 2021–2022 school year) reports that only 49% of public schools provided diagnostic mental health services and only 38% provided mental health treatment services to students (NCES, 2024b). Given the high rates of mental health challenges among today's students, continued growth in the area of school mental health is urgent. *And so, we ask: What would it mean for schools to be places in which students and educators perceive positive mental health in themselves and their peers?*

STOP AND REFLECT

1. If you work in a school, what would you need to experience positive mental health there? What would your students need? What would it take for this to become a reality?
2. Thinking back to your own experiences in school, how was the mental health of students and educators promoted? How could this have been improved upon?

Introducing the Dual-Factor Model of Mental Health

Social, emotional, and behavioral well-being and poor mental health are sometimes thought of as mutually exclusive. However, a growing body of research suggests a dual-factor model of mental health (Magalhães, 2024; Suldo & Shaffer, 2008). This model suggests that although there are strong associations between subjective well-being and mental health concerns (i.e., those with severe mental health concerns generally have lower subjective well-being), they are not mutually exclusive (e.g., Magalhães, 2024; Suldo & Shaffer, 2008). Said differently, only measuring levels of mental health concern does not provide direct information about someone's subjective well-being (i.e., how they appraise their own well-being). Consider, for example, a person who is apathetic or indifferent—they may not demonstrate mental health concerns but may also not experience subjective well-being.

What does this all mean for work in schools? We suggest three primary considerations that inform our guidance and recommendations throughout this book:

1. **Promotion work is a valuable investment.** Promoting mental health in schools helps students and educators to productively cope with the stresses of life, learn to their full potential, and positively contribute to their communities. It can also prevent the onset of mental health concerns. It is estimated that every $1 invested in social, emotional, and behavioral promotion work saves society $11 in future costs related to substance use, delinquency, and sexual risk behaviors (Belfield et al., 2015), all of which are associated with poorer mental health.

2. **Prevention work is needed.** Even with optimal mental health promotion efforts, some individuals will still be susceptible to mental health concerns. Prevention efforts can help to identify these concerns early and prevent them from intensifying or causing enduring distress. Schools are opportune sites for this work given that they serve the vast majority of children and adolescents. Preventing mental health concerns from emerging, intensifying, or going unnoticed will also likely improve students' academic outcomes (a key benchmark for schools).

3. **Responsive supports should focus on both reduction of symptoms and strategies for promoting well-being.** Reducing concerning symptoms does not ensure well-being. Therefore, response strategies need to include those that promote well-being. Examples include building coping and social skills to strengthen relationships in students' lives. These skills will help to improve well-being and provide support for coping when symptoms arise.

Educators' Roles in Promoting School Mental Health

Educators play a key role in supporting the mental health of their students. In a 2023 national survey of teachers, more than half of participants (57%) reported helping students with mental health challenges at least a few times a week (Lin et al., 2024). More than one-quarter of participants (28%) reported helping students with mental health needs daily. The importance of educators' actions in promoting mental health in schools cannot be overstated. Yet the majority of educators are not trained as mental health professionals. School mental health, however, is promoted through educators' everyday interactions with students and families, classroom climate, and collaboration with colleagues regarding concerns and proactive supports. Educators are an important source of referral to mental health supports for students (Green et al., 2022) and are uniquely positioned to recognize concerns and refer students for additional support. Although caregivers hold tremendous expertise about their children, they do not have the concentrated knowledge about specific developmental periods that educators do, nor the accumulated experience with dozens or hundreds of students (Whitcomb, 2017). Thus, educators' knowledge and large amounts of time spent with students can help them to recognize when mental health concerns may be present and impacting students' success and well-being. Conversations with caregivers, school mental health professionals, or administrators can be pivotal in connecting students to needed supports or services.

The presence of school mental health professionals varies greatly school-to-school. Across the United States, recommended ratios of school mental health professionals to students are rarely achieved (American School Counseling Association, 2025; National Association of School Psychologists, 2025; School Social Work Association of America, 2025). Schools and districts also invest in school mental health professionals with varied training, and for educators less familiar with this training, their roles and expertise may be less clear. Table 1.2 summarizes common school mental health professional roles as well as the minimum required training and common areas of focus for each of these professionals. As can be seen in the table, there is considerable overlap across roles related to delivering services and interventions across multi-tiered systems of support, establishing relationships with families and community partners, and providing direct counseling services to specific students. Notably, school psychologists are the only providers listed in this table that are credentialed to administer psychological assessments (e.g., intelligence tests given as a part of special education evaluations).

It is also important to note that since 2015, U.S. schools have also been allowed to hire independently licensed mental health professionals (e.g., licensed professional counselors, licensed clinical psychologists, licensed clinical social workers; Frey et al., 2022). Unlike the school mental health professionals listed in Table 1.2, these professionals are qualified to provide clinical services, diagnose mental health conditions, and bill Medicaid for services in most states. However, they are not required to have any school-based experience to become licensed. Therefore, it is important for schools to consider the needs in their setting when hiring new school mental health professionals.

In addition, because schools are often not meeting recommended ratios for school mental health professionals to students, roles may evolve over time or be more constrained. We encourage educators to seek out information about the roles and responsibilities of any school mental health

TABLE 1.2. Roles and Minimum Training of Various School Mental Health Professionals

Role name	Minimum required training	Common areas of focus
School counselor[a]	Masters in school counseling with a practicum in a school setting	• Work with students to address academic, mental health, college preparation, and career preparation goals
School psychologist	Education Specialist (EdS) in school psychology with a practicum in a school setting	• Conduct psychological assessments • Provide direct service (e.g., counseling) to a caseload of students • Consult with school staff and administrators regarding social, emotional, and behavioral needs • Support school-wide services (e.g., universal screening, mental health literacy) • Collaborate with families and community partners
School social worker	Masters in Social Work (MSW), including school-specific course work and practicum	• Deliver services and interventions across tiers of intervention • Foster relationships between families, school, and community to strengthen school climate • Provide direct counseling support to a caseload of students

Note. Based on Frey et al. (2022).
[a]Schools may also have other counselors with similar areas of focus (e.g., school adjustment counselors).

professionals in their settings. For example, in one setting, a school psychologist may only conduct psychological assessments, and all counseling referrals are routed to the school social worker. In a different setting, the school psychologist might see students with Individualized Education Plans (IEPs) for counseling services whereas the school counselor might facilitate small skills groups for students in need of social or emotional support but not yet evaluated for special education services.

Organization of This Book

Using a public health model, we organize this book into three sections: promotion, prevention, and response (National Academies of Sciences, Engineering, and Medicine, 2019a). This model aligns with best practices in schools, which focus on universal instruction for all students, and more targeted and intensive supports for students demonstrating additional need (e.g., Sugai & Horner, 2009; Walker et al., 1996). Although educators might be most familiar with the language of multi-tiered systems of support (MTSS), Response to Intervention (RTI), or Tiers 1, 2, and 3 (i.e., the "triangle" image), we made an intentional choice to organize this book into sections on promotion, prevention, and response. This was for multiple reasons. First, educators sometimes misperceive Tier 2 or Tier 3 services as requiring specialized training (e.g., special education, school psychology) and thus being out of their purview for implementation. **In this book, all of the strategies shared are available for educators to use. They do not require specialized training.** Next, mental health can be supported universally by both promotion and prevention efforts. What differentiates promotion and prevention efforts is their respective goals, rather than who receives the supports. Promotion efforts are implemented to develop skills that promote mental health and well-being, such as self-regulation, self-efficacy, goal setting, and positive relationships (National Academies of Sciences, Engineering, and Medicine, 2019a). Prevention efforts aim to prevent mental health concerns from emerging, intensifying, or going unnoticed. Stated differently, whereas promotion efforts seek to increase positive behaviors, prevention efforts seek to prevent or minimize negative symptoms. Last, response strategies are provided to support students demonstrating mental health need. In this book, we specifically focus on strategies that can be used in the general education setting without any specialized or clinical training. Although these strategies will likely be most useful with individuals who are demonstrating mental health challenges or have been diagnosed with a mental health disorder, this does not prevent educators from using the strategies more broadly. The three sections of this book and their respective chapters are summarized in Figure 1.2.

The aim for this book is for it to be applicable to educators working in schools, regardless of their role. The strategies shared across its three sections do not require specialized training. Instead, promotion, prevention, and response are within the purview of all educators. We hope to equip educators with a range of strategies to promote mental health in their settings; prevent concerns from emerging, intensifying, or going unnoticed; and skillfully respond to those mental health needs that are impacting learning.

Chapters 2–5 focus on school mental health *promotion*. This section investigates universal efforts to develop skills that promote the mental health and well-being of school community members. We focus specifically on facilitating mental health and well-being by promoting a positive school climate, facilitating whole-child instruction, fostering social and emotional learning, and supporting educator mental health. Next, Chapters 6–9 address *prevention*. This section discusses universal strategies to prevent mental health concerns from emerging, intensifying, or going unnoticed.

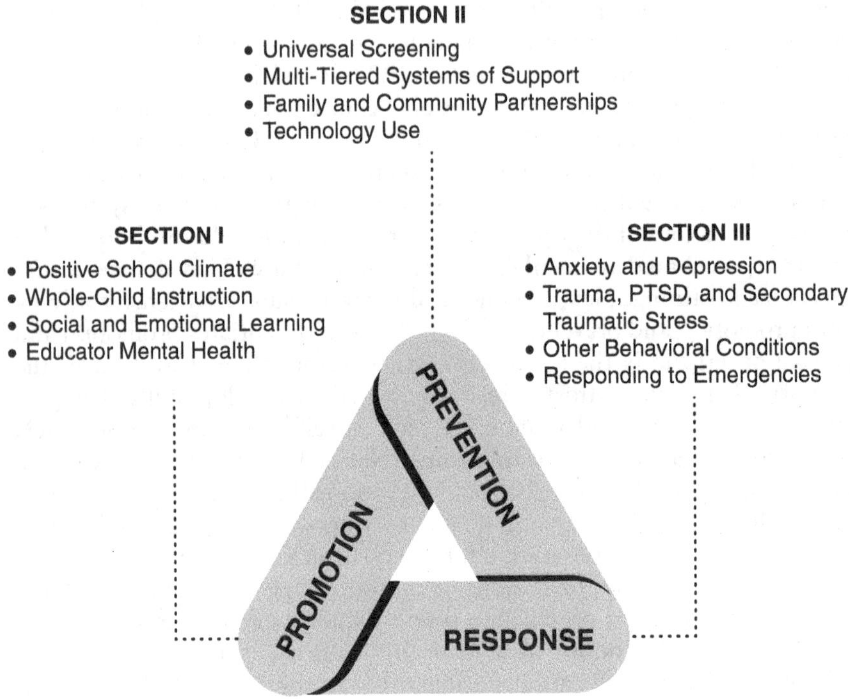

FIGURE 1.2. Promotion, prevention, and response.

We specifically address four types of school mental health prevention work: universal screening, multi-tiered systems of support, family and community partnerships, and intentional use of technology. Finally, Chapters 10–13 focus on *response* to mental health needs. These chapters include strategies educators can use to support students demonstrating mental health need in the school setting. We specially review strategies that do not require specialized or clinical training and can be implemented by an educator. We discuss how symptoms of various mental health concerns may present in the classroom, the skills students might be developing through evidence-based treatment, and how educators can augment this skill-building in their classrooms. Specifically addressed are anxiety and depression; trauma; posttraumatic stress disorder (PTSD) and secondary traumatic stress; and other behavioral conditions. The section concludes with a chapter on responding to emergencies, equipping educators with knowledge and skills to use when emergencies arise. Throughout the book, we aim to build educators' understanding and agency needed to support their students while validating their nonclinical role in responding to mental health need. Each chapter includes evidence-based strategies that are shown to improve mental health for both individuals and school communities, vignettes illustrating key points, and reflection questions prompting educators to pause and consider applications in their own settings and work.

We wrote this book to increase educators' knowledge, skills, and confidence with which to promote, prevent, and respond to mental health in their schools. Each educator working in a school has an important role in promoting school mental health, and there is substantial research to support a range of strategies that promote school mental health. Although entire books have been dedicated to each of the chapters we have included, we aim to show how these supports can be used to provide a range of mental health promotion, prevention, and response efforts in schools and classrooms. Next, we share some key strategies for selecting where to focus one's efforts. Rather than becoming overwhelmed by the many different ways one could improve their practice, we aim for readers to select a few recommendations that are most relevant and feasible in their settings. Concrete guidance for doing so is provided.

Planning for Success

This book is intended to enhance educators' current practice and well-being. We are not asking educators to do more—instead, we present research and practical strategies to inform educators' daily interactions and instruction. It is our hope that the knowledge and recommendations in this book build educators' confidence and agency with which to promote mental health in their settings through their interactions, decision making, and instructional practices. Inevitably, educators will witness or experience mental health concerns in their students, colleagues, or themselves—and we hope this book equips them with knowledge and strategies with which to respond to those concerns. But how might educators choose where to focus their efforts? How can they avoid becoming overwhelmed by the many options or possibilities?

Implementation science is a field of research focused on how interventions get implemented with fidelity (i.e., implemented as they were intended or designed to be; Lyon, 2017). Implementation science tells us that if we try to do too many new things at once, we will not be able to do any of them well. Here, *quality* over *quantity* matters. Implementing new practices often requires replacing, or unlearning, previous practices (Evidence for Learning, 2020; McKay et al., 2018), many of which may be ingrained habits (Hobbiss et al., 2021). We encourage educators to offer themselves grace as they navigate this change process.

Educators can increase their chances for success by proactively considering the goodness-of-fit of planned changes. This allows educators to prioritize those changes that are most feasible and actionable in their setting. Congruence theory (Nadler & Tushman, 1980) offers a framework for considering the goodness-of-fit of a proposed change. Specifically, congruence theory refers to the goodness-of-fit between the *work* that needs to be done, the *people* who need to do the work, the formal *structure* of the system, and the *culture* of the system. Even when educators are considering implementing a new practice on their own, proactively considering congruence can help them to identify potential barriers to successful implementation. This, in turn, allows them to adjust their plan or strategy to increase chances for success. Consider the following questions related to goodness-of-fit:

- **Work:** Is this a priority for our setting? Is there data indicating need (e.g., student, family, community, staff perceptions of need)?
- **People:** Are there sufficient personnel to implement this initiative? Do personnel have the necessary knowledge and skills to implement, or is professional learning needed?
- **Structure:** Are the resources necessary for implementation available (e.g., data systems, curriculum, time)? Is the initiative aligned with school or district priorities?
- **Culture:** Is the initiative aligned with community values? Are there positive attitudes about the initiative (e.g., staff buy-in)?

After considering goodness-of-fit, one might choose to pursue an idea as is, modify the idea (e.g., change the timetable, seek out professional learning), or put aside the idea for the time being. None of these decisions are wrong and proactively identifying that an idea is not set up for success frees up resources to focus on something else. Educators' time and energy are finite resources. Being strategic allows educators to make the most of their time and energy to support students, colleagues, and their own mental health.

Let's consider two different scenarios to see how congruence theory can help educators to check goodness-of-fit and strengthen plans for implementation.

> Consider Jamie. Jamie is a third-grade teacher at a small elementary school. The school does not use a consistent SEL program across grade levels, but Jamie would like to build her students' emotion regulation, conflict resolution, and social skills. Jamie is contemplating implementing weekly SEL mini-lessons during her morning meeting. Next, consider Ryan. Ryan is a high school history teacher. He is concerned that his students are having difficulty planning for long-term assignments, and the associated stress this is causing. Ryan is considering incorporating instruction on goal setting, organization, and tracking progress with the next long-term assignment.

In Figures 1.3 and 1.4, we show how Jamie and Ryan each consider the goodness-of-fit of their planned changes. We also show how Jamie proactively strengthened her plan for implementation based on her informal assessment of goodness-of-fit whereas Ryan confirmed he was ready to move forward.

Context: Third-grade grade general education classroom
Idea: SEL mini-lessons during morning meeting to build social and emotional skills

Consideration	**Answer**
Work: Is this a priority for our setting? Is there data indicating need?	Yes, administrators are supportive of SEL instruction. Students would benefit from proactive instruction in emotion regulation, social skills, and conflict resolution.
People: Are there sufficient personnel to implement this initiative? Do personnel have the necessary knowledge and skills to implement, or is professional learning needed?	Yes, Jamie can implement on her own. She feels comfortable reviewing lesson plans and implementing them.
Structure: Do we have the necessary resources to implement? Is the initiative aligned with school or district priorities?	Jamie's school does not use a consistent SEL program across grade levels. She has found some freely available materials aligned with standards and her goals for students but has not yet vetted these with others in her setting (colleagues, administrators).
Culture: Is it aligned with community values? Are there positive attitudes about the initiative?	Administrators are supportive of educators providing SEL instruction. Jamie believes families will also be supportive but does not have concrete evidence of this.
Plan	Jamie plans to proceed with modifications. Her modifications are to run the plan by her administrator and grade-level colleagues to see if they have any feedback. She decides to also include information about the mini-lessons in her weekly newsletter to families to proactively share what she is teaching and increase opportunities for students to practice the skills at home.

FIGURE 1.3. Jamie's proactive planning for implementation by considering goodness-of-fit. Questions adapted from Chafouleas and Koslouski (2026).

Context: Eleventh-grade history teacher	
Idea: Executive functioning instruction to reduce student stress	

Consideration	Answer
Work: Is this a priority for our setting? Is there data indicating need?	Yes, students are getting overwhelmed as deadlines approach and turning in incomplete or late work. The students' distress is causing Ryan to question whether he needs to lower his expectations. Ryan is frustrated by the students' incomplete and late work.
People: Are there sufficient personnel to implement this initiative? Do personnel have the necessary knowledge and skills to implement, or is professional learning needed?	Yes, Ryan can implement on his own. In previous years, he has taught ninth-grade history and provided graphic organizers and intermediate deadlines to students to help with planning, organization, and tracking progress. He feels he has the skills to adapt these materials to match the eleventh-grade assignments.
Structure: Do we have the necessary resources to implement? Is the initiative aligned with school or district priorities?	Yes, Ryan will need to invest some extra time to prepare materials for the next unit, but feels this investment will be worthwhile for both him and his students' learning and mental health.
Culture: Is it aligned with community values? Are there positive attitudes about the initiative?	Yes, the school community has high expectations for student achievement. Ryan's plan also aligns with the school's focus on providing responsive, tiered supports.
Plan	Ryan plans to proceed as planned.

FIGURE 1.4. Ryan's proactive planning for implementation by considering goodness-of-fit. Questions adapted from Chafouleas and Koslouski (2026).

As shown in Figure 1.3, Jamie anticipates that she will be able to implement SEL mini-lessons on her own during her morning meeting. She has identified freely available lesson plans that align with established standards and address her goals for students. She realizes that sharing her plan with her administrator and grade-level colleagues would allow for her to proactively identify other considerations. Jamie also realizes that although she assumes families will be supportive, providing proactive information in her weekly newsletters may reduce confusion about what she is teaching and increase opportunities for students to practice the skills at home. Based on this quick assessment, Jamie decides to proceed with small modifications (sharing the idea with her administrator and grade-level colleagues; planning to include information about SEL mini-lessons in her weekly newsletter to families).

Recall that Ryan is concerned about the challenges his students are having planning for long-term assignments, and the associated stress this is causing. In considering goodness-of-fit (Figure 1.4), Ryan recognizes that he has data indicating need and the idea aligns with school and family priorities in his setting. He also realizes that he has previous instructional materials that he can draw upon and adapt for his eleventh graders. Based on this information, Ryan decides to move forward with his plan.

As shown in the examples of Jamie and Ryan, a quick assessment of goodness-of-fit can help educators to foresee potential strengths and challenges to implementation. Although not shown in the examples, it can also help them to prioritize among multiple ideas. After considering the goodness-of-fit of multiple ideas, educators can choose to focus on those that will be most feasible for implementation. In the appendix of this book, we provide reflection questions for educators to consider recommendations or practices that resonate throughout the book, evaluate goodness-of-fit, and action plan for meaningful and sustainable change. We encourage readers to engage with this resource as they navigate this book.

RELATED RESOURCES

School Mental Health Quality Guides

www.schoolmentalhealth.org/resources/school-mental-health-quality-guides

Offers guidance for strengthening each component of a comprehensive school mental health system.

The Landscape of School-Based Mental Health Services

www.kff.org/mental-health/the-landscape-of-school-based-mental-health-services

Provides an overview of school-based mental health services offered in U.S. schools as well as who provides these services and how they are funded.

Mental Health and Schools: Best Practices to Support Our Students

www.bakercenter.org/application/files/5616/8235/2328/Baker_Center_-_Mental_Health_and_Schools_Report_-_April_2023.pdf

Provides an overview of school mental health services, including case studies and implications for policy and practice.

SECTION I
PROMOTION

Introduction to Section I

We begin this book by focusing on mental health promotion, meaning universal efforts to develop skills that promote mental health and well-being, such as self-regulation, self-efficacy, goal setting, and positive relationships (National Academies, 2019a). Rather than focusing on preventing mental health concerns (i.e., reducing something), these efforts focus on promoting mental health and well-being (i.e., increasing something).

It may be helpful to draw upon an analogy here. Consider physical health for a moment. There are many actions individuals can take to promote their physical health: healthy eating habits, engaging in physical activity, and scheduling routine medical and dental care. In addition, the environment can be cultivated to promote physical health. For example, clean air, fresh drinking water, and access to green space all promote physical health.

The same is true regarding mental health. There are numerous individual actions and malleable environmental conditions that can promote mental health and well-being. Schools can promote mental health and well-being by cultivating students' and educators' relationships, social and emotional skills, and sense of connection within and beyond the school. Specific efforts in schools include promoting a positive school climate (e.g., by facilitating strong relationships, sense of safety and belonging, and opportunities for meaningful participation), attending to the many interrelated facets of student development (i.e., facilitating "whole-child" instruction), fostering social and emotional learning, and supporting educators' mental health. Each promotes positive mental health for students, educators, and school communities by increasing sense of belonging and positive relationships, for example. Therefore, we devote the first section of this book to sharing ways that educators can promote mental health in their school settings, knowing this investment pays dividends through increased positive mental health and well-being.

As shown in Figure I.1, this section contains four chapters focused on how educators can promote mental health: Promoting Positive School Climate (Chapter 2), Facilitating Whole-Child Instruction (Chapter 3), Fostering Social and Emotional Learning (Chapter 4), and Supporting Educator Mental Health (Chapter 5). In Chapter 2, we focus on school climate. We introduce four different facets of positive school climate: (1) *strong relationships*, (2) *sense of safety*, (3) *sense of belonging*, and (4) *opportunities for meaningful participation*. We describe how each of these facets contributes to a positive school climate and provide strategies for educators

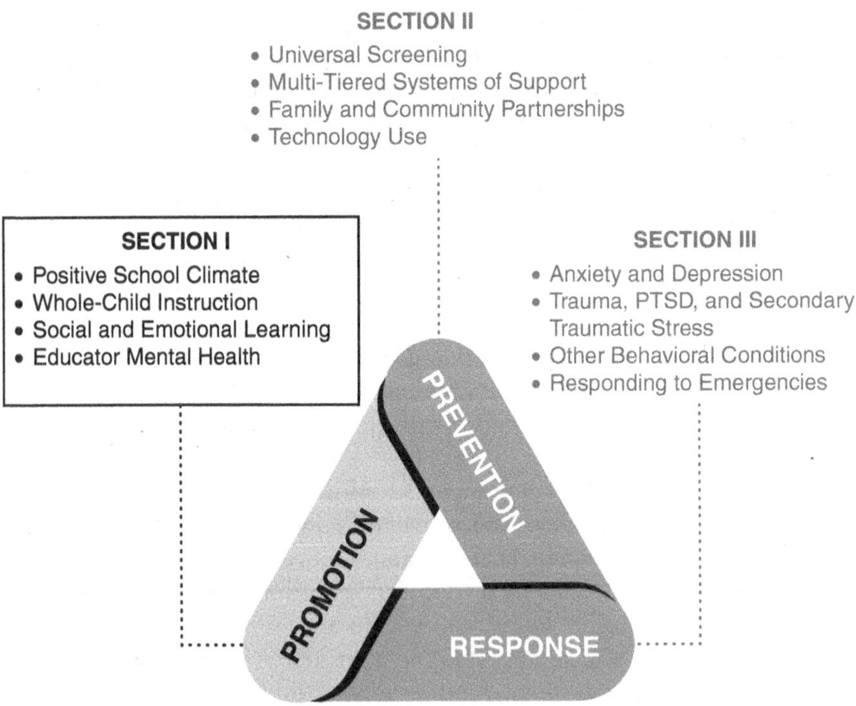

FIGURE I.1. Section I: Promotion.

to contribute to a positive school climate in their settings. Throughout the chapter, we invite educators to reflect upon the relationship between school climate and mental health for their students as well as for themselves and their colleagues.

In Chapter 3, we turn our attention to whole-child instruction. Schools are increasingly recognizing that academic learning is affected by students' physical, social, emotional, and behavioral development, as well as their contexts. We begin by defining "whole child" and discussing the various developmental pathways and contextual factors that affect student mental health and success. Next, we introduce three existing frameworks for supporting holistic needs and development in schools. Last, we share freely available tools for evaluating current use of whole-child policies and practices. Throughout, we offer reflection questions to guide educators' thinking about the various influences on student learning, mental health, and development, as well as strategies for increasing attention to whole-child instruction in their settings.

In Chapter 4, we zoom in to focus on a specific aspect of whole-child development: social and emotional learning. We discuss SEL's role in promoting mental health by equipping students with important life skills. The chapter is organized into three sections: (1) an overview of social and emotional learning (SEL) definitions, current research on the effectiveness of SEL, and best practices in teaching SEL; (2) potential controversies regarding SEL and the importance of contextually relevant SEL programming; and (3) tips for maximizing SEL instruction using differentiation.

In our final chapter in this section, Chapter 5, we focus on educator mental health. Student achievement is directly related to educator mental health and well-being (Granziera et al., 2023). Therefore, promoting educator mental health and well-being is a valuable and necessary investment. In this chapter, we invite readers to consider their own mental health, and the mental health of other adults within their school communities. First, we make a case for why educators' mental health is important, both for educators' own professional outcomes as well as their students' outcomes. Then, we draw on a framework from organizational psychology to explore how the balance between available resources and the demands that educators experience relates to their mental health. We discuss the ways that self-care and community care impact educators' mental health and conclude with individual and collective strategies to foster educator mental health.

While reading Section I, we encourage educators to consider the ways in which they already promote their own mental health and well-being, as well as that of those around them (e.g., students, colleagues, friends, family), and ways in which they would like to strengthen these practices. We remind readers that the suggestions offered in this book are not expected to be implemented overnight. Whereas some ideas may resonate immediately for personal action, others will require more planful efforts to implement. We encourage educators to choose the ideas that resonate most with them and are feasible for implementation in their contexts. Small steps in the right direction, over time, will generate many positive effects for educators and their school communities. To guide educators' efforts, each chapter will include evidence-informed recommendations, vignettes illustrating key points, and reflection questions prompting educators to pause and consider applications in their own setting and work. We also encourage educators to use the Action Planning Reflection Questions in the appendix to strategically consider next steps for application to their setting.

CHAPTER 2

Promoting Positive School Climate

KEY IDEAS

1. A positive school climate can promote the mental health of school community members.
2. In a positive school climate, school community members experience strong relationships, a sense of safety, a sense of belonging, and opportunities for meaningful participation.
3. Each school community member's identity shapes how they experience and contribute to a school's climate.

Consider Mariame, Tyler, and Devon. These students are all juniors in high school. They are all in Advanced Placement (AP) classes and have been best friends since freshman year. Yet when asked to complete a school climate survey, Mariame and Tyler rate the climate as very positive, whereas Devon rates it as poor. Mariame and Tyler spend most of their free time in drama club, alongside a lot of other students from their AP classes. But Devon is on the varsity baseball team and has few classes with his teammates. He lifts weights with the team before school, and his teammates often tease him for being such a "nerd." Yet when he goes to his AP class of the day, he feels like an imposter, and rarely participates in class discussions. His classmates seem to breeze through their work, and he spends hours every weekend studying just to keep up. Devon feels like he lives in two worlds at school and doesn't fully belong to either one.

Now consider Mr. McMillian and Mr. Owens, two of the AP teachers in the school. On a recent staff survey of school climate, Mr.

McMillian rates the climate as poor, whereas Mr. Owens rates it positively. Although they have the same number of classes to prepare for, their experiences in the school are very different. Mr. McMillian, in his second year at the school, struggles with behavior management. He feels lonely and ineffective, and he's not sure who he can reach out to for help. Mr. McMillian is struggling with low self-efficacy and anxiety. On the other hand, Mr. Owens, a veteran teacher who also coaches the successful debate team, feels confident, and rates the climate as very satisfactory.

The Relationship between School Climate and Mental Health

As demonstrated in the opening vignette, both personal and professional identities of each school community member shape how they experience the same school. Take a moment to reflect on the different schools that you have attended, worked in, or visited. In which schools did you feel safest, happiest, and most understood? Affective memories provide important insight into the *climate* of school communities. Just like the weather and climate often impact how people feel and engage in activities within their environment, the metaphorical school "climate" refers to the atmosphere of a school—how school *feels* to community members.

In the 1960s, researchers started investigating the role of organizational climate on students' academics and development (Wang & Degol, 2016). Today, the concept of *school climate* is a broad term operationalized in many ways across policy, research, and daily practice. School climate is both a psychological and social experience. It is informed by a variety of hard-to-measure affective and attitudinal factors, such as beliefs, values, attitudes, expectations, and norms (Aldridge & McChesney, 2018; La Salle et al., 2021). For the purposes of this chapter, we draw on a definition of positive school climate provided by Voight and colleagues (2015): "Experiences of safety, connectedness to school, opportunities for meaningful participation, and quality of relationships between students and staff" (p. 252).

How does a positive school climate relate to mental health? Historically, the field of psychology has tended to focus on investigating things that can go wrong with mental health. Around 2000, a turning point took place in psychological research and discourse: the funding and institutional support for studies exploring *positive psychology*, including topics such as the psychology of health, well-being, and positive experiences (Seligman, 2019). For example, Fredrickson (2013) introduced the concept of *broaden-and-build*, which suggests that positive emotions expand individuals' focus, motivation, and energy. Positive emotions are a powerful resource for teaching and learning and can have demonstrable benefits for attention and memory (LeBlanc et al., 2015).

Emotions are also contagious. *Social contagion* refers to the ways that individuals' affect and motivation impact one another within social networks (Burgess et al., 2018). After living through a pandemic, educators likely have negative connotations of the word *contagion*, but contagion has a positive side too: consider how contagious laughter can be! In fact, researchers have found that laughing together has positive impacts on teachers (Mawhinney, 2008). Teachers' humor styles impact student emotions (Bieg et al., 2019), and principals' sense of humor can positively impact teachers' job satisfaction and school climate (Şahin & Tabak, 2020). In other words, the way that each member of the school community feels can be influenced by the emotions of others in the community.

Researchers have demonstrated that mental health and school climate are closely intertwined. In a systematic literature review of 48 research studies, Aldridge and McChesney (2018) found that adolescents' sense of safety and school connectedness, and the strength of their relationships with teachers and peers, were associated with better mental health outcomes. Other studies have demonstrated the connection between school climate and mental health among elementary students (Kohoulat, 2015; Leadbeater, 2015) and middle school students (Franco et al., 2023) as well as the impact of positive climates on educators' own mental health (Collie et al., 2012; Gray et al., 2017; Grayson & Alvarez, 2008).

In this chapter, we unpack four different facets of positive school climate: (1) *strong relationships*, (2) *sense of safety*, (3) *sense of belonging*, and (4) *opportunities for meaningful participation*. In Table 2.1, we provide a brief description of each of these facets. Next, we describe how each of these facets contributes to a positive school climate and school mental

TABLE 2.1. Four Facets of School Climate

Facet of school climate	What does this look like in a positive school climate?
Strong relationships	Members of the school community trust one another
Sense of safety	Members of the school community feel protected from threats
Sense of belonging	Members of the school community are appreciated as their authentic selves
Opportunities for meaningful participation	Members of the school community are purposefully engaged in the school's activities and have a role in shaping the school's goals

health. As Thapa and colleagues (2013) explain, "Both the effects of school climate and the conditions that give rise to them are deeply interconnected, growing out of the shared experience of a dynamic ecological system" (p. 359). By engaging in efforts to foster a positive school climate, educators can promote both their own mental health and that of their colleagues and students.

Facet 1: Strong Relationships

The foundation of a positive school climate is strong relationships, characterized by trust, among members of the school community. To put it simply: a positive school climate requires trust among administrators, educators, students, and families (and each dyad therein; Tschannen-Moran, 2020). One of the most important ways that educators can help to facilitate a positive school climate is by building trusting relationships with other adults in the school. Trust among adults leads to positive outcomes for *both* educators and students (Bryk & Schneider, 2002). When the adults in a school have positive relationships with one another, they set the stage for positive relationships among students and between educators and students.

Research shows that teachers and students experience a wide range of emotions within the context of school-based relationships (Goetz et al., 2013; Stark et al., 2023) and that these emotions can easily transfer among members of the school community (Goetz, 2021). Trust allows community members to practice healthy levels of vulnerability and emotional authenticity as they navigate the varied emotions they naturally experience in their day-to-day work (Tianqi & Jinhao, 2024; Tschannen-Moran, 2020). When school community members trust each other, they can ask for help when things become challenging and celebrate with each other when things go well.

STOP AND REFLECT

1. Think about a professional colleague whom you trust.
2. What did it take for you to trust this person? Why do you trust them?

How might educators foster trust among adults in the building? One way to build trust is to demonstrate curiosity toward colleagues' professional work. Each member of the school community has a different role and approach to fulfilling it. Often, these roles are complex and hard to understand—even for the person in that role. Educators can build trust by asking colleagues about their work responsibilities and the types of support they need. Rather than jumping right to solutions, educators can ask questions and seek to understand their colleagues' experiences. By demonstrating curiosity, educators show that they appreciate their colleagues and take their work seriously. Gratitude and appreciation for those with different roles within the school community affirms the importance of each community member and validates that the success of the community depends on a diverse range of skill sets.

A strategy that can be helpful for building trust and appreciation is known as the 2 × 10 method. When educators find a student difficult to reach, McKibben (2014) suggests spending two minutes per day for 10 consecutive days getting to know them, focusing on "small talk" or nonacademic topics. Educators might also use this strategy to engage with colleagues who they do not know well or with whom they have a challenging relationship. This strategy can be used to build or restore trust and promote mental health. In addition, educators might consider initiating conversations about colleagues' loved ones and life outside of work—asking colleagues about their children, hobbies, or pets. Conversations with colleagues that recognize other aspects of identity (i.e., outside of *educator*) can be a powerful way to build trust and support. Consider what might happen if the veteran teacher from the opening vignette, Mr. Owens, made an effort to check in briefly with Mr. McMillian a few times a week:

> During a staff meeting, Mr. Owens notices Mr. McMillian scrolling on his phone, checking football scores. Mr. Owens strikes up a conversation about last night's heartbreaking playoff game, and they discover their mutual love for the local professional basketball team. Throughout the following weeks, Mr. Owens stops by Mr. McMillian's room every few days to commiserate about the team's unsuccessful playoff journey. One day, Mr. Owens notices that a few of his debate team members are in Mr. McMillian's class. He mentions that they have an upcoming debate about pay for college athletes and invites Mr. McMillian to come. Mr. McMillian shows up and stays after to congratulate the students. The interaction with the team leads him to share his own experiences playing college basketball. Over time, conversations like these help Mr. McMillian to build stronger relationships with a few key students, and the behavior management dynamics in his classroom slowly start to improve.

In future chapters, we will dive more deeply into practices that educators can use to foster meaningful, positive relationships with their students and between students, especially when students or educators are struggling with their mental health. Practices that support positive relationships include teaching social and emotional skills (see Chapter 4), providing tiered systems of support (see Chapter 7), and building partnerships with students' families (see Chapter 8).

STOP AND REFLECT

1. Identify one collegial relationship that you'd like to strengthen within your school community.
2. What can you do this week to help build trust with that person?

Facet 2: Sense of Safety

A second aspect of school climate that relates to school community members' mental health is their *sense of safety*. In a positive school climate, members of the school community feel protected from threats. These threats may be physical, such as the risk of gun violence or fights, or psychological threats, such as bullying and discrimination. When school community members frequently experience threats to their safety, it is difficult to maintain a positive school climate that supports community members' mental health. In a positive school climate, school community members can teach and learn without being distracted by fear for their physical or emotional safety.

To establish a positive school climate and promote the mental health of all community members, it is crucial to proactively plan for the psychological impact of threats to physical safety. Later in the book we devote an entire chapter to responding to emergencies (Chapter 13). These response efforts include proactive planning for emergencies. These efforts play an important role in establishing a positive school climate by proactively addressing potential threats and skillfully responding when they occur.

Another way to foster a sense of safety is to enact culturally responsive, transparent, and restorative behavioral practices. Behavior management systems promoting a *zero tolerance* approach are intended to enhance school safety through tightly monitoring and controlling behavior. However, these types of systems can easily threaten community members' expression of identity, agency, and motivation to engage in school activities. In fact, in a survey of over 10,000 teachers in Virginia, Huang and Cornell (2021) found that teachers' support for zero tolerance policies was associated with lower perceptions of school safety. Educators can play a role in promoting a sense of safety by exploring how their school's behavior management systems may disproportionately support or threaten the safety of members of the school community based on their linguistic, cultural, racial, sexual, or gender identities.

STOP AND REFLECT

1. How was challenging behavior addressed in your home or school growing up?
2. How did this relate to your sense of safety as a child?

Behavior management systems that promote a sense of safety are characterized by restorative practices; buy-in from families, educators, and students; transparency; and consistency. Establishing consistent and transparent policies and practices regarding behavior and emergencies is an important step toward increasing a sense of safety in schools. The efficacy of these policies goes back to the first facet of school climate: strong relationships. School community members are unlikely to feel safe without strong relationships. Educators who have strong relationships with their students are more likely to recognize signs that a student is considering engaging in risky or unsafe behavior and are more likely to successfully deescalate unsafe behavior. What makes a school feel safe differs based on each community members' life experiences, identity, and positionality in the school community (Voight et al., 2015). Strong relationships allow educators to have open discussions with students about what they need to feel safe in school.

Relationships among educators and students' families are also important for establishing a sense of safety. Family members may understand nuances in the politics and activities of the neighborhood in which the school is situated, and educators' access to this information can help them support safety policies and initiatives at school. To illustrate: In 2023, 13% of high school students reported that they missed school because they felt unsafe within or traveling to school (Center for Disease Control, 2024a). When school community members have strong relationships with members of the broader community in which the school is located, they can collaborate to address threats to safety arising both inside and outside of the school. For example, through community partnerships, Washington, DC Public Schools developed and implemented the Safe Passage program, which draws on the support of adults in local community organizations to help students get to and from school safely. There are similar programs in many major cities, including New York and Chicago.

Strong relationships also help school communities make informed choices about their chosen strategies for promoting safety and security within their schools. For example, in efforts to increase school safety, many schools choose to hire police or security staff. For some school community members, however, the presence of such staff may increase feelings of threat based on negative prior interactions with law enforcement in their neighborhoods and communities (American Civil Liberties Union [ACLU], 2017). Strong relationships among school community members can support decision making regarding the strategies that are most likely to promote a sense of safety for members of the community. Individual educators cannot control the systematic injustices that lead to some neighborhoods feeling less safe, or those who feel safe within various neighborhoods. However, educators can work to build trust and community within their schools, which can help to increase community members' sense of safety. By promoting a sense of safety, educators help support all community members' mental health.

STOP AND REFLECT

1. What do you think currently threatens a sense of safety for members of your school community?
2. How might you help address these threats?

Facet 3: Sense of Belonging

Sense of belonging is impacted by how much an individual feels their identity is valued or appreciated within the school and perceives that there is a place for it within the school community. Thus, a third facet of school climate is community members' *sense of belonging*. In a positive school climate, members of the school community are appreciated as their authentic selves. Sense of belonging and sense of safety are deeply intertwined. If school community members feel physically or emotionally unsafe, it is unlikely they will experience a sense of belonging—and vice versa. For example, consider the experiences of sexual minority youth in U.S. schools. In 2023, 3 in 10 LGBTQ+ high school students in the United States reported being bullied at school and 2 in 10 reported missing school because of safety concerns (CDC, 2024a). On the other hand, Colvin and colleagues (2019) found that sexual and gender minority youth who experienced their school climate as more positive reported lower levels of anxiety and depression.

Students' and educators' backgrounds—including race, ethnicity, and disability status—can shape one's sense of belonging depending on how those identities fit within their broader school and community. Sense of belonging is not only about what one's identity is, but also how it is received within the school community. For example, consider racial identity. Voight and colleagues (2015) found that within schools, students of different racial and ethnic identities experienced school climate differently, suggesting the presence of "microclimates" (p. 254). The extent to which schools recognize and affirm community members' identities has important implications for mental health. A sense of belonging among community members fosters the mental health of all.

Educators can promote school community members' sense of belonging by increasing representation of diverse identities, providing opportunities to learn about identity in class, and participating in the development and implementation of policies regarding respect and discourse around identity. For example, educators can increase representation by strengthening the extent to which they highlight different identities within their curriculum and the school building (e.g., displayed art, music played, communication styles). To improve opportunities to build a sense of belonging, educators might make changes to the school curriculum and environment to better reflect the identities of those in their school community. During instruction, educators can provide activities in which students reflect upon their own identity and learn about that of their peers and educators. They can also invite students to bring aspects of their own culture into the classroom. When opportunities arise, educators might also consider participating in the development and implementation of both classroom level and schoolwide level policies and norms that promote respect for diverse identities within the school community. This may include efforts to reduce discrimination embedded within disciplinary policies, increase freedom to communicate using one's preferred language and modality, and establish systematic and fair processes for resolving conflict. Spaces that allow community members to be authentically themselves are also beneficial. To promote a sense of belonging, Darling-Hammond and DiPaoli (2020) describe the need for "identity-safe spaces" within schools. These can include clubs, affinity groups, physical displays, and curricular content.

Consider the experiences of Mariame, Tyler, and Devon from the opening vignette. Even though Devon's teachers perceived him as a successful student-athlete, Devon struggled to find a sense of belonging within his school. What could teachers do to help him find his place?

> Devon's AP calculus teacher pulls him aside to talk after class on a day when she notices that he is particularly withdrawn. She praises him for his excellent work in her class and asks if there's anything she can do to help him continue succeeding—and, maybe, to help him speak up just a bit more in class discussions. Devon tells her that he is studying a lot in the evenings and weekends, and that he's just really tired. She tells him that this is common for many of the successful student athletes in her classes, all of whom have to juggle a demanding schedule. She mentions that she checks in with two student athletes from the soccer team on Thursdays at lunchtime and invites him to drop by anytime. Devon stops by the next week and quickly begins to develop a friendship with the other two students. They even meet up a few times outside of school to prepare for big exams. Knowing that these students are also navigating two different worlds within the school helps Devon feel more secure in his own identity within the school.

STOP AND REFLECT

1. Think about a student who, like Devon, may struggle to find their place within your school.
2. What's one thing you could do to help increase this student's sense of belonging?

Facet 4: Meaningful Opportunities to Participate

The final facet of school climate is *meaningful opportunities to participate.* In a positive school climate, members of the school community are purposefully engaged in the school's activities and have a role in shaping its goals. Meaningful participation will look different for each student, educator, and community member. At its foundation, *meaningful opportunities to participate* is the idea that all students have access to academic opportunities at an appropriate level of instruction, supports for both academics and behavior, and opportunities to engage with a variety of students and adults. Meaningful opportunities for educators to participate are also essential to a positive school climate. For example, special educators and teachers of English language learners should be included in content or grade-level meetings (or both) and included in ways that draw on their expertise.

Meaningful opportunities to participate in the school community foster self-determination among community members. Schools that lack a positive climate often have limited opportunities for students and educators to have agency—choice and voice. When students lack a sense of agency, they are less likely to feel good in school, trust their teachers, or engage in academic activities. Similarly, when educators feel that their work is constrained by top-down policies and they have little meaningful decision making within their classrooms, they are unlikely to be motivated to engage in the work fully. Having opportunities to celebrate meaningful events and to raise concerns when things are not going well are crucial for a positive school climate, and ultimately, for educator and student mental health.

STOP AND REFLECT

1. What does meaningful participation look like for you within your school community?
2. How could you increase opportunities for student agency (choice and voice) in your classroom?

If we return to the analogy of climate as the "weather" or "atmosphere" of a school, we recognize that as an individual educator, it can feel like school climate is beyond one's control: Isn't the "weather" beyond the agency of the individual? Educators often work in schools where the climate is not inclusive of their students' identities or their own identity. The need to engage in constant advocacy and education regarding such inclusion can be exhausting.

As we invite educators to engage in efforts to improve the climate of their school communities, we also encourage educators to reflect on their own locus of control (i.e., what is within their control versus what is outside of their control). Doing so can help educators focus their attention on factors within their control while releasing feelings of personal responsibility for those factors that are outside of their control. As discussed throughout this chapter, there are many small actions that educators can take to strengthen relationships, safety, belonging, and meaningful participation in their schools—but these changes take place over time.

Conclusion

In this chapter, we explored four facets of school climate, each of which has an important association with mental health: *strong relationships*, *a sense of safety*, *a sense of belonging*, and *meaningful participation*. We discussed how each of these facets is experienced differently among members of the school community, and we provided ideas for what educators can do to facilitate a positive school climate within their own community.

RELATED RESOURCES

National School Climate Center
https://schoolclimate.org
Offers resources and publications regarding school climate.

SchoolSafety.Gov
www.schoolsafety.gov/school-climate
Provides downloadable guides to improving school safety and climate.

School Climate Domain Assessment Tool
www.wested.org/resource/promoting-safe-and-supportive-learning-environments-a-school-climate-domain-assessment-tool
This resource from WestEd and the California Center for School Climate helps educators assess various domains of their school's current climate.

CHAPTER 3

Facilitating Whole-Child Instruction

KEY IDEAS

1. Attending to the "whole child" means supporting students' academic, physical, social, emotional, and behavioral development holistically.
2. Student mental health and development is affected by contextual assets and barriers.
3. By attending to the whole child in context, educators can promote students' mental health and development.

> Recall a night when you did not get enough sleep. How did it affect you? Did it impact your patience with others? How was your frustration tolerance when things went wrong? Were you eager to engage in complex problem-solving tasks or strenuous physical activity?

Sleep, one facet of physical health, can affect individuals across many other domains: academically, socially, emotionally, and behaviorally, for example. Many students (and school staff) do not get adequate sleep (CDC, 2024a; Paruthi et al., 2016). Inadequate or disrupted sleep can be caused by chronic health conditions, mental health concerns (e.g., anxiety, attention-deficit/hyperactivity disorder; see Chapters 10 and 12), and contextual factors. Students and educators may have family or work responsibilities that reduce the amount of time they have to sleep, or be awoken by noise or other disruptions, for example. Research on sleep suggests several negative consequences of chronically inadequate sleep in children, adolescents, and adults, including difficulties with memory and attention (e.g., Leger et al., 2024; Liu et al., 2024) and increased mental health symptoms (Morin et al., 2021; Short et al., 2019).

Sleep is just one of many examples of influences on mental health and student development. Schools are increasingly recognizing that academic learning is affected by students' physical, social, emotional, and behavioral development, as well as students' environments. This is often referred to as attending to the "whole child." Several scholars have advocated for educating the whole child by considering student development holistically (e.g., Chafouleas & Iovino, 2021; Darling-Hammond & Cook-Harvey, 2016; Osher et al., 2020). In this chapter, we first discuss various developmental pathways and contextual factors that affect student mental health and success. Then we discuss existing frameworks for supporting holistic needs and development in schools, including Comer's (2004, 2020) School Development Program; full-service community schools; and the Whole School, Whole Community, Whole Child model (Lewallen et al., 2015). We then share freely available tools for implementing the Whole School, Whole Community, Whole Child model. These include tools for learning more about and evaluating current use of whole-child policies and practices. Throughout, we offer reflection questions to guide educators' thinking about the various influences on student learning, mental health, and development, as well as strategies for increasing attention to the whole child in their settings.

Developmental Pathways

As shown in Figure 3.1, students develop along multiple pathways: academic, social, emotional, behavioral, and physical. Reviewing these developmental pathways can help educators to consider student development holistically. As described in the opening vignette, difficulties or delays in any of these areas can affect student mental health and school success. Let's take a moment to define each of these developmental pathways.

Academic development refers to students' progress in building academic, cognitive, and executive functioning skills, such as literacy, mathematics, memory, task initiation, and organization. *Physical* development relates to a student's health, including progress toward developmental milestones, the presence or absence of chronic health conditions, and any medical needs. *Social* development refers to how students interact, which might be demonstrated through their social skills and relationships with peers and adults. *Emotional* development encompasses how students feel, including their ability to recognize and regulate their emotions, self-esteem, and overall emotional well-being. Last, *behavioral* development refers to how students act, and is demonstrated through positive and productive contributions to their communities, controlling impulses, and interacting kindly with others. Each developmental pathway offers unique contributions to student development,

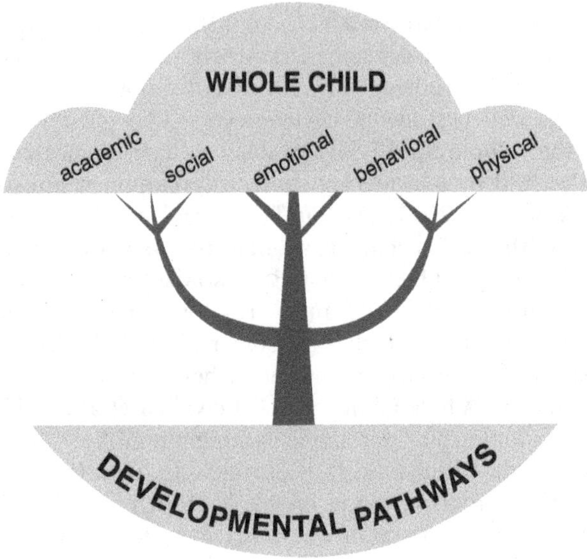

FIGURE 3.1. Developmental pathways.

but also affects other aspects of development. Take, for example, a student with a chronic health condition that results in frequent school absences. This aspect of their physical development will likely have implications for their academic, social, and emotional development. The student may fall behind academically or feel less connected to their teachers and peers, for example. By considering these various aspects of student development together, educators are better equipped to educate the "whole child."

STOP AND REFLECT

1. Consider a student with very strong social skills and average academic skills. How might each set of skills affect the students' peer relationships or academic progress?
2. Consider a student with underdeveloped emotional and academic skills, but strong physical development. How might the students' underdeveloped skills be related? How might you use the student's strengths to build underdeveloped skills?

Contextual Influences on Student Mental Health and Development

In addition to considering various aspects of student development, it is also important to consider how students are affected by contextual assets and barriers in their environments. It may come as no surprise to school staff that a student's home, school, and community environment affect their learning. In the late 1970s, Bronfenbrenner (1979) proposed an ecological systems theory. This theory showed that children develop within nested systems of family, neighborhoods, schools, and social policies and practices, for example, all of which evolve over time. During the COVID-19 pandemic and extended periods of remote instruction and learning, the impact of contextual assets and barriers on students' learning may have been particularly evident to school staff (Fahle et al., 2023; Fortuna et al., 2020). But what exactly is meant by contextual assets and barriers, and how do they affect student mental health and school success?

One term used to describe contextual assets and barriers is *social determinants of health*, or the conditions in which students, families, and staff learn, grow, and play (U.S. Department of Health and Human Services, n.d.). Social determinants of health have lifelong influences on health and well-being. Examples include economic stability, education, social and community context, health and clinical care, neighborhood and physical environment, and food (Henrikson et al., 2019). Economic stability refers to income, financial support, debt, and liabilities impacting families. Education refers to past and present educational opportunities available to both children and adults within a family. Health and clinical care includes the availability and quality of care to prevent or manage health conditions. Neighborhood and physical environment refers to the safety of a family's living conditions and neighborhoods, as well as availability of open space, reliable transportation, parks, and playgrounds. Finally, food refers to the ability to access and afford sufficient, nutritious food. For example, food insecurity, family and community violence, and low levels of social support are all associated with increased mental health concerns (Cain et al., 2022; Miliauskas et al., 2022 Mohammad et al., 2015; Zablotsky et al., 2024). Whereas contextual barriers can cause or exacerbate mental health challenges, contextual assets (e.g., social support, economic stability, quality education) can buffer against mental health challenges (Compton & Shim, 2015; VanBronkhorst et al., 2024; Zablotsky et al., 2022). Additional examples of contextual assets and barriers are shown in Table 3.1.

STOP AND REFLECT

Are there contextual assets and barriers that are overwhelmingly present among students and families in your classroom or school?

1. Could these assets be used to increase community?
2. How does your setting currently support any contextual barriers in students' lives (e.g., food insecurity, unmet health-care needs)?
3. How could barriers be addressed in more systematic ways (e.g., school food pantry, list of community resources distributed to all families)?

TABLE 3.1. Whole-Child Development Reflection Questions

Domain name	Definition/examples	Sample reflection questions
Developmental pathways		
Physical	Health, physical development, chronic conditions, medical needs	• How is this student's health? • How well-rested or tired do they generally appear? • Do they have a known chronic health condition?
Academic	Literacy, mathematics, science, social studies, cognitive skills, academic enablers (e.g., executive functioning)	• In comparison with their peers, how is this student's learning? • In what subjects do they excel? • What subjects are more challenging? • How is their executive functioning?
Social	Social skills, positive relationships with peers and adults	• How would you describe this student's social relationships? • Do they seem to have at least one friend? • How would you describe this students sense of belonging among peers? • How often are they sought out by peers?
Emotiona	Emotional well-being, self-esteem	• How would you describe this student's emotional well-being? • On average, how content do they seem? • How would you describe this student's self-esteem? • How would you characterize this student's mental health?
Behavioral	Positive and productive contributions, following rules, controlling impulses, interacting kindly with others	• How would you describe this student's behavior? • What types of feedback does this student generally receive about their behavior? • What strengths does this student have with regards to their behavior? • What skills could this student be taught to strengthen their engagement and belonging in the classroom?
Contextual assets and barriers		
Economic stability	Employment, income, expenses, debt, medical bills, financial support	• To what extent does the student's family have stable and consistent employment and income? • To what extent does the student's family experience challenges paying their bills or have high levels of debt? • To what extent is this student and their family able pay for their basic needs as well as enrichment, leisure, or vacation expenses?

(continued)

TABLE 3.1. *(continued)*

Domain name	Definition/examples	Sample reflection questions
Education	Early childhood education, high school graduation, language, literacy, vocational training	• What was the quality of this student's early childhood education experiences? • To what extent is the student's family multilingual? Is the family fluent in the language spoken at school or in the community? • To what extent is reading a part of the home environment?
Social and community context	Discrimination, incarceration, social integration, support systems, loneliness, community engagement, immigration and refugee status	• To what extent does this student and their family have strong social support? • What community organizations, teams, religious organizations, or close-knit neighborhoods are they a part of? • To what extent are extended family members involved in caretaking for the student? • Do the student and their family members have citizenship? Are they undocumented, refugees, or asylum seekers?
Health and clinical care	Access to health care, health coverage, provider availability, provider linguistic and cultural competency, quality of care	• To what extent does the student have access to high-quality health care? • To what extent can this care be accessed to address preventative, acute, or chronic health-care needs? • To what extent does the student receive regular dental care? • To what extent does the family have quality medical insurance? • To what extent does the student have access to any necessary medications or adaptive equipment?
Neighborhood and physical environment	Safety, crime, and violence; environmental conditions, housing quality, housing instability, transportation, parks, playgrounds, walkability	• How consistent and safe is the student's neighborhood? • To what extent does the student and their family have access to reliable transportation? • To what extent does the student and their family have access to open space (e.g., parks, nature)? • To what extent does the student and their family live in an area with high risk of a climate disaster (e.g., hurricane, forest fires, poor air quality)?

(continued)

TABLE 3.1. *(continued)*

Domain name	Definition/examples	Sample reflection questions
Food	Hunger, food insecurity, access to healthy options	• To what extent does the student and their family have access to sufficient, and healthy, food? • To what extent does the student or their family forgo meals because there is not enough food?
Whole child		• Considering the categories and questions above, how might specific aspects of this student's development or context be impacting other areas? • Have you gained any new insights into factors that might be affecting this student's learning, mental health, or engagement? • With these whole-child understandings, what next steps might you take to support this student's learning, mental health, or engagement?

Note. We do not expect educators to know the answers to all these questions. The purpose, instead, is to prompt your reflection on the various factors that could be impacting your students' learning, mental health, and engagement.

Table 3.1 also includes questions to guide educators' reflection on how various developmental pathways and contextual assets and barriers may affect your students. In reviewing these questions, educators are not expected to know all of the answers, and specific answers do not always have positive or negative implications for students. Instead, these questions are intended to guide educators' thinking about the complex and multifaceted influences on student development and success. When considering student challenges in one's classroom or school, we encourage educators to think broadly about potential causes and how support might be provided to address the root cause of challenges. Consider how various domains may be interacting, buffering, or compounding risk, and how the school can build skills or resources that address the root cause of identified challenges.

Frameworks for Addressing Integrated Needs in Schools

In this section, we will share three frameworks for addressing integrated needs in schools: (1) the Comer School Development Program, (2) full-service community schools, and (3) the Whole School, Whole Community, Whole Child model (Lewallen et al., 2015). We begin with the Comer School Development Program. As early as the 1960s, Comer et al. (2004) worked with schools to improve their support of student development. Comer et al. (2004) found that when educators and schools were supported to understand and support student development holistically, student achievement and well-being improved. Using a robust and sustained consultation model called the School Development Program, Comer supported schools in fostering the physical, cognitive, language, social, ethical, and psychological development of students. Still in existence, the School Development Program works to build educators' skills in collaboration, consensus decision making, and no-fault problem solving with goals to increase educator efficacy and competence (Lunenburg, 2011; Yale Child Study Center, 2024). Comer has found that this work requires mindset shifts and transformative leaders to implement and sustain it over time. When done well, research and practice evidence have indicated that attention to multiple pathways of student development holds potential to strengthen student success, achievement, and well-being (Cantor et al., 2019; Comer, 2020; Diamond, 2010; García & Weiss, 2016).

More recently, full-service community schools have emerged as an example of schools providing robust attention to developmental pathways and contextual assets and barriers in students' lives. These schools work to become a hub within their communities, providing a strong core instructional program, extended school days (e.g., longer days and school years) with a variety of enrichment activities, and a full range of health, mental health, and social services (Lubell, 2021). Akin to the School Development Program (Comer et al., 2004), full-service community schools typically embrace four pillars: (1) integrated student supports, (2) expanded learning time and opportunities, (3) family and community engagement, and (4) collective leadership and practice (Maier et al., 2017). Implementation generally takes 5–10 years, with schools often achieving partial implementation in 3–4 years (Maier et al., 2017). Full-service community schools develop strong partnerships with families and community agencies to increase support and services available to students and families. Although they are intensive to develop, cost-benefit studies have identified that full-service community schools generate financial savings through increased academic achievement (Economic Modeling Specialists Inc., 2012) and reduced likelihood of delinquency, incarceration, teen pregnancy, and poor long-term health (DeNike & Ohlson, 2013). Yet the substantial investment of time, resources, and personnel to create full-service community schools makes them relatively rare in the United States.

Next, we transition to the Whole School, Whole Community, Whole Child (WSCC) model (Lewallen et al., 2015). This is perhaps the most actionable whole-child model available at this time. The model (shown in Figure 3.2) offers a promising, evidence-informed framework for considering integrated needs in school settings. At the center of the WSCC model is

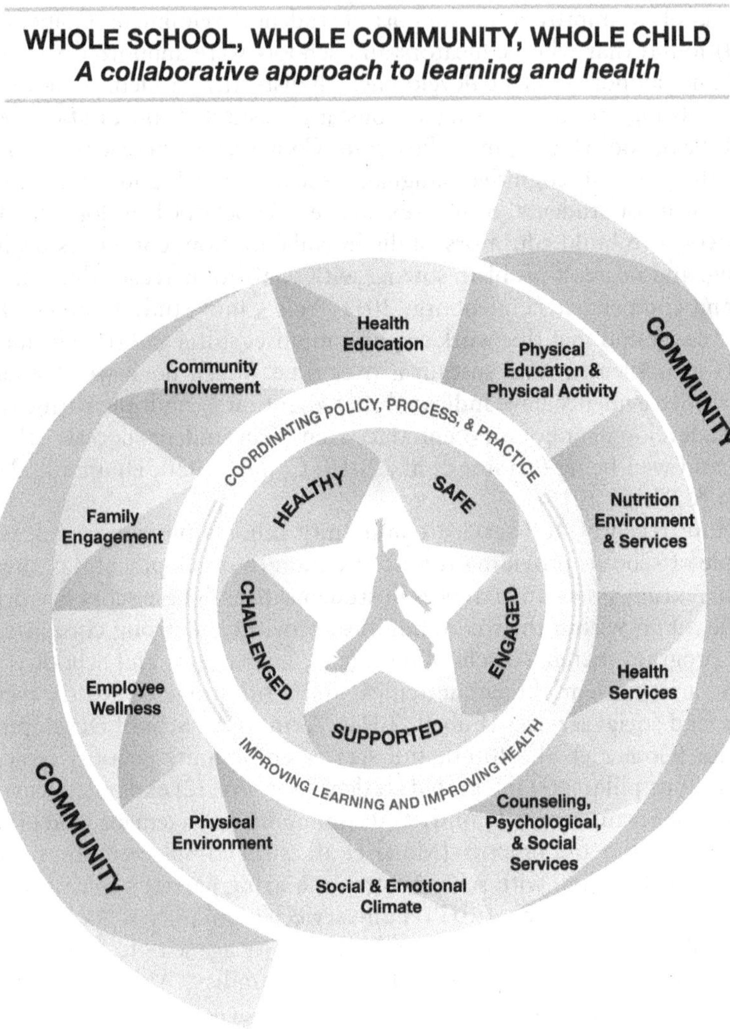

FIGURE 3.2. The Whole School, Whole Community, Whole Child model.

a challenged, healthy, safe, engaged, and supported student. Think back to Chapter 2 on school climate—these are many of the student attributes and outcomes that positive school climates seek to foster. The model advocates for schools to consider 10 domains that contribute to healthy students and positive whole-child outcomes: health education; physical education and physical activity; nutrition environment and services; health services; counseling, psychological, and social services; social and emotional climate; physical environment; employee wellness; family engagement; and community involvement. It sets forth that these domains be addressed through school policies, practices, and processes (Lewallen et al., 2015). It also recognizes that this work is best facilitated when supported by, and embedded in, the local community. The WSCC model is not prescriptive. Instead it is intended to be implemented through evidence-based policies and practices that fit local context. Although allowing for contextually-aligned implementation, this requires greater planning on the part of schools and districts.

The WSCC model draws attention to the physical, social, emotional, and behavioral development of students as well as recognition of their context. Traditional school mental health supports align most directly with the domains of social and emotional climate; counseling, psychological, social services; and employee wellness, but a healthy school environment across all of these domains is likely to contribute to student and staff mental health. Table 3.2 provides a description of each of the WSCC domains.

Importantly, the WSCC model pushes schools toward coordinated and integrated, rather than siloed, work (Rooney et al., 2015). In looking at the WSCC model, it is likely that schools are already engaged in many WSCC-aligned practices. Therefore, a key question is how to integrate this work to streamline efforts, maximize resources, and avoid duplication (Chafouleas & Koslouski, 2026). Often, various school personnel are underinformed about the efforts of others within their building. For example, best practices in SEL and health and physical education overlap (Society of Health and Physical Educators [SHAPE] America, 2018). Thus, school mental health professionals and health and physical education teachers may be working toward similar goals. Without knowledge of each other's work, however, opportunities for collaboration and mutually beneficial outcomes may be missed. Integration and de-implementation of redundant initiatives, or those not achieving intended outcomes, can free up resources for more promising or urgent work (Chafouleas & Koslouski, 2026). Although the WSCC model is intended to be implemented at the school or district level, individual educators can support student learning and mental health by using evidence-based WSCC practices.

Several tools have been created to assist schools in implementing the WSCC model, which are summarized in Table 3.3. The WSCC Practice Briefs, published by the University of Connecticut's Collaboratory on School and Child Health, offer concise summaries of the research supporting each WSCC domain as well as evidence-based practices for educators and schools to consider. These practices are organized by the level of resource demand required for implementation (low, medium, and high resource), recognizing that schools may have fewer or greater resources that they can dedicate to any one initiative. In addition, in the absence of a schoolwide effort to implement the WSCC model, the WSCC Practice Briefs can inform educators' individual practices and interactions to support positive student outcomes.

TABLE 3.2. Ten Domains of the Whole School, Whole Community, Whole-Child Model

Domain	Description
Health education	Structured learning experiences in which students acquire knowledge to engage in health-informed decision making and adopt lasting healthy behaviors
Physical education and physical activity	Includes (1) physical activity before, during, and after school; (2) physical education; (3) staff involvement; and (4) family and community engagement
Nutrition environment and services	Focuses on developing students' abilities to make healthy nutritional decisions
Social and emotional climate	Refers to the psychosocial aspects of student experiences
Counseling, psychological, and social services	Consists of school-based prevention and response services that address students' social, emotional, and behavioral (SEB) health
Health services	Consists of supports provided to promote the physical health of students in the school setting
Physical environment	Describes the school building and physical space around the school, school grounds, and the land on which the school is built, as well as how safe people feel in that space
Employee wellness	Focuses on the health and well-being of school employees to promote a positive school environment for all school personnel and students
Family engagement	Refers to a collaboration between families and school personnel with the goal of fostering positive outcomes for student learning, health, and development across domains
Community involvement	Refers to partnerships between school and community groups and/or community-based organizations

Note. Adapted from Chafouleas and Koslouski (2026).

Tools are also available to help schools evaluate their WSCC-related policies and practices. Assessment can be done at the domain level (e.g., assessing counseling, psychological, and social services or social and emotional climate) or across all 10 WSCC domains. Available tools include the Wellness Assessment Tool: WSCC Policy (Koriakin et al., 2020), and WellSAT WSCC in Practice (*www.wellsat.org*).

Finally, for schools considering schoolwide implementation, the WSCC Practice Blueprint leads school-based teams through 10 activities to

TABLE 3.3. Tools to Support Implementation of the WSCC Model

Tool name	Tool purpose
WSCC Practice Briefs	Provides concise summaries of the research supporting each WSCC domain as well as evidence-based practices to consider
WellSAT WSCC Policy	Affords users the opportunity to evaluate their school and district policies for alignment with the WSCC model
WellSAT WSCC in Practice	Allows users to assess their current practices for alignment with each of the WSCC domains and to identify areas for strengthening
WSCC Practice Blueprint	Offers 10 activities to lead school teams through a process of learning the WSCC model, identifying potential directions for strengthening practices in their setting, and action planning for implementation

Note. At the time of this writing, all of these tools were freely available online.

learn about the WSCC model, assess their current practices, identify areas for improvement, and develop an action plan for sustainable implementation. A key consideration in the WSCC Practice Blueprint is to balance existing and planned initiatives with available resources to maximize the likelihood of successful execution. The WSCC Practice Blueprint also has school teams consider de-implementation, whereby they examine whether any current practices are not achieving intended outcomes, or the resources used to implement them would be better used elsewhere. Finally, before action planning, school teams consider the *goodness-of-fit* of potential initiatives with their school environment, including the presence or absence of staff buy-in toward the idea, fit with community priorities, and available resources for any necessary professional learning or ongoing implementation support (see Chapter 1). The WSCC Practice Blueprint draws upon implementation science and the authors' combined experience in schools to maximize the potential for sustainable change (Chafouleas & Koslouski, 2026). The WSCC Practice Blueprint is freely available from *https://csch.uconn.edu.* A parallel WSCC Policy Blueprint is also available for school and district administrators interested in assessing and strengthening their policies to attend to the whole child.

STOP AND REFLECT

1. Explore a tool from Table 3.3 to learn more about evidence-based practices that support the whole child.
2. Consider assessing your current use of evidence-based practices using the WellSAT WSCC in Practice. This tool will alert you to whole-child practices you are already using and provide insight on areas for strengthening your practice.

Conclusion

Attending to the whole child can improve student outcomes across academic, physical, social, emotional, and behavioral indicators. Although some may argue that these domains are not all relevant or within the purview of schools to support, evidence suggests that students are more engaged and successful when schools attend to their holistic development. The WSCC model offers one framework for schools to consider and organize this work. The idea is not to do more, but instead to integrate, streamline, and strengthen existing work (Chafouleas & Koslouski, 2026). We encourage educators to identify one to three next steps for using the frameworks and resources shared in this chapter to strengthen whole-child support in their settings. Educators might choose to learn more about a specific aspect of development, assess their current use of whole-child practices, or use the reflection questions in Table 3.1 to reflect upon various influences on their students' learning and mental health. In the next chapter, we focus on social and emotional learning, one strategy for promoting students' social, emotional, and behavioral development and mental health.

RELATED RESOURCES

Healthy People 2030
https://odphp.health.gov/healthypeople
Offers an overview of social determinants of health and how they affect outcomes.

Whole Child Project
https://csch.uconn.edu/whole-child-project
Provides guidance for implementing a whole-child approach in schools through both policy and practice.

Whole School, Whole Community, Whole Child (WSCC)
www.cdc.gov/whole-school-community-child/about/index.html
Includes an explanation of the WSCC model and offers strategies for using it in schools.

CHAPTER 4

Fostering Social and Emotional Learning

KEY IDEAS

1. Social and emotional learning (SEL) instruction can promote mental health by equipping students with life skills.
2. Educators, families, and community partners should work together to identify SEL programming that is aligned with shared expectations for emotional expression and social skills.
3. Differentiated SEL instruction allows diverse learning needs to be accommodated, potentially reducing the need for more intensive supports.

> Sam is in fifth grade. For the most part, he gets along with his peers and is making gains in reading, writing, and math. He is outgoing, thoughtful, and generous. Yet Sam easily becomes frustrated and overwhelmed. He will give up on his work, loudly expressing his frustration and resisting help. At times, he uses inappropriate language in front of his peers and refuses to reengage. His teacher, Ms. Patel, feels that she has tried everything. She sometimes loses her patience, needing to walk away from Sam. Ms. Patel often feels defeated in her efforts to support Sam and frustrated by the ways in which he disrupts the classroom and others' learning.

Consider for a moment: With what skills might Sam benefit from support in strengthening? How about Ms. Patel? In this chapter we provide an overview of social emotional learning and its role in school mental health. It's organized into three sections: (1) an overview of SEL definitions, current research on the effectiveness of SEL, and best practices in teaching SEL;

(2) potential controversies regarding SEL and the importance of contextually relevant SEL programming; and (3) tips for maximizing SEL instruction using differentiation.

Defining SEL

The term *social and emotional learning,* or SEL, has become ubiquitous in schools, yet there is no widespread consensus on what SEL is. For example, Berg et al. (2017) identified more than 136 SEL frameworks, and Jones et al. (2019) indexed more than 200 SEL-related skills across frameworks. The acronym *SEL* is sometimes used on its own, and at other times used to describe certain types of skills, programs, interventions, or policies. For the purposes of this chapter, we draw educators' attention to two of the most commonly used SEL frameworks: that of the Collaborative for Academic, Social, and Emotional Learning (CASEL) and the Ecological Approaches to Social Emotional Learning (EASEL) Laboratory at Harvard University. CASEL (n.d.) defines SEL as

> the process through which all young people and adults acquire and apply the knowledge, skills, and attitudes to develop healthy identities, manage emotions and achieve personal and collective goals, feel and show empathy for others, establish and maintain supportive relationships, and make responsible and caring decisions. (p. 1)

In line with this definition, CASEL outlines five core SEL competencies: self-awareness, self-management, social awareness, relationship skills, and responsible decision making. The EASEL Laboratory at Harvard University (Jones et al., 2021) defines SEL in terms of six domains: cognitive, emotional, social, values, perspectives, and identity. Table 4.1 provides a more complete definition for each of the CASEL and EASEL domains along with example skills captured within each domain.

Both the CASEL and the EASEL frameworks have been used to guide policy, research, and programming to support students' mental health. Although SEL programming alone does not constitute a comprehensive school mental health system, SEL programming plays an important role in promoting student mental health. By SEL programming, we mean (1) targeted instruction in social and emotional skills, (2) work to improve school and classroom climate through improved norms, expectations, and practices, or (3) efforts to develop student mindsets, including perceptions of themselves, others, and school (Jones et al., 2021). In schools, SEL programming aims to promote positive relationships, emotionally safe

TABLE 4.1. SEL Competencies and Example Skills

Skills	Example skills
CASEL	
Self-awareness: The ability to understand one's own emotions, thoughts, and values and how they influence behavior across contexts.	Identifying emotions, recognizing personal strengths, examining personal biases, developing sense of purpose
Self-management: The ability to manage one's emotions, thoughts, and behaviors effectively in different situations and to achieve goals and aspirations.	Regulating emotions, goal setting, planning and organizing, demonstrating personal and collective agency
Social awareness: The ability to understand the perspectives of and empathize with others, including those from diverse backgrounds, cultures, and contexts.	Perspective taking, empathy, identifying diverse social norms, expressing gratitude
Relationship skills: The ability to establish and maintain healthy and supportive relationships and to effectively navigate settings with diverse individuals and groups.	Collaborative problem solving, communication skills, cultural competency, offering and seeking support when needed
Responsible decision making: The ability to make caring and constructive choices about personal behavior and social interactions across diverse situations.	Demonstrating curiosity, identifying potential solutions and associated consequences, ethical responsibility
The EASEL Project	
Cognitive: attention control, inhibitory control, working memory and planning skills, cognitive flexibility, and critical thinking	Ignoring distractions, controlling impulses, setting and achieving goals, managing multiple priorities, analyzing and using information to make decisions
Emotion skills: emotional knowledge and expression, emotional and behavioral regulation, and empathy/perspective taking	Recognizing and regulating one's emotions, understanding the emotions of others, demonstrating empathy
Social skills: understanding social cues, conflict resolution/social problem solving, and prosocial/cooperative behavior	Interpreting other people's behavior, navigating social situations, interacting positively with peers and adults
Values: ethical values, performance values, civic values, and intellectual values	Acting upon a concern for justice and fairness; striving to perform to one's highest potential; pursing knowledge and truth; participating in community life and serving the common good
Perspectives: How one interprets and responds to events and interactions throughout their day	Displaying gratitude, optimism, openness, and enthusiasm or zest
Identity: How one understands and perceives themselves and their abilities, such as their knowledge and beliefs about who they are and their ability to learn and grow	Developing self-knowledge and sense of purpose, demonstrating self-efficacy and self-esteem

environments, and students' skill development, all of which are important protective factors that buffer against mental health risks (National Academies of Sciences, Engineering, and Medicine, 2019a).

Many of the skills taught through SEL programming hold promise to reduce mental health symptomology. For example, children, adolescents, and adults who perceive they have meaningful relationships experience higher levels of mental health (Holt-Lunstad et al., 2010). Thus, supporting students' development of social skills equips them with tools to build and sustain meaningful relationships that may improve their mental health. Likewise, several mental health disorders—such as anxiety, depression, and conduct disorders—include challenges with emotion regulation (Berking & Wupperman, 2012; Paulus et al., 2021). Thus, proactive instruction in emotion regulation strategies may help to prevent or reduce the severity of mental health concerns. Increased emotion regulation, problem-solving, and relationship skills—all skills taught using SEL programming—are associated with reduced risk for substance use and dependence (Posamentier et al., 2022). Thus, SEL programs are a valuable, proactive piece of comprehensive and tiered school mental health supports. We include SEL in the promotion section of this book because of its specific focus on developing skills that promote mental health, such as self-regulation, self-efficacy, goal setting, and positive relationships (National Academies of Sciences, Engineering, and Medicine, 2019a).

STOP AND REFLECT

1. Which of the skills listed in Table 4.1 do you currently teach in your setting?
2. What additional SEL skills your students need?
3. How might you embed instruction of these additional skills into your existing classroom structures, routines, or lessons?

Current Research on the Effectiveness of SEL

Research on SEL programs has proliferated over the past two decades (Cipriano et al., 2023), and several systematic reviews and meta-analyses have been conducted (e.g., Cipriano et al., 2023; Durlak et al., 2011; Taylor et al., 2017; Wigelsworth et al., 2022). Given the range of SEL definitions and programs available, it is not surprising that these reviews highlight the heterogeneity of studies that have been conducted (e.g., various programs and skills taught, varied length of lessons and curriculum; Cipriano et al., 2023; Cipriano et al., 2024). That said, compelling evidence has been found in support of universal school-based SEL interventions. In a meta-analysis of 258 studies, Cipriano et al. (2023) found that, in comparison with peers who did not participate in universal school-based SEL interventions, students who did demonstrated significant improvement in academic achievement, school functioning, social and emotion skills, peer relationships, and prosocial behaviors. Students also experienced reductions in emotional distress and externalizing behaviors. In a smaller meta-analysis of 90 SEL studies implemented within the United States, Cipriano et al. (2024) found that SEL programs benefited U.S. elementary and secondary students equally well. Although some analyses have indicated no follow-up effects of SEL interventions (e.g., sustained effects at least six months later; Cipriano et al., 2024), others have found follow-up effects at six months (Cipriano et al., 2023) and even long-term effects on health, employment, and financial stability into adulthood (e.g., Taylor et al., 2017). Next steps in SEL research include identifying the optimal frequency and duration of SEL instruction and if and how outcomes might differ across various populations of students.

Distinguishing between Whole-School and Classroom-Based SEL

Consistent with the ambiguity in how to define SEL, there is variation in the scope of SEL instruction. In general, the literature tends to distinguish between classroom-based SEL and whole-school SEL (Wigelsworth et al., 2022). Classroom-based SEL is typically initiated by the classroom teacher. Although it generally focuses on direct instruction of social and emotional skills, it may also include efforts to improve classroom climate. Classroom-based instruction can vary in terms of content (e.g., prepackaged program versus local curriculum; SEL skills taught) and structure (e.g., frequency and length of lessons). In general, classroom-based instruction is not integrated with a larger school vision or mapping of instruction across grade levels or settings within the school (e.g., related arts, cafeteria, hallways).

Whole-school SEL approaches take a more systematic approach to SEL instruction through consistent instruction across school years and contexts (Wigelsworth et al., 2022). There is substantial variation in what this can include, however. For example, whole-school SEL approaches can include common SEL curriculum implemented across grade levels, schoolwide assemblies, staff professional development, or extracurricular activities (Wigelsworth et al., 2022). Whole-school SEL approaches might also include revision to school climate policy or collaboration with families and outside agencies. A recent review suggested that whole-school approaches generally produce stronger student outcomes than classroom-based approaches, but the reason for this is not yet well understood (e.g.,

What aspects of the whole-school approach contribute to improved outcomes?; How do they strengthen outcomes achieved through classroom SEL instruction?; Wigelsworth et al., 2022).

In general, classroom-based and whole-school SEL programming are considered Tier 1 interventions because they are provided to all students in the general education setting. Table 4.2 lists several tools to help educators compare existing Tier 1 SEL programming and frameworks. At the time of this publication, these resources were all freely available on the web.

Best Practices in SEL Instruction

Across both CASEL's and the EASEL project's frameworks, there is a clear understanding that social and emotional skills should be directly taught to students, rather than expecting students to learn them implicitly. Best practices in SEL instruction include (1) sequenced and coordinated activities that foster skill development, (2) active learning that allows students to become proficient in new skills, (3) focused time dedicated to cultivating one or more social and emotional skills, and (4) explicit defining and

TABLE 4.2. Example Resources for Comparing SEL Frameworks and Programs

Resource	Description	URL
CASEL's Program Guide	Repository of evidence-based PreK–12 SEL programs; can filter and compare multiple programs	*https://pg.casel.org*
Navigating SEL from the Inside Out: Preschool and Elementary Focus (Jones et al., 2021)	Comparison of 33 preschool and elementary SEL programs, including the SEL skills taught and learning modalities used	*https://wallacefoundation.org/report-series/navigating-social-and-emotional-learning*
Navigating SEL from the Inside Out: Middle and High School focus (Jones et al., 2022)	Comparison of 18 middle and high school SEL programs, including the SEL skills taught and learning modalities used	*https://wallacefoundation.org/report-series/navigating-social-and-emotional-learning*
ExploreSEL	Maps SEL frameworks and skills, allowing users to visualize skills taught in various frameworks and how frameworks overlap and diverge	*http://exploresel.gse.harvard.edu*

development of skills (Cipriano et al., 2023; Durlak et al., 2011; Jones et al., 2021). Within SEL lessons, it is recommended that skills are *taught, modeled, practiced by students*, and *discussed or reflected upon* (Jones et al., 2021). Over time, instruction focuses on teaching students the components of a new skill, opportunities to practice the skill, and generalization to new settings and scenarios (Jones & Kahn, 2017; Jones et al., 2021). Using these best practices, SEL intends to build students' independent use of a variety of skills and strategies across situations and the lifespan.

SEL skills have a developmental progression (Denham, 2018). Skills build upon one another: skills learned in early childhood assist with the development of more complex skills in elementary school, which then support the development of increasingly complex skills in middle and high school. For example, developing the skills of emotion recognition and emotion regulation during childhood are prerequisites to students learning to resolve challenging social conflicts in adolescence (Jones et al., 2021). That is, to resolve challenging social conflicts, students (and adults) first need to be able to recognize and regulate their own emotions before they can work collaboratively with others to resolve conflicts.

Some social and emotional skills are also particularly salient during certain developmental stages and in certain social contexts. For example, emotion recognition, emotion regulation, and empathy are taught and valued in U.S. elementary schools (e.g., Denham, 2018; Jones et al., 2021). In early adolescence, many students seek to develop a group-based identity based on gender, race, ethnicity, sexuality, or interests. In addition, hormonal fluctuations with the onset of puberty can lead middle school students to make decisions based on emotion rather than logic, but increased cognitive abilities also provide opportunities for adolescents to evaluate the consequences of different decisions (Jones et al., 2022). In later adolescence, students often work toward a more individuated personal value system and identity across contexts (e.g., school, work, extracurriculars; Denham, 2018; Jones et al., 2022; Nagaoka et al., 2015; National Academies of Sciences, Engineering, and Medicine, 2019b). Figure 4.1 lays out a developmental continuum of social and emotional skills from elementary school through high school, demonstrating both the progression of skills over the course of development as well as stage-salient skills.

Educator SEL

In addition to developing the social and emotional skills of students, it is important to recognize that these skills are also learned and malleable within educators. This is important because educators' social and emotional skills and competence affect both their instruction of student SEL

Early elementary	Later elementary	Middle school	High school
• Inhibitory control • Transitioning between tasks • Labeling feelings • Taking turns (e.g., sharing)	• Planning, organizing, and goal setting • Social awareness and perspective taking • Developing more sophisticated friendships • Resolving conflicts • Engaging in ethical behavior	• Exploring group-based identities • Navigating increasingly complex friendships • Gaining peer acceptance • Resolving conflicts • Beginning to explore identity outside of one's family	• Exploring individuated identity in multiple contexts (e.g., school, home, work) • Developing a personal value system • Increasing autonomy from adults • Exploring romantic or sexual relationships

FIGURE 4.1. Example developmental continuum of social and emotional skills from elementary through high School. Content based on Jones et al. (2021, 2022).

and their daily interactions with students (Jones et al., 2022). Educators with reduced emotion regulation skills—due to underdeveloped skills or contextual stressors—may have greater difficulty responding to students with curiosity, empathy, or patience (Sutton & Harper, 2009). As also discussed in Chapter 2 on school climate, students' interactions with educators are likely to affect their relationships with adults at school as well as their perceptions of psychological safety. Educators' implicit and explicit modeling of social and emotional skills also influences how students develop these skills (e.g., through positive or negative modeling; Gimbert et al., 2023). It is likely that educators who feel less confident in their abilities to teach SEL are going to be less proficient in doing so (Brackett et al., 2011). Unfortunately, to date, educators have not routinely been trained in providing SEL instruction (Hon et al., 2023; Schonert-Reichl et al., 2017). High school teachers, in particular, report receiving less training in SEL instruction than early childhood and elementary teachers (Bridgeland et al., 2013). Improvement in SEL instruction in schools hinges, in part, on investment in the skills and the capacity of educators to teach SEL (Schonert-Reichl et al., 2017). This will require a greater emphasis on SEL in educator preparation programs and national priorities.

Controversy Related to SEL

These efforts may be hampered, however, by national discourse regarding SEL. In recent years, there has been substantial controversy about SEL programming in schools, most often centered around misunderstandings about what SEL is and is not (Abrams, 2023; Sullivan, 2022; Standford & Meisner, 2023). SEL was conflated with critical race theory, and conservative groups began raising questions about students being taught about gender identity, social justice, and oppression (Abrams, 2023; Standford & Meisner, 2023). Bills in at least eight states sought to ban or limit SEL (Abrams, 2023). Some definitions of SEL are more explicit about culture, equity, and social justice than others. For example, *transformative SEL* (Jagers et al., 2018; Jagers et al., 2019), a term developed by CASEL, refers to SEL that explicitly addresses power, privilege, prejudice, discrimination, social justice, empowerment, and self-determination. Simmons (2019) argues that failing to consider racism, power, and privilege within SEL instruction can perpetuate white supremacy and racial injustice. However, to date, most SEL programs do not include lessons on identity, power, or social injustice (Ramirez et al., 2021). More commonly, they provide guidance and resources for ensuring that materials and content are relevant to students of all backgrounds and identities (Ramirez et al., 2021).

Data from a nationally representative survey of parents suggests that the vast majority support SEL instruction in their children's schools (Tyner, 2021), and that controversy arose around misunderstandings about what SEL is. Administrators report that when sitting down with families opposed to SEL and showing them the skills taught (e.g., self-regulation, teamwork, time management), families agreed that these skills should be taught in schools (Standford & Meisner, 2023). Survey data suggests that the term *life skills* resonates more positively with families and may help to reduce confusion and ambiguity (Tyner, 2021). It has also been suggested that drawing connections between SEL and equity may fuel polarization, and SEL might instead be described as a means to strengthen learning for all students (Abrams, 2023).

STOP AND REFLECT

1. How is SEL programming or instruction perceived by families in your setting?
2. In what ways does communication with families about SEL instruction in your setting take place? How might this be strengthened?
3. How might you use communication with families to strengthen students' generalization of skills into home and community settings?

Contextually-Relevant SEL

Amid this controversy, there is risk of perpetuating inequities and marginalization by not examining SEL programs closely. Norms and expectations related to emotion and behavior vary greatly across cultures as well as within cultures by age, gender, and other aspects of identity (e.g., Mesquita, 2022; Savina & Wan, 2017). Norms and expectations evolve over time, and children and families often navigate and negotiate multiple sets of cultural norms (e.g., in multicultural families; those practicing more than one religion; in various settings).

Emotional norms and expectations vary across cultures. One way to reflect upon cultural variation in emotional experience and expression is by considering cultures that value *in*dependence and those that value *inter*dependence. Cultures valuing independence tend to socialize children to openly express their emotions, to seek high-intensity positive emotions, and to develop self-esteem, independence, and self-efficacy (Savina & Wan, 2017). On the other hand, cultures valuing interdependence tend to socialize children to regulate their emotions in the interest of maintaining group harmony, to strive for emotional calmness, and to meet social expectations (Savina & Wan, 2017). Consider how students from each of these cultures might respond to being praised in the classroom. In general, students socialized in independent cultures respond favorably to praise as it contributes to their self-esteem. Conversely, students socialized in interdependent cultures may become shy or embarrassed when publicly praised because it differentiates them from the group (Savina & Wan, 2017).

Shifting to social or behavioral skills, consider expectations for eye contact between students and adults. In some cultures, eye contact is viewed as a sign of respect and children are taught to look adults in the eyes when listening or engaged in a conversation. In other cultures, however, eye contact from children is viewed as a sign of disrespect. Instead, children are taught to look down to demonstrate respect toward adults. Without an understanding of these expectations, educators may perceive students as lacking social skills or label them as rude or disrespectful. With this knowledge, however, educators can explicitly teach students about the varied expectations across settings or contexts, assisting students in developing social understanding and perspective taking that will benefit them in a multicultural society.

STOP AND REFLECT

1. What emotions and behaviors were more or less acceptable during your own childhood?
2. Can you identify how your experiences with emotions and behavior may influence your expectations for student behavior?

In increasingly diverse schools and classrooms, students are socialized in a wide range of social and emotional norms and values in their homes and communities, some of which may not align with those of the school. Thus, it is critical that educators reflect on whether SEL instruction reflects the cultural norms and values of the students, families, and local community (Jones et al., 2022). Collaborating with families and community partners is an opportune way to evaluate SEL programming so that it is affirming, relevant, supportive, and beneficial across student backgrounds and identities (Jones et al., 2021). Including families in this process is also likely to dispel some of the myths and uncertainty about SEL that has fueled controversy.

As stated by Jagers et al. (2018), "Schools are cultural institutions and advance (consciously or unconsciously) dominant racialized cultural norms, values, and practices" (p. 9). Unexamined, they can alienate or punish students and staff for not conforming to these norms (Coomer, 2019). It is important that educators be careful not to use SEL to require student compliance, to stifle emotions and behavior, or to pathologize emotional experiences that do not conform to specified norms (Coomer, 2019).

STOP AND REFLECT

1. What purpose does teaching social and emotional skills serve in schools?
2. What steps can you take to avoid alienating or pathologizing students whose social and emotional skills differ from school norms?

Maximizing SEL Instruction through Differentiation

In addition to considering how social and emotional development and expectations might vary cross-culturally, it is also important to consider how students' learning needs may affect their acquisition of these skills. Despite overall positive outcomes associated with SEL programming (e.g., Cipriano et al., 2023), many students are still struggling socially, emotionally, and behaviorally in schools (Child and Adolescent Health Measurement Initiative, 2023; U.S. Department of Education, 2022). What actions can educators take to maximize positive SEL outcomes for all students?

Differentiating Tier 1 SEL instruction can help educators to meet the diverse needs of learners with whom they are working. Differentiated instruction recognizes that not all students learn the same, and that proactive and varied instructional techniques can maximize learning opportunities (Tomlinson et al., 2003). Tomlinson (2014) suggests that differentiation can be achieved by adjusting content, process, products, or learning environments. *Content* refers to what students are expected to learn; *process* refers to the activities used to teach the content; *product* refers to how students demonstrate their learning; and *learning environments* refers to the classroom atmosphere.

Recent reviews (Jones et al., 2021; Jones et al., 2022) suggest that SEL programs use similar instructional activities as those used in academic lessons. For example, in early childhood, SEL programs most commonly teach skills through children's books, songs, teacher-led puppet demonstrations, or movement (i.e., kinesthetic) activities. In elementary grades, SEL programs use discussion, worksheets, and writing activities to teach social and emotional skills. Particularly toward later elementary grades, didactic instruction (i.e., teacher-directed instruction or explanations) is also used (Jones et al., 2021). Middle school lessons primarily consist of discussion, didactic instruction, worksheets, visual displays (e.g., charts or posters), writing tasks, and vocabulary lessons (Jones et al., 2022). Last, high school SEL programs primarily rely on discussion, writing tasks, visual displays, skill practice, role-play, and worksheets. In high school, there is also a marked increase in student-led discussions in comparison to middle school SEL lessons (Jones et al., 2022).

Rappolt-Schlichtmann et al. (2023) identified four common barriers to SEL instructional activities that students may experience: (1) physical, sensory, and cognitive accessibility, (2) emotional accessibility, (3) language, text, and discourse, and (4) executive functioning. As discussed later in greater detail, each of these areas presents opportunities for differentiating instruction to support the strengths and learning of all students. *Physical, sensory, and cognitive accessibility* refers to how students sense, perceive, explore, and navigate the learning environment. When lessons only provide a single representation (e.g., audio without captions, visual representations without explanation), students may have difficulty accessing or interpreting the information. Physical, sensory, and cognitive accessibility can be improved through multimodal representations and multisensory lessons, for example. *Emotional accessibility* refers to supportive emotional conditions that promote engagement. Students may feel uncomfortable in an activity that does not reflect salient parts of their identity or emotional experiences. Students may also have varying levels of comfort with individual, small group, and large group tasks, affecting their emotional experience and engagement. Therefore, emotional accessibility seeks to create lessons that optimize student learning by reducing emotional roadblocks. Staying curious about students' emotional responses to lessons or having them track their emotions across the school day can yield insight about how they are engaging with various content. *Text, language, and discourse* refers to the words, symbols, numbers, and icons used to teach SEL. Writing or discussion tasks may present challenges for second-language learners or students with varied learning profiles. SEL instruction also includes a great deal of receptive and expressive language that can pose barriers for students. Therefore, educators might consider pairing verbal and nonverbal cues, previewing advanced vocabulary at the beginning of a lesson, or providing sentence frames or graphic organizers to increase accessibility related to text, language, and discourse. Finally, *executive functioning* refers to requirements for goal setting, strategizing, progress monitoring, and responding to feedback inherent to SEL and academic instruction (Rappolt-Schlichtmann et al., 2023). Unstated or implicit goals can be unclear for students, and may cause educators or peers to perceive students as careless or unmotivated (Rappolt-Schlichtmann et al., 2023). Executive functioning supports—such as graphic organizers, visual timers, or scaffolded self-monitoring instruction—can support students in accessing these parts of the curriculum.

Although substantial attention has been dedicated to differentiating academic instruction over the past 20 years, the same level of attention has not yet been given to differentiated SEL instruction (Stark et al., 2024). As we will discuss in Chapter 7, a subset of students will likely also need additional small group or individualized social or emotional support, oftentimes provided by a school mental health professional or aide. Yet how can we differentiate *universal* SEL instruction to reach more students in the general education setting? Universal interventions are put into place to reduce the need for more targeted interventions (small group, 1:1), yet we know one size does not fit all. Rather than only responding with more targeted interventions for those not responding to a universal intervention, could we differentiate universal instruction to increase the number of students that benefit from it? An example might be helpful here.

> Recall Sam, introduced at the beginning of the chapter. Sam has many social and emotional strengths: he is outgoing, funny, thoughtful, and generous. As previously described, he also has difficulty regulating his emotions in the face of setbacks. Sam's challenges with emotion regulation and self-esteem are compounded by a history of trauma. He has inconsistent communication with his father, who is incarcerated, and has caretaking responsibilities for his younger sister while his single mother works and battles a substance use disorder.
>
> Sam receives special education services related to a specific learning disability in the area of reading. He struggles to read grade-level materials. His handwriting is poor and labored, and writing tasks are often a source of frustration. Sam is aware that he is not achieving at the same level as many of his peers and is often embarrassed when reading or writing in front of his classmates.
>
> Consider how Ms. Patel might differentiate academic instruction for Sam. Perhaps she provides instructional-level texts and the option to type written responses. During group work, she might assign Sam roles that draw upon his strengths in oral language (e.g., reporting

back to the large group) while reducing opportunities for frustration or embarrassment in front of his peers. Could these same differentiated supports be provided for SEL instruction?

Using Tomlinson's (2014) categories of differentiation, Table 4.3 lists several possibilities for differentiating SEL instruction. Keep in mind that differentiated instruction aims to increase accessibility for all students, including those who would benefit from extension. Educators are always balancing a goal to develop students' skills across the curriculum while working to present a tolerable level of challenge and frustration, which may change lesson-to-lesson. In the case of Sam, Ms. Patel might differentiate differently each day, or each lesson, based on specific goals and how Sam is doing. Keep in mind that when stressed, students (and colleagues) generally have a narrower window of tolerance, or range of emotional experiences that they can comfortably experience, process, and integrate (Siegel, 1999). When calm, the same students and colleagues will have a wider window of tolerance, or capacity to tolerate challenge, frustration, and setbacks, and thus can be stretched further in their learning (Siegel, 1999).

STOP AND REFLECT

1. Consider a SEL lesson you have taught in the past, or one that you might teach (e.g., deep breathing, mindful attention, perspective taking).
2. How might you differentiate this lesson's content, process, product, and learning environments? (see Table 4.3)

In considering differentiated SEL instruction, educators need to also be mindful about how they are augmenting universal instruction. In general, a good starting place is to use the same universal content or curriculum, but to teach it in a small group or one-on-one. This allows the student repeated exposure to the same materials, language, and skills with increased opportunities for practice and feedback. Decisions to implement something different from the universal curriculum should be thoughtful. Implementing something different means that the student will be learning new language and skills on top of what they are already learning in the universal curriculum. If the targeted intervention is implemented by a school mental health professional outside of the classroom, the classroom teacher may be unaware of the curriculum language and elements, and therefore not well positioned to reinforce learning in the classroom. This is not to say it cannot or should not be done: there are certainly circumstances when a more clinical or specific intervention is warranted. In these cases, educators should work to establish common language and expectations among

TABLE 4.3. Example Differentiation of SEL Instruction

Type of differentiation	Definition	Example differentiation	Rationale
Content	What students are expected to learn	Students identify self-directed SEL goals.	Provides choice to increase relevance and engagement; allows for varied emotional experience and expression.
		Students learn varied emotion regulation strategies.	Allows for selection of strategies that match development, cultural norms, and personal preferences.
Process	Activities used to teach the content	Material presented via leveled text, video, and demonstration.	Allows learners to access material through various modalities; supports those reading below grade level and English-language learners.
		Material is recorded and stored for students to revisit; related books added to classroom library.	For students with processing or memory challenges, or English-language learners, opportunities to review the material can reinforce learning. Providing related materials in the classroom library can also extend students' learning.
Product	How students demonstrate their learning	Students have a choice of preparing brochures, skits, commercials, or magazine articles to demonstrate learning.	Provides choice to increase relevance and engagement; allows for those with oral, written, or interpersonal strengths to demonstrate learning in various ways.
		Graphic organizers, sentence frames, or sentence starters are provided to assist students in expressing their knowledge or experiences.	Helps students to understand what is expected, and allows them to focus on essential content rather than sentence construction or other task-adjacent skills (e.g., organizing ideas coherently).
Learning environments	Psychosocial learning environment and classroom atmosphere	Students can choose to work individually or in a small group.	Some students prefer to work individually or not to share their emotional experiences with peers. Others prefer to work with peers and benefit from the dialogue and co-creation of knowledge that occurs in groups.
		Students can choose to work at their desks, in the hallway, or a quieter area in the classroom.	Allows students who are sensitive to noise or distractions to choose a more conducive working environment; allows for flexible seating and movement to meet varied sensory needs.

all adults working with the student to optimize student learning and outcomes.

> Let's return to Sam and consider three possible scenarios. In the first, differentiated instruction allows him to access the universal SEL curriculum to the point that he does not need additional social, emotional, or behavioral support outside of the classroom. He makes progress with regulating his emotions, and Ms. Patel learns to recognize signs of Sam's mounting frustration sooner. Ms. Patel differentiates for Sam and his classmates across the curriculum, and Sam's self-esteem slowly shows signs of improvement in the classroom. In a second scenario, Sam might demonstrate need for some additional support with emotion regulation, and join a skills group with the school psychologist, who uses the same language and SEL curriculum to reteach and reinforce Sam's classroom instruction. With repeated exposure and additional practice to supplement instruction in the classroom, Sam is demonstrating gains in emotion regulation and self-esteem. Last, in a third scenario, Sam did not respond to instruction in the skills group. After ensuring sufficient implementation and exposure (e.g., the lessons were implemented and Sam attended those sessions), Sam is referred for weekly one-on-one sessions with the school psychologist, who will work with him using a specialized emotion regulation curriculum. The school psychologist plans a meeting with Ms. Patel and Sam's mom to share the program language, goals, and guidance for reinforcing Sam's learning across settings.

To summarize, for some students, differentiated classroom instruction can promote access to the universal curriculum, reducing the need for additional, more intensive supports. For others, differentiated classroom instruction will promote access to learning that can be reinforced and supplemented with additional indicated supports.

Conclusion

In this chapter, we first provided an overview of SEL definitions, current research on its effectiveness, and best practices in teaching it. Then, we discussed potential controversies regarding SEL and the importance of contextually relevant SEL programming. Finally, we shared recommendations for maximizing SEL instruction using differentiation. We dive deeper into tiered social, emotional, and behavioral supports in Chapter 7. In the meantime, we recognize that this meaningful work to support students can also elicit many emotions for educators like Ms. Patel. In the next chapter, we turn to educator mental health in greater depth.

RELATED RESOURCES

Collaborative for Academic, Social, and Emotional Learning
www.casel.org
Includes descriptions of what SEL is, how it might be used in schools, and existing SEL programs.

EASEL Lab
https://easel.gse.harvard.edu
Provides comparisons of existing SEL frameworks as well as reports summarizing the most common early childhood, elementary, middle school, and high school SEL programs.

Greater Good Science Center
https://greatergood.berkeley.edu/education
Offers several blog posts, videos, and related resources related to building social and emotional skills in the classroom.

CHAPTER 5

Supporting Educator Mental Health

KEY IDEAS

1. Educators' mental health impacts both student and educator outcomes.
2. Educators' mental health is shaped by personal, professional, and sociopolitical events and circumstances.
3. Both individual and collective efforts are important for promoting educators' mental health.

> Julie has been teaching for four years. Last night, she and her partner of two years had a serious fight, stemming from concerns about finances. This morning, she and her co-teacher are introducing a new, project-based science unit. Although her students are excited about the project, the adjustment to a new seating arrangement and the new pedagogical approach has resulted in some particularly challenging behaviors. Just as she is reminding students of the classroom expectations, Julie hears her administrator come over the loudspeaker: "Staff and students, there has been an intruder. Please follow the emergency procedures." Julie's breath catches in her chest. Amid everything going on, she forgot that there was a lockdown drill scheduled for today. It has only been a few years since she experienced an actual lockdown at her previous school. Even though she knows this is just a drill, she finds it hard to focus and remember what she is supposed to do next. As her co-teacher directs students to sit against the classroom wall, Julie takes deep breaths, trying to maintain her composure.

Overview of Educator Mental Health

In the past four chapters we have defined school mental health, described school climate, provided an overview of whole-child instruction, and discussed social and emotional learning. In this chapter, we invite readers to turn their focus toward their own mental health, and the mental health of other adults within their school communities. We begin with a case for attending to educators' mental health. We then explore how the balance between educators' professional responsibilities and access to the resources necessary to meet them relates to their mental health. We discuss the ways that self-care and community care impact educators' mental health, and then conclude with strategies to foster mental health among educators.

As the opening vignette illustrates, educators' mental health is impacted by a variety of overlapping contexts: their personal and professional contexts and the sociopolitical context around them. Educators will all experience times of personal strain that impact their mental health (Dunn, 2021). Challenging personal experiences—such as the loss of loved ones, relational stress, financial challenges, and physical illnesses or injuries—impact the way that educators act and feel when they show up in their school communities. At the same time, positive personal experiences—such as fulfilling nonprofessional activities and relationships—support educators' mental health before they enter the building.

Regardless of what is happening in their personal lives outside of school, the climate of the school community also affects educators' mental health (Acton & Glasgow, 2015). Educator well-being is impacted by the extent to which the school climate feels welcoming or hostile toward one's identities (Hong, Cross Francis, et al., 2024). When educators work in communities in which they feel safe, appreciated, effective, and known, the resulting sense of community can be a protective factor for their mental health.

Finally, educators' mental health is impacted by the broader sociopolitical context surrounding their personal and professional lives. Perhaps the clearest example of this is the detrimental impact of the COVID-19 pandemic on educators' physical and mental health (Baker et al., 2021; Kim, Oxley, et al., 2022). Additionally, despite efforts to address systemic sources of discrimination across the United States, educators' work is situated in a broader context still deeply marked by systemic racism and ableism (Baglieri & Lalvani, 2019; Bailey et al., 2021), which has negative implications for all educators, regardless of their own identity (McGhee, 2021). The sociopolitical context in which schools are situated impacts educators' well-being in disparate ways, depending on how their identity and their students' identities are perceived. For example, in the current social and political context, the rights of gender and sexual minorities are being actively threatened (ACLU, 2025; Miller, 2019). The ability to show up within schools as one's authentic self is not something that all educators (nor students) can take for granted. This, of course, has implications for educators' mental health.

STOP AND REFLECT

1. How have aspects of each of these layers (personal, school, sociopolitical) positively impacted your mental health?
2. How have aspects of each of these layers (personal, school, sociopolitical) negatively impacted your mental health?

The Importance of Supporting Educator Mental Health in Schools

Sometimes, efforts to enhance school mental health focus solely on student mental health and not that of educators. In the following sections, we provide three arguments for why policies and practices that promote educator mental health are crucial to the success of the school community overall. We demonstrate that educators' well-being is related to a wide variety of positive outcomes for both students and educators and is therefore an integral part of school mental health (Dreer, 2023; Lee et al., 2023; Lever et al., 2017).

Educators' Mental Health Impacts the Quality of Instructional Opportunities and Relationships

Educators' mental health shapes their instructional decisions and interactions with students. For example, McLean and Connor (2018) found that educators experiencing higher levels of depression provided less frequent positive student feedback than educators not experiencing it. Implementing evidence-based practices like the provision of positive and constructive feedback to students requires access to higher-order thinking skills, which can be harder to access when experiencing intense negative emotions or stress (Blanchette & Richards, 2010; Eysenck et al., 2007; Plass & Kalyuga, 2019). In fact, Wong and colleagues (2017) found that educators who reported higher levels of stress also reported using less effective teaching strategies and lower levels of student engagement in their classes. When educators are emotionally exhausted, it can be harder to respond effectively to challenging student behavior (Chang, 2009) or to implement evidence-based behavioral practices with fidelity (Garwood, 2023). As discussed in

Chapter 4, educators are important models of social and emotional skills for their students. Students depend on educators to model skills such as emotional regulation and self-management (Gimbert et al., 2023; Lee et al., 2023). If educators are emotionally exhausted, it may be harder to model these competencies and skills.

Thankfully, the opposite is also true. Educator well-being is buoyed by strong relationships with students and colleagues within their communities (Roffey, 2012). Some researchers have demonstrated that educators who feel successful *are* more successful (e.g., that self-efficacy is linked with instructional quality; Holzberger et al., 2013). When educators experience positive emotions in the classroom, they feel more successful in the moment (Stark et al., 2023) and provide higher-quality instructional opportunities to their students (Burić & Frenzel, 2023). Educators' emotions can serve as a powerful resource within their professional work. For example, educators may hide or display emotions to demonstrate care for students, to encourage students who are struggling with content, and to engage students in instructional material (Stark & Bettini, 2021). In sum, educators' mental health plays an important role in building student relationships and providing effective instructional opportunities.

Educators' Mental Health Relates to Collaborative Relationships

Educators' mental health also plays an important role in educator collaboration. In today's schools, students' access to high-quality instructional opportunities depends on the ability of the educators in the building to effectively collaborate (Ronfeldt et al., 2015). With increased use of multi-tiered systems of supports, growing numbers of students qualifying for special education, and expanding needs for English language learning programming and supports, educator collaboration is crucial for student success. Educators can no longer operate in siloed classrooms in which one teacher provides the same instruction to all students. As schools build differentiated systems designed to provide targeted or individualized support for students, educator collaboration within these systems is crucial.

Educators' mental health and their ability to collaborate are directly related. When the adults in a school trust and feel safe with one another, they are more likely to share resources and step in to support each other as needed (Hallam et al., 2015). Relationships among adults within a school can help educators to share resources and navigate the stress associated with changes to school policies (Datnow, 2018). Emotional connections among the adults in a school play an important role in collaboration and adult mental health outcomes. For example, Jacobsson and colleagues (2016) studied educators' perceptions of the effectiveness of their teams and levels of emotional exhaustion and work satisfaction. Unsurprisingly, educators who viewed their teams as more effective were less exhausted and more satisfied. Developing connections with educators who share similar values, beyond their own school communities, can also play an important role in educators' mental health. For example, Mawhinney and colleagues (2024) describe how the creation of an activist network helped to support the mental health of educators of color by providing a trusting space to debrief experiences of isolation and marginalization within their respective schools.

Educator Mental Health Impacts Workforce Sustainability

Finally, educator mental health affects workforce sustainability. When educators' mental health is threatened by high levels of stress and burnout, they often leave their roles, schools, or the entire profession. A 2024 Pew Research survey reported that 77% of K–12 educators felt that their job was frequently stressful and 68% said it was overwhelming. When compared with U.S. workers overall, educators in the survey also reported lower job satisfaction (Lin et al., 2024). Although educator stress levels appear to have decreased since the COVID-19 pandemic, one out of every six educators reported they were somewhat or very likely to leave their job by the end of the school year (Steiner et al., 2025). In fact, a 2023 survey from the federal government suggested that 86% of public school leadership teams struggled to hire enough educators for the 2023–2024 school year (NCES, 2023). In a 2024 analysis, researchers at the Learning Policy Institute estimated that it can cost school districts $25,000 to replace a teacher due to the costs of recruitment, hiring, and training. In other words, investments in supporting educators' mental health are crucial for the overall well-being and sustainability of the school community and educator workforce.

STOP AND REFLECT

1. Which of the three arguments for the importance of supporting educator mental health resonates most with you?
2. Why else do you think supporting educator mental health is important?

Strategies for Supporting Educators' Mental Health: Balancing Resources and Demands

One useful framework for thinking about how to support educators' mental health from organizational psychology is Bakker and Demerouti's (2007) Jobs Demands Resources Model of workplace stress. Bakker and Demerouti assert that professionals experience stress when the demands of their jobs do not align with the resources available to them. In other words, to support educators' mental health, schools need to examine the balance between the demands placed on the educator (e.g., the professional responsibilities associated with their role) and the resources available to them to meet those demands. This means that supporting educators' mental health is *not* about providing a certain type or number of resources: it is about ensuring that the resources educators have access to match the unique demands they face.

One way to conceptualize resources is to think about *social* resources and *logistical* resources (Bettini et al., 2020; O'Brien et al., 2019). Social resources are the relationships that educators have with individuals who can provide informational or emotional support. For example, a social resource might be a formal coaching relationship or an informal relationship with a close colleague who provides advice and a space to vent. Logistical resources include curricular materials, protected planning time, and teaching supplies. Logistical resources might also include interdisciplinary planning time or access to online professional learning opportunities, which can also facilitate access to social resources.

STOP AND REFLECT

1. Consider your professional responsibilities. What social or logistical resources help you to complete these responsibilities?
2. What additional social or logistical resources would be beneficial to you?

Consider how the resources that educators need may vary across their roles. A special educator's mental health might be particularly buoyed by the social and informational support provided through weekly protected check-ins with a special education administrator. On the other hand, a math teacher struggling with low self-efficacy in a certain math intervention might gain confidence through the support of a district-level math coach. Two history educators teaching the same curriculum might benefit from different types of professional learning: one might be overwhelmed with classroom management concerns whereas the other might be experiencing stress regarding how to facilitate discussions about difficult topics. Access to professional learning in which educators have agency and choice is important for educator mental health (Cann et al., 2024). When educators have access to resources that are differentiated and aligned with the specific demands of their roles, they are less likely to experience feelings of high stress and overwhelm, which have a negative impact on their mental health.

As discussed at the beginning of the chapter, educators' mental health can be impacted by circumstances at the personal, school, and sociopolitical levels. The resources that educators need vary both according to their role (including the type of students they serve) as well as according to their own identity and personal circumstances. For example, as educators gain experience, they often find that they need different resources as a veteran educator than they did as a novice educator. Major life events, like parenthood or geographical relocation, can also cause shifts in the types of resources educators need to fulfill their professional responsibilities and maintain their well-being. Understanding mental health as a function of the balance between resources and demands can help educators to advocate for differentiated, targeted resources for themselves and their colleagues. It can also help school leaders justify investments in resources that vary among educators, as well as with educators individually over time, as each educator's own positionality, needs, and personal experiences change.

STOP AND REFLECT

1. How have your own needs shifted over the course of your career?
2. What resources do you need that your colleagues might not?

Approaches to Supporting Educator Mental Health: Balancing Self-Care with Collective and Systemic Efforts

Advocacy on behalf of oneself and others is an important skill for all educators. School systems are not inherently built to protect or maintain educators' mental health. Nor are they built to distribute resources and responsibilities equally among staff members. Educators may benefit from strong advocacy skills, both on their own behalf and on behalf of other members of the school community, to sustain their work and a successful school environment.

Constantly engaging in advocacy efforts can be exhausting. Even with concerted efforts to rectify resource inequities, many educators still work in challenging conditions (Educators for Excellence, 2023) caused by the large-scale inequities in how U.S. schools are structured and funded (Allegretto et al., 2022). Amid their ongoing activism, educators need strategies and mechanisms for sustaining a sense of purpose and enjoyment within systems where resources are insufficient. In the next section, we describe the need for both *self-care* and *community care*.

Educator Self-Care

Often, educators are encouraged to practice self-care as a strategy to maintain their mental health. Self-care can mean different things to different people, and may include physical, social, emotional, or spiritual practices. Self-care practices are important and associated with positive outcomes for educators' mental health. For example, Latino et al. (2021) found that practicing yoga for 8 weeks improved educators' mental health. Self-care practices do not need to be time-consuming. For example, many educators benefit from spending a few moments engaged in self-care through mindfulness activities. Mindfulness has a lot of different definitions, but a definition commonly used in educator intervention research comes from Kabat-Zinn (2003), who defines it as "the awareness that emerges through paying attention on purpose, in the present moment, and nonjudgmentally to the unfolding of experience moment by moment" (p. 143). In a systematic review of mindfulness interventions, Hwang and colleagues (2017) found that engaging in mindfulness meditation can reduce educator stress, burnout, depression, and anxiety—and it can also increase educators' self-compassion. Mindfulness-based interventions can also help educators regulate their emotions (Emerson et al., 2017). Like other forms of self-care, mindfulness can help promote educators' sustainability.

Self-care practices such as yoga and mindfulness activities serve to remind educators of the importance of work-life balance. With long school hours (including work activities that occur before and after school), and years of being socialized into identities that venerate service and sacrifice, placing a pause on work and engaging in *any* other type of activity can be difficult for some educators. One tool that might help educators engage in reflection regarding their own balance, and relevant self-care activities, is an exercise called Assessing Your Life Balance (Robertson & Microys, 2001). This tool helps users reflect upon their own self-care practices and identify areas of strength and potential growth.

Self-care is not selfish; rather, by enhancing educator sustainability, self-care benefits both the educator themself as well as their broader community. Yet even when educators know that self-care is important, they may feel guilty about prioritizing their own self-care or may receive mixed messages from school administrators about doing so (Gearhart et al., 2022). In addition, encouragement to practice self-care can subtly promote a dangerous (and inaccurate) message that educator mental health is simply a function of one's own choices. In messaging about the importance of self-care, the onus is sometimes put on the individual educator to keep themselves alive and well in a systematically unjust system that is not designed to protect them. Messaging about self-care sometimes minimizes the need to dismantle unjust systems—*if educators get Friday donuts and a gift card to a spa, do class sizes really need to change? Does the number of paraprofessionals really need to increase?* As an antidote to the sometimes-harmful narratives around self-care, some scholars and activists have highlighted the concept of *community care* or *collective wellness*.

Embedding Self-Care within Community Care

The concept of *community care* or *collective wellness* acknowledges that one's well-being is wrapped up in the collective's well-being. The Mapping Collective Wellbeing project's (2023) website explains:

> While the term wellbeing is often interpreted as individual wellness, collective wellbeing speaks to interconnection and our shared capacity to flourish together. Collective wellbeing provides a shared sense of purpose. It reveals the interrelatedness of the parts and frames an understanding of the whole.

Collective well-being highlights the strengths that each community member can bring to supporting the well-being of others. It positions all community members as both people who can provide help and people who need help. To build collective well-being, members of the community need to demonstrate ongoing curiosity about the strengths and gifts that they each bring to the community and also be willing to acknowledge the areas in which they each need support (van Woerkom, 2021).

How might educators foster collective well-being? One way is to develop a gratitude practice, which can have a positive collective influence on educators and their students (Howells, 2015). Creating gratitude lists, or the practice of writing down things that one is grateful for, is associated with decreased stress and depression (Komase et al., 2021). For example, Chan (2010) asked educators to spend 15 minutes per week, for 8 weeks, writing down three good things that happened during each week, and to reflect on the questions, "What did I receive? What did I give? What more could I do?" (p. 144). Educators who participated reported higher life satisfaction afterward as compared to before. The researchers also found that educators with higher levels of gratitude had higher levels of personal accomplishment and lower levels of emotional exhaustion and depersonalization. A similar practice is to simply pause at the end of each day to reflect on what went well that day, which can help invoke positive feelings and a sense of calm after a stressful day of teaching (Turner & Theilking, 2019).

Another way to foster collective well-being is to double down on sustaining relationships. We invite educators to identify one relationship within their school building and one relationship outside of it that sustains them. Invest in these relationships: show these individuals that you appreciate them and schedule times to connect. Turner and colleagues (2022) asked a group of five educators in Australia to consciously provide social support to another teacher in their life for 15 days and to journal about what they did. Teachers reported that providing support to another teacher—through simple acts, such as bringing them a cup of coffee or lunch, helping to problem solve technological issues, covering recess duty, or just making time to chat—also increased their own sense of well-being.

Finally, as described in the opening of this chapter, educator mental health is not only impacted by events happening within one's personal or professional spheres but also by the social and political environments in which they are situated. In the United States, school systems are situated within social and political environments marked by systematic racism and ableism. Educators can engage in a variety of political actions to change these systems. Engaging in political actions to foster educational equity may be beneficial for educators' mental health. These actions can be as simple as increasing one's own political education. For example, educators might consider learning about organizations that are actively fighting for educational justice by following them on social media, subscribing to newsletters or listservs, reading books, or consuming media that focuses on how these groups are changing systems. By learning from others who model advocacy, activism, and vision, educators can support their own mental health and that of their colleagues. Although mental health is easily impacted by awareness of negative current events, it can also be impacted by positive news or inspiration. By building their political knowledge, educators can remind themselves that they are located within a bigger system.

Consider how self-care and community-care practices might relate back to the opening vignette. After school, Julie both engages in self-care and draws on her community for support:

> Directly after school, Julie heads to the gym. She isn't feeling up for a heavy workout, but it is gloomy outside and she knows she feels better when she takes time to exercise. While she walks on the treadmill, she listens to a comedy podcast that her friend recently shared with her. She walks for half an hour and feels better afterward. Later that night, she texts one of her former colleagues from the school where she experienced the lockdown. "Had a drill today," she shares.
>
> "Scary! We had one last week and I was a mess. I'm glad you're safe," her former colleague texts back. A few minutes later, the colleague adds, "Want to chat about it?" Julie still wants to get some grading done and doesn't feel up for chatting. But just knowing that her former colleague understands and validates how she feels makes a big difference. "Thanks, I'm all right," she texts. "Just feels good to know I'm not alone."

Differentiating between Clinical Mental Health Concerns and Professional Stress

Before closing this chapter, we want to pause briefly to acknowledge that sometimes taking care of one's own mental health does in fact mean making the difficult decision to change roles, schools, or even careers (Lee & Thomas, 2024). It also means recognizing the difference between clinical mental health concerns and professional stress, the latter of which most individuals experience at various points in their careers. We encourage educators to proactively seek out professional supports for their mental health if they are experiencing mental health concerns. Many educators do experience clinical levels of anxiety and depression (Agyapong et al., 2022). And, just like students, many educators have endured traumatic experiences that may impact their mental health (Merrick et al., 2019). The longer that individuals wait to address these concerns, the more difficult they can be to solve. Seeking support from a mental health professional is a sign of strength and commitment to yourself and your community. If you are experiencing an ongoing mental health concern, know that you are not alone, and that there are professionals prepared to support you in developing tools to foster both sustainability and well-being in your life.

Conclusion

In this chapter, we have made three research-based arguments for why educators' mental health is crucial to the overall success of school communities. We have provided a framework to help educators consider how improving the balance of resources and demands in their roles can promote their mental health. We have also discussed the role of the individual and the community in supporting educators' mental health. We encourage readers to remember that their own mental health is a crucial aspect of the mental health ecosystem within their schools, and that taking time to invest in their own self- and community care is time well spent. As we close this chapter, we invite readers to spend a few moments completing the SWOT chart provided in Figure 5.1 to reflect on their own mental health.

STRENGTHS	WEAKNESSES
• What are the things you're currently investing in to support your own mental health? • What's working well about what you're currently doing to support your mental health?	• What personal, professional, or sociopolitical factors are currently barriers to your mental health? • What gets in the way of your efforts to protect and enhance your own mental health?
OPPORTUNITIES	**TENSIONS**
• What areas for growth can you identify to better support your own mental health? • What resources are available to you that you could try to access?	• What challenges might you face as you try out new mental health strategies or practices? • What is coming up in your life in the next few weeks or months that you might need to adjust your practices for?

FIGURE 5.1. SWOT chart: Educator mental health.

RELATED RESOURCES

Headspace
www.headspace.com/educators
Headspace provides evidence-based meditation and mindfulness tools, mental health coaching, and therapy services. At the time of this writing, educators are eligible for a free subscription.

Edutopia Teacher Wellness Collection
www.edutopia.org/topic/teacher-wellness
Edutopia's curated list of readings and videos on the topic of teacher well-being.

National Education Association (NEA) Student and Educator Mental Health Collection
www.nea.org/student-success/great-public-schools/student-educator-mental-health
Provides research, resources, and policy ideas pertaining to educator (and student) mental health.

SECTION II
PREVENTION

Introduction to Section II

Now that we have shared several considerations and strategies for promoting mental health and well-being in schools, we transition to the next part of our framework: *preventing* mental health concerns from emerging, intensifying, or going unnoticed. There is no question that promotion efforts help to improve mental health. Yet mental health concerns will still exist for some individuals, and there are actions educators can take in schools to prevent them from intensifying or going unnoticed. Generally, the earlier mental health concerns are identified and treated, the more efficient and effective treatment will be. Untreated, many mental health concerns intensify and create greater suffering for individuals, their families, and their communities. Thus, we now turn our attention to efforts educators can take to prevent mental health concerns from emerging, intensifying, or going unnoticed.

Prevention efforts can be implemented universally to reduce the likelihood of mental health concerns emerging, intensifying, or going unnoticed. As shown in Figure II.1, there are many prevention strategies that can be used in schools. For example, prevention efforts can include universal mental health screening to identify mental health needs early and prevent them from intensifying. School-based prevention efforts often also include multi-tiered systems of support to provide varied levels of support to students that can prevent intensification. In addition, proactive partnerships with families can be used to identify mental health concerns early and connect students to necessary support. Prevention efforts might also include partnerships with community agencies to increase the amount and types of resources available to students and families. Last, schools might engage in prevention efforts related to technology, aiming to use it as a resource and prevent negative mental health effects for students and educators.

We begin this section by introducing universal screening as an important way to prevent mental health concerns from intensifying or going unnoticed. Universal screening refers to quickly assessing all students (or educators) for certain indicators and then following up with those experiencing concerning symptoms. For example, medical professionals often ask patients to read rows of letters to identify anyone who may need a more comprehensive vision exam. This is a quick, population-wide way of catching vision problems early, and preventing them from going untreated. In the same way, social, emotional, or behavioral screeners aim to identify individuals in need of additional support. In Chapter 6, we discuss

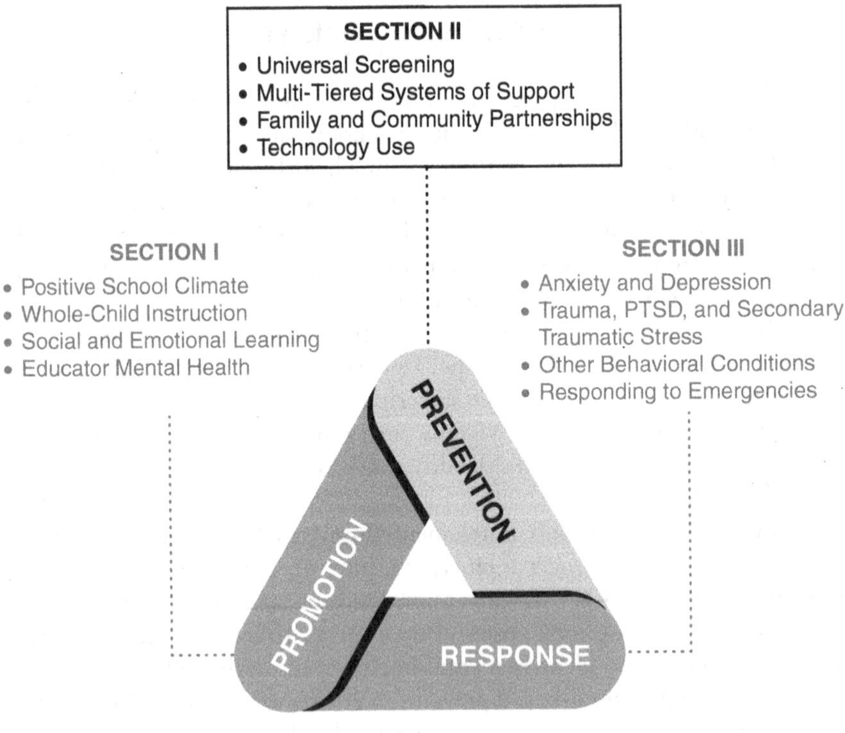

FIGURE II.1. Section II: Prevention.

the characteristics, strengths, and limitations of existing universal screening instruments. We will review current use of universal screening in U.S. schools and considerations for implementing universal screening. Sample data reports and guiding questions are provided to facilitate educators' understanding, interpretation, and use of universal screening data in their settings. Throughout the chapter we discuss different ways in which universal screening data can be used to improve student mental health and classroom instruction.

In Chapter 7, we transition to discussing multi-tiered systems of support (MTSS) as a mechanism for preventing mental health concerns from developing or intensifying. MTSS is a framework for organizing all available interventions within a school or community into various "tiers," or levels of support. Tier 1 interventions are universal and available to all in the school (e.g., general education social and emotional learning curriculum). Tier 2 interventions are more targeted and provided to those displaying need for additional support (e.g., small group social skills instruction). Finally, Tier 3 interventions are the most intensive and are often delivered 1:1 or using specialized curriculum (e.g., counseling services). Our goal is to provide educators with an overview of MTSS, including its history, potential benefits in supporting student and educator mental health, and potential implementation challenges. We invite educators to consider their own roles within these systems and how students may "move" in and out of more intensive tiered supports as their strengths and needs change over time.

Chapter 8 discusses the importance of family and community partnerships in preventing mental health concerns from emerging, intensifying, or going unnoticed. Partnerships with families allow for early identification of mental health concerns as well as efficient implementation of interventions to address these concerns. Community partnerships can increase resource capacity by bringing external providers into the school setting and allowing for referrals to community supports. In addition to increased mental health service supports (e.g., counseling), partnerships with community agencies also allow for connections to resources that facilitate mental health and well-being (e.g., extracurricular activities, resources to meet basic needs). In Chapter 8, we introduce different meanings of "partnership," and strategies for strengthening relationships with family and community members. We share recommendations for partnerships with families regarding student mental health, drawing specifically on the concept of cultural reciprocity to guide thoughtful and empathetic conversations with families about the sensitive topic of mental health. We also address the important role of educators in connecting families to community-based mental health resources. We conclude by sharing an activity in which educators can map resources available within their own school's community. We intend for this activity to equip educators with information to share with students and families, as needed. Educators are some of the strongest referral providers in students' lives and we cannot overstate the importance of this role in preventing mental health concerns from intensifying.

In the final chapter of this section, Chapter 9, we transition to discussing the role of technology in students' and educators' lives. We specifically discuss the potential positive and negative impacts of technology on mental health. We provide guidance for using technology as a resource to prevent mental health concerns from emerging or intensifying. We also share potential threats of technology to student and educator mental health to raise awareness and guide positive change. Throughout, we illustrate the delicate balance needed for the use of technology as a resource and provide educators with multiple recommendations for promoting healthy technological habits with their students.

Again, we cannot overstate educators' roles in supporting student (and colleague) mental health. We aim to equip educators with knowledge, skills, and empathy with which to prevent mental health concerns from emerging, intensifying, or going unnoticed. To maximize learning, each chapter includes a vignette that illustrates key points and reflection questions prompting educators to pause and consider applications in their own setting and work. In the following chapters, we encourage educators to choose one to three actions or recommendations to consider integrating into their practice to allow for sustainable growth and change. Educators can consider using the Action Planning Reflection Questions in the appendix to guide their efforts.

CHAPTER 6

Universal Screening

KEY IDEAS

1. Using universal screeners can prevent mental health concerns from getting worse and students from "falling through the cracks."
2. Screeners are designed to be brief, so additional data are often needed to drive decisions about specific supports.
3. Educators can use mental health screening data to inform their interactions and instruction in the classroom.

> Consider Lilah. Lilah is a freshman in high school who excels across the curriculum. She is on the student council and babysits on weekends. Lilah has a close group of friends and a supportive home environment. She is seemingly thriving in her transition to high school. Yet she experiences significant anxiety about measuring up, meeting others' expectations, and balancing her many commitments. Lilah often has trouble sleeping because her mind is racing. She worries that a poor test grade will ruin her chances of attending a competitive college, and that she's not doing enough to build a strong resume. Lilah does her best to push these thoughts away during the day, using humor and care for others to deflect attention away from herself. Teachers and classmates regularly commend Lilah's hard work, engagement, and leadership.

Universal screening is a promising approach for identifying emergent mental health needs, allowing for these concerns to be addressed before they become more severe. It is a key strategy in preventing concerns from going unnoticed or "falling through the cracks" and is considered to be an essential feature of multi-tiered systems of support (Brown-Chidsey & Bickford, 2016). Universal screening means that all students, regardless of any known risk factors, are assessed to identify those in need of support (NCSMH, 2023). Available mental health screeners include those that assess for anxiety, depression, suicidality, substance misuse, and inattention among other concerns. Screening for these concerns has been linked to positive outcomes such as increased identification of mental health need and connection to mental health services (Husky et al., 2011; Peetz, 2024). For students like Lilah, universal screeners may surface potentially concerning symptoms or experiences that are otherwise unknown to school staff and families.

Screeners are designed to be brief, some including as few as one to three questions, so they can be quickly and feasibly implemented. Screeners include guidance for school personnel to identify those students who may be in need of additional evaluation or support. This guidance is generally based on national norms (e.g., cut scores) as well as items that are associated with significant risk (e.g., planned violence or suicide attempt; Substance Abuse and Mental Health Services Administration [SAMHSA], 2019a). For example, the Patient Health Questionairre-2 (PHQ-2; Kroenke et al., 2003) includes two questions that ask students how often they have had little interest or pleasure in doing things over the past two weeks and how often they have felt down, depressed, or hopeless during that time. Students indicating either on more than half the days or nearly every day are flagged for follow-up by school personnel or external referral. Because of their brief nature, screeners are not designed to provide diagnoses. Instead, they identify students who may be experiencing mental health challenges so that school personnel can follow up with additional assessment, intervention, or referral to community partners. Examples of several existing mental health screeners are listed in Table 6.1. As can be seen in the table, universal screeners vary in their scope (e.g., one topic, multiple topics), length, informant (student, educator, caregiver), and age range.

In this chapter, we first discuss the characteristics, strengths, and limitations of existing universal screening instruments. Then, we review current use of universal screening in U.S. schools and considerations for implementing universal screening. Finally, we share sample data reports and guiding questions to facilitate educators' understanding, interpretation, and use of universal screening data in their settings.

Characteristics, Strengths, and Limitations of Existing Universal Screening Instruments

Existing school-based mental health screeners have several strengths and limitations. As illustrated by the examples thus far, many screeners focus

TABLE 6.1. Example Universal Mental Health Screeners Used in Schools

Name	Domain(s) assessed	# of items	Age range	Informant	Administration time	Languages
Center for Epidemiological Studies Depression Scale for Children (CES-DC; Faulstich et al., 1986)	Depression	20	6–23	Student	5–10 min	Multiple languages
Children's Hope Scale (Snyder et al., 1997)	Hope	6	8–16	Student	2 min	English only
Columbia Suicide Severity Risk Scale (C-SSRS; Posner et al., 2011)	Suicide risk	6	All ages	Student	1–2 min	Available in >150 country-specific languages
CRAFFT 2.1 Questionnaire (Knight, 2020)	Substance misuse	9	12–18	Student	1–2 min	Available in 35 languages
Generalized Anxiety Disorder–7 (GAD-7; Spitzer et al., 2006)	Anxiety	10	11–17	Student	5 min	Available in 50 languages
Student Risk Screening Scale Internalizing and Externalizing (SRSS-IE; Drummond, 1994)	Internalizing and Externalizing Behaviors	12	Elementary	Educator	1–2 min per student	English only
		13	Middle/ high school			
Students' Life Satisfaction Scale (SLSS; Huebner, 1991)	Life satisfaction	7	8–18	Student	>5 min	Spanish, Portuguese, German

Note. As the time of this writing, all screeners included in this table were freely available online.

on one area of concern (e.g., anxiety, depression). The data generated from these screeners will likely need to be combined with other screening data or information to gain a more complete understanding of students' mental health and well-being. Although a brief anxiety screener may suggest that a student (such as Lilah) is experiencing significant anxiety in their daily life, it is unlikely to identify the causes of that anxiety. Additional data and follow-up conversations with the student and their caregivers are likely needed to identify sources or triggers of the anxiety and appropriate supports. If, for example, the student is experiencing anxiety due to challenges learning to read while their peers are reading proficiently, a reading intervention may be more effective than (or at least needed in tandem with) a psychological intervention. If, instead, the student is experiencing anxiety related to their family's housing instability, potential interventions would look quite different. Therefore, it is crucial to use brief mental health screeners in conjunction with additional screening and diagnostic information. Screeners provide important entry level information for identifying student mental health strengths and concerns.

To identify mental health concerns and remain brief, many mental health screeners focus on symptomology without gathering information about students' mental health strengths (e.g., emotional well-being, coping strategies). This raises a couple of concerns. First, a singular focus on symptomology may influence the perceptions of raters (e.g., students, teachers, caregivers). For example, if a behavior screener focuses on severe externalizing behaviors (e.g., aggression) and a student receives elevated ratings, the rater's thinking and subsequent interactions with the student may be affected. Despite their best intentions, an educator might inadvertently invest less time in supporting the student academically or discipline them more quickly than other students. In the case of student self-report, students might internalize feelings of shame or hopelessness. In addition, the absence of items related to students' strengths reduces opportunities to draw upon these strengths when addressing concerns. For example, although a screener might indicate that a student is struggling with symptoms of depression, it generally does not collect information about any (potentially positive) coping strategies the student is using.

Another concern related to screeners' traditional focus on symptomology is that the absence of symptomology does not always indicate that students are doing well (e.g., Suldo & Shaffer, 2008; Suldo et al., 2016). They might be apathetic or indifferent, for example. In addition, as shared in Chapter 1, distress and emotional well-being are not mutually exclusive. Suldo (2008) and Suldo and colleagues (2016) have identified four general classifications of students that demonstrate varied levels of risk and need: complete mental health (high subjective well-being, low psychopathology), vulnerable (low subjective well-being, low psychopathology), symptomatic but content (high subjective well-being, high psychopathology), and troubled (low subjective well-being, high psychopathology). Collecting information on student perceptions of well-being can be important to understanding the nuances of student need and appropriate supports. If, for example, a student is endorsing symptoms of anxiety (i.e., psychopathology) but also high levels of subjective well-being, supports might look different than for a student endorsing high levels of anxiety and very low levels of subjective well-being. Lastly, because universal screeners are administered to all students, collecting information about well-being allows schools to identify leaders, role models, and peer mentors to support students who are struggling. Solely collecting data on symptomology indicates the number of students that are experiencing specific symptoms, but does not give any further information on strengths that could be leveraged.

STOP AND REFLECT

1. What universal screening tools have you seen used (e.g., depression, vision, hearing, reading)?
2. What pros and cons of universal screening can you identify?

Use of Universal Screening in U.S. Schools

Although there has been a proliferation of social, emotional, and behavioral screening instruments in recent years (Kim & Choe, 2022), they are not yet widely used in schools. Whereas 70–80% of schools report using universal academic (literacy) and health (vision, scoliosis) screeners, only 9% report using social, emotional, or behavioral screeners, including mental health screeners (Briesch et al., 2022). A study by Briesch and colleagues (2022) found that elementary and secondary school administrators were equally likely to use universal social, emotional, and behavioral screeners, and the most commonly used screeners assessed social skills, behavioral risk, self-esteem, anxiety, aggression, and depression. The researchers also found that generally, screening related to social skills and behavioral risk were more common at the elementary level, whereas screening for depression and substance use were more common in secondary schools.

In the absence of widespread use of universal mental health screening, schools overwhelmingly rely on educator referral to identify students in need of additional support. However, it can be difficult for educators to accurately gauge students' mental health need. Research suggests that educator referral results in underidentification of students in need of support (e.g., Dowdy et al., 2013; Husky et al., 2011; Splett et al., 2018). A study by Splett and colleagues (2018) found that in comparison to those already receiving social, emotional, or behavioral support, a universal mental health screener identified an additional 18% of students in need of support. In particular, educators often underestimate the severity of student anxiety or depression, more commonly referring students exhibiting disruptive or inattentive behaviors (Loades & Mastroyannopoulou, 2010; Splett et al., 2018). Overlooking these students can have consequences including intensifying depression, anxiety, or suicidality (Hill et al., 2016; Mullen, 2018; Petito et al., 2020). Thus, universal screening is an important means of proactively and efficiently identifying students in need of support (Koslouski et al., 2024; Moore et al., 2023).

Why is universal SEB or mental health screening not yet widely used in schools? Identified barriers include lack of awareness of existing screeners, funding constraints, and difficulty accessing measures (Bruhn et al., 2014; Wood & Ellis, 2022). Family and community objection to universal mental health screening in schools may also pose barriers (Chafouleas et al., 2010; Stanford, 2023). In some instances, students, families, and communities feel that it is not appropriate for schools to assess students' mental health and raise concerns about student or family privacy (e.g., Palmer et al., 2025). A final concern relates to schools' capacities to provide indicated services (Burns & Rapee, 2021; Chafouleas et al., 2010; Palmer et al., 2025). As previously described, universal screening may increase the number of students identified as in need of support. Schools may anticipate that they cannot meet this increased need. This begs the question of whether it is more helpful or harmful for students and families to know about potential mental health needs in the absence of available school-based supports or referrals. Proactive partnerships with community providers who can provide school- or community-based services may help to reduce this concern.

Considerations for Universal Mental Health Screening in Schools

As shown in Table 6.2, there are several guidance documents available for those interested in implementing universal screening in their schools. Although varying in their recommended number of steps, these guidance documents suggest thoughtful and intentional planning before implementing universal mental health screening. This planning might include identifying goals, researching and selecting an instrument(s), determining a screening schedule (e.g., screening frequency), providing training to those completing the screeners and interpreting resultant data (e.g., teachers), and establishing active or passive consent procedures. Once screening procedures have been implemented, follow-up steps include organizing and interpreting data, using data to inform intervention, and evaluating progress.

TABLE 6.2. Example Resources to Guide Implementation of Universal Mental Health Screening in Schools

Title	Publication year	Authors	Description
Best Practices in Social, Emotional, and Behavioral Screening: An Implementation Guide. Version 2.0	2020	Romer et al.	This guide focuses on the preparation phases of implementing universal mental health screening. Topics include selecting a tool, consent procedures, and planning for data collection and use. (33 pages)
Ready, Set, Go, Review: Screening for Behavioral Health Risk in Schools	2019	SAMHSA	This resource offers detailed guidance on researching, planning, implementing, and evaluating universal mental health screening efforts. A unique consideration is potential funding mechanisms for universal screening. (89 pages)
School Mental Health Quality Guide: Screening	2023	NCSMH	This guide first defines and offers rationale for conducting universal mental health screening. It then shares nine action steps for planning to implement universal mental health screening in a school or district, beginning with assembling a team and concluding with addressing barriers. (25 pages)
School-Wide Universal Screening for Behavioral and Mental Health Issues: Implementation Guidance	2016	Noltemeyer et al.	This resource provides guidance for establishing a school leadership team to coordinate universal mental health screening, selecting an instrument(s), planning and executing screening, using results to inform instruction, and evaluating outcomes. (28 pages)

In general, educator or caregiver (e.g., parent) reporting is recommended when assessing the social, emotional, or behavioral development of children in preschool and early elementary school, whereas student self-reporting is recommended beginning around age 8 (Conijn et al., 2020; Nowinski et al., 2021). Previous research suggests that educators and parents tend to underestimate students' internalizing symptoms, such as experiences of anxiety or depression (Lagattuta et al., 2012; Loades

& Mastroyannopoulou, 2010; Makol & Polo, 2018); thus, student self-reporting is thought to be necessary to fully identify students in need of support. In cases where educator reporting is used, enough time needs to elapse after the start of the school year (e.g., 6–8 weeks) for educators to get to know the students so they are able to provide accurate data.

Schools should carefully consider their student population when selecting measures. Many screeners have been normed with samples that do not match the diversity of U.S. schools, and may not include specific subgroups of students at all (SAMHSA, 2019a). Indicators of mental health and distress vary across cultures (Hodes et al., 2018; Levy & Spurgeon, 2016). Therefore, screeners may not detect the distress of some students or may misidentify particular behaviors or symptoms as signs of distress or concern (SAMHSA, 2019a). One way to address this issue is to include caregivers or community cultural liaisons in measure selection decisions. Soliciting family and community input on topics of concern for universal screening and perceptions toward mental health (e.g., a large concern for today's students; a private, family concern) can also help to inform these decisions. Schools should consider the various types of student diversity in their school, including racial, ethnic, gender identity and expression, disability, and linguistic needs. For example, as shown in Table 6.1, many screeners are available in additional languages, which may be useful to ensuring student access to universal screening. Schools should also research the student populations with which particular tools have been validated, and use this information in measure selection (e.g., selecting a measure validated with a sample that reflects their student population, if possible) and data interpretation (e.g., understanding that screeners may be less accurate with populations for whom it has not been validated or normed).

When considering mental health screening, schools may also want to think about screening for social determinants of health or trauma exposure. As described in Chapter 3, social determinants of health refer to the conditions in which students, families, and staff learn, grow, and play (U.S. Department of Health and Human Services, n.d.). More specifically, social determinants of health refer to the contextual assets and barriers in students' lives including economic stability, education (e.g., access to early childhood education), social and community context (e.g., social support, discrimination), health and clinical care (e.g., access to preventative care), neighborhood and physical environment (e.g., quality of housing conditions), and food (e.g., food security; Henrikson et al., 2019; Koslouski et al., 2024). Because these contextual assets and barriers are closely associated with student mental health and academic success (Spencer, 2018; Xiao et al., 2023), screening for these assets and barriers may provide valuable information to schools. For example, in the absence of additional information, if a student is exhibiting irritable and noncompliant behavior each morning, a behavior plan might be put in place. But, if screening data showed the student was experiencing food insecurity, and thus arriving at school hungry each morning, educators might hypothesize the root cause of the behavior as hunger and facilitate access to breakfast at school each morning.

The practice of universally screening for contextual assets and barriers has begun to emerge in pediatric medical settings (Morone, 2017; Sokol et al., 2019). This screening aims to connect children and families to needed social services (e.g., assistance with employment, housing, or food; Henrikson et al., 2019; Morone, 2017; Sokol et al., 2019). Early evidence from this work suggests reduced family social need and improved mental and physical health of children (Gottlieb et al., 2016). Although some have suggested schools as opportune sites for this type of screening (e.g., Sokol et al., 2019), potential positive or negative consequences (e.g., connection to services, undesired disclosure, perceived invasion of family privacy) that could result from such screening has not yet been thoroughly investigated (Koslouski et al., 2024).

There are divergent opinions on the appropriateness of schools screening for trauma exposure. On the one hand, this information can alert schools to students who may need support and may facilitate access or referral to necessary supports. On the other hand, more than 75% of U.S. adolescents report having experienced a potentially traumatic event (Swedo et al., 2024), and only a subset of these students will experience persistent symptoms of traumatic stress (American Academy of Pediatrics, 2014; Garner et al., 2021; Hambrick et al., 2019). As such, screening for trauma exposure may overidentify students in need of support and lead to negative unintended consequences. For example, students who are not exhibiting symptoms of traumatic stress may receive labels based on screening data that negatively affect their interactions with educators or their perceptions of themselves. Cole and colleagues (2005, 2013), authors of guidance on becoming a trauma-informed school, object to universal trauma screening in schools. Instead, their perspective is that schools should use trauma-informed practices with all students and watch for signs of traumatic stress to identify students in need of additional support.

Interpreting and Using Universal Mental Health Screening Data

A crucial step after administering a universal mental health screener is to interpret and use the resultant data. It is likely that a school mental health professional, administrator, or multidisciplinary team will first organize and review the data. This is important as they hold specific expertise with which to analyze the data for both individual students and the school as a whole. School- or grade-level data review can inform systemic changes and reduce burden on educators by providing a first look at the data. In addition, educators may also be provided with student- or classroom-level data reports. Educators can learn valuable information from these reports to inform their decision making. Next, we provide a sample classroom-level data report and guidance for interpreting and using the data.

Figure 6.1 shows a classroom-level data report summarizing a universal social and emotional screener administered to Ms. Flores's class. The report includes student names, ID numbers, and student ratings in the areas of sadness, worry, positive affect, and social connections. Using this report, Ms. Flores might consider which students need additional supports or referrals, which students might be identified as peer leaders, and any classwide interventions that might be warranted. For example, using this data, Ms. Flores might decide to work on fostering social connections classwide because more than half of her students are indicating potential need in this area. Ms. Flores might also follow up with a school mental health professional or administrator about students endorsing concerning levels of sadness or worry (⚠). Lastly, Ms. Flores might strategically pair students such that those scoring positively (+) across all categories are partnered with those endorsing concerns to allow for peer modeling of coping strategies, positive affect, and relationship skills.

Educators should collaborate with their administrators and school mental health professionals regarding plans to share student-level data with students or families. Due to privacy and ethical concerns (e.g., The Family Educational Rights and Privacy Act [FERPA], 1974), classwide data reports of this nature should not be shared with students or families. Instead, deidentified summary data might be shared with students to illustrate classwide goals or to provide a rationale for a classwide intervention. Educators should ensure that these summaries and associated class discussions do not identify any individual students but instead focus on classwide trends and action steps. In the case of Ms. Flores's data shown in Figure 6.1, she might share with her class that several students are hoping to increase the quality and quantity of their friendships and that the class will be engaging in a number of fun, community-building activities to strengthen their connections with one another.

Receiving these data reports can be overwhelming. Next, we review six questions to assist educators' interpretation of data reports and informed decision making. These six questions can be used to interpret and make decisions about many different types and presentations of data. After introducing these questions, we will illustrate how Ms. Flores might use them to process the data in Figure 6.1.

Classroom: Flores
Grade: 9
Date: October 2025

Student name	ID	Sadness	Worry	Positive affect	Social connections
Carlos	103578	+	+	+	?
Liam	106921	+	⚠	+	+
Aria	101043	+	+	+	+
Muhammad	108456	?	?	+	⚠
Lilah	102198	+	⚠	+	+
Alexander	105763	+	+	⚠	?
Mateo	109320	+	+	+	+
Ava	104085	+	+	+	+
Sofia	107369	+	?	+	⚠
Ethan	105621	?	+	+	⚠
Leila	103894	+	+	⚠	?
Jasmine	101470	+	+	?	?
Shanice	106052	+	+	+	+
Jayden	102893	+	+	+	+
Grace	107316	⚠	+	+	⚠
Keisha	105047	⚠	+	?	⚠
Jamal	101682	+	+	+	⚠
Hannah	109435	+	+	+	?
Malik	102167	+	+	+	+
William	108794	+	+	+	?

⚠ = area of concern, screening data suggest the need for follow-up

? = an area of potential concern, screening data suggest the need for monitoring

\+ = an area of little concern or strength, screening data suggest continuing as is

FIGURE 6.1. Example universal screening classroom data report.

1. **What is my question?** Data reports can be used to answer many different questions. The first step is to determine what question you are trying to answer in this specific viewing of the data. For example, are you interested in how a specific student is doing? Are you interested in classwide trends to inform continued practices or new interventions? Are you curious how different subgroups of students (e.g., by race, gender identity, special education status) responded? We encourage you to approach the data with one question at a time, but to return with additional questions.

2. **What does the data indicate in regard to my question?** Once you have determined your question, analyze the data in relation to your question. For example, if you have a question about a specific student, you

might view the individual student data report or the line of the class-level report specific to that student. If you have a question about classwide trends, you will be looking for patterns across students, perhaps including specific areas of strength and challenge.

3. **What additional data, information, or conversations might inform my understanding of what the data are telling me?** As previously discussed, screening data are intended to provide an efficient snapshot of how an individual is doing. Additional data, information, or conversations may help to meaningfully explain or contextualize the data. Would a review of attendance data, grades, or disciplinary referrals be helpful? Would conversations with specific colleagues, caregivers, or the student be useful in interpreting the data? Determine who should have these conversations and arrange to review additional data sources.

4. **Are there alternative explanations of what the data are telling me?** Let's return to the example of a student displaying irritable and noncompliant behavior each morning. If this student were to complete a social and emotional screener, the data might indicate high levels of frustration, irritability, or worry. Yet this does not paint the full picture. Consider potential alternate explanations for the data (e.g., incomplete information, faulty data collection) to rule these out or adjust your interpretations of the data. You might consult with colleagues to brainstorm some of these alternative explanations or gather more information.

5. **What next steps are needed?** Once you have interpreted what the data are telling you, it is time to determine next steps. At this stage, you will want to consider timing in the school year (e.g., beginning vs. end) to identify reasonable next steps. These might include further assessment, a conversation with the student or their caregiver, a classroom intervention, or referral for school- or community-based services. In determining next steps, consider feasibility (e.g., Will I be able to do this?) and potential barriers. For example, how might you set up a classroom intervention for success or effectively facilitate a difficult conversation with caregivers? Figure 6.2 includes some tips for facilitating difficult conversations with students and families.

6. **How can I track progress or improvement?** After determining and implementing next steps, you will want to track progress or improvement related to the area of concern. Depending on the identified next steps, this might be documenting conversations and referrals made as well as any follow-up actions taken by others. If you decide to implement an intervention in the classroom, you will want to assess the effectiveness of the intervention in some way. Then, you might consider either repeating the screener that informed the initial decision or progress monitoring in some other

Let's imagine that you work in a school that uses universal mental health screening to assess for symptoms of depression and suicidality in students. You facilitated data collection in your homeroom and the school psychologist promptly reviewed the screening results. They shared with you that two students endorsed suicidality and that they have already met with those students to conduct a risk assessment and safety plan. The school psychologist has also reached out to the caregivers of both students to alert them to the concern and facilitate access to supports. The school psychologist wanted you to be aware, however, because of your close relationships with the students and upcoming parent-teacher conferences.

What do you do next?

First, we encourage you to take a moment to process the information yourself. Hearing that two of your students reported suicidality can be distressing and bring up a number of emotions in oneself. Take a moment to process this information and these emotions.

Next, we encourage you to collaborate with the school psychologist on next steps. Will you acknowledge the information with your students or their caregivers if they do not bring it up? How will you respond if they introduce the topic?

When talking with individual students, we encourage you to be mindful of other students that may be within earshot, to thank the student for sharing what they have been struggling with, and to continue to encourage them to access formal and informal supports (e.g., counseling, medical care, church groups, positive social experiences).

When talking with caregivers, we again encourage you to be mindful of others that may be within earshot to protect the student and family's privacy. We encourage you to validate the caregiver(s)' emotions, which may include confusion, worry, anger, frustration, or fear. We also encourage you to be honest about the observations you have had in the classroom (e.g., related to work completion, affect, any changes in behavior or relationships). Lastly, as best you can, encourage caregivers to access formal and informal supports (i.e., both for the student directly and the caregivers as they process the information and support their child).

FIGURE 6.2. Tip box: Discussing concerning data with students or caregivers.

way. For example, Ms. Flores might resurvey her class in 8–10 weeks to assess how many students are reporting strong social connections to determine if her interventions have been helpful and if continued targeted work is needed.

Let's imagine Ms. Flores uses these six questions to process the data shown in Figure 6.1.

In Table 6.3, we illustrate how Ms. Flores might use these questions to answer one specific question she has about the data. We emphasize, however, that Ms. Flores could answer many more questions with the data and we encourage educators to do the same with data they have in their settings. We also point out that Ms. Flores's answers are not right or wrong—there are many ways to approach, interpret, and act upon data. Instead, this is an example to illustrate how an educator might use these six questions to interpret and act upon universal screening data in their setting.

Conclusion

Universal screening can be an important component of a comprehensive school mental health system. Universal screeners can help to prevent mental health concerns from going unnoticed and allow for intervention before concerns become more severe. Because screeners are designed to be brief, follow-up assessment, data collection, and conversations will be needed to identify next steps. Educators can use universal screening data to inform decisions for individual students, small groups, or entire classrooms. Next, we turn to multi-tiered systems of support, discussing interventions that can be used to assist students exhibiting mental health need to prevent them from intensifying.

RELATED RESOURCES

Center on Multi-Tiered Systems of Support
https://mtss4success.org
Provides infographics and briefs describing universal screening procedures and data-based decision making.

School Health Assessment and Performance Evaluation System—Assessment Library
https://theshapesystem.com/assessmentlibrary
Offers short summaries of available screening tools, which can be filtered by domain of interest, student age, and cost.

Comprehensive, Integrated Three-Tiered Model of Prevention (Ci3T)
www.ci3t.org/screening
Includes overview and training videos on universal screening as well as information about several social, emotional, and behavioral screening tools.

TABLE 6.3. Example of How to Use the Six Questions to Make Data-Based Decisions

Guiding question	Ms. Flores's answer
1. *What is my question?*	Ms. Flores is curious how her high-achieving students are doing. She has seen and heard a lot about the high levels of stress and pressure experienced by high-achieving students and wants to make sure that she's not overlooking any of these students.
2. *What do the data indicate in regard to my question?*	Ms. Flores looks at the results for Lilah, Jayden, and Malik. Although it appears that Jayden and Malik are doing well on these indicators, Lilah has reported a concerning level of worry.
3. *What additional data, information, or conversations might inform my understanding of what the data are telling me?*	A couple of additional data sources could be helpful for interpreting these data. First, Ms. Flores would like to have a brief conversation with Lilah about the results to confirm her experiences of substantial worry and to ask if there are specific ways she can support Lilah. Ms. Flores would also like to briefly check in with her colleagues that also have Lilah in class to see how she is doing in their classes. Finally, Ms. Flores plans to review Lilah's recent grades and performance in her class to look for any significant changes.
4. *Are there alternative explanations of what the data are telling me?*	Ms. Flores brainstorms two alternative explanations for what the data are telling her. First, although Ms. Flores approached the data with a question about her high-achieving students, the worry Lilah is reporting may not be tied to academics or achievement. Instead, there could be family or social stressors at play, or generalized worry that extends beyond any specific stressor. Second, in conjunction with her quick check-in conversation with Lilah, Ms. Flores can rule out a measurement error in which Lilah intentionally or unintentionally selected answers that do not reflect her experiences or a programming error in which the data were incorrectly summarized in Ms. Flores's report.
5. *What next steps are needed?*	Through a brief and thoughtful conversation with Lilah, Ms. Flores confirms that Lilah is experiencing high levels of worry. Ms. Flores reaches out to the school psychologist and guidance counselor to determine next steps. Lilah's guidance counselor is able to meet briefly with Lilah the following day to learn more about what is going on and to offer supports. She will also reach out to Lilah's caregivers to share the concern and collaborate on next steps. Ms. Flores continues to keep an eye on Lilah for any concerning changes in behavior, and decides to offer all of her students one late pass for an assignment of their choosing, which can be used when other commitments or stressors prevent them from giving their full effort to one of her assignments.
6. *How can I track progress or improvement?*	Ms. Flores plans to quickly check in with Lilah and her guidance counselor every couple of weeks to see how things are going and if there are any additional supports she can offer. The guidance counselor will use an anxiety screener to monitor Lilah's symptoms over time and to determine whether additional community-based referrals are needed.

CHAPTER 7

Multi-Tiered Systems of Support

KEY IDEAS

1. Tiered levels of support help prevent mental health concerns from intensifying.
2. Multi-tiered systems of support include tiered interventions, systematic decision-making procedures, and progress monitoring.
3. Schoolwide collaboration is needed for tiered systems of support to be effective.

Luca often pushes papers off his desk during math class, which makes other students laugh. His teacher, Ms. Jackson, is frustrated—the behavior demonstrates Luca's own disengagement, and it distracts other kids as well. Ms. Jackson decides it is time to try something new. Twice a week, she has students break up into stations. She rotates between stations, making sure she sees Luca's group for at least 15 minutes. She provides Luca with extra attention and positive feedback during his time at her station, and her teacher assistant floats among the other groups to monitor the computer station, the games corner, and the independent workstation. As Ms. Jackson spends more time working with small groups, she realizes that Luca and a few of the other students who don't qualify for special education services really benefit from additional instruction on some of the foundational concepts. She also notices that Luca is very quiet during small groups—almost shy! She is surprised at how this slight change in support impacts his experiences and engagement in the classroom. Over the next month, Ms. Jackson tracks Luca's progress and sees that he is completing more assignments without shutting down and is shouting out less frequently. She feels less frustrated and is happy to see Luca's increased engagement during class.

Differentiated Supports and Mental Health

Each member of the school community needs different types of resources and support to maintain their mental health. The resources and support will shift over time, depending on personal lives outside of school, interpersonal dynamics within the school, and broader societal events and contexts. To meet these various needs, many schools are developing and implementing tiered systems of support. In this chapter, our goal is to provide educators with a bird's-eye view of different tiered systems of support, including how they developed, their potential benefits, and possible implementation challenges. We invite educators to consider how tiered supports might impact student and educator mental health, and what their own roles are within these systems.

Tiered systems of support are closely linked to the public health model of prevention in which practitioners proactively recognize needs and strategically align resources to meet those needs (Weist et al., 2014). These systems vary in their areas of focus: some offer tiered supports in academic content areas such as English or math skills, whereas others provide tiered supports for the development of social, emotional, and behavioral skills. Each of these tiered systems can help promote positive mental health outcomes in schools. For example, Kelm and McIntosh (2012) found that implementing tiered systems of behavioral support increased educators' self-efficacy by helping them to respond more systematically and equitably to challenging student behaviors. Regarding student outcomes, Eiraldi and colleagues (2019) found that the number of office discipline referrals declined in two urban K–8 schools when evidence-based, tiered mental health supports were implemented with fidelity. Similarly, Weist and colleagues (2022) found that implementing an integrated system of schoolwide tiered mental health supports reduced office discipline referrals and in-school suspensions in elementary schools. Taken together, research on tiered systems of support demonstrates their positive impact on both student and educator mental health outcomes.

Special Education as the Original Tiered System of Support

There are many types of tiered systems of support, including *multi-tiered systems of support (MTSS)*, *Response to Intervention (RTI)*, and *Positive Behavioral Interventions and Supports (PBIS)*. Before we begin to unpack the differences and similarities across them, we first need to acknowledge the original system through which differentiated academic and behavioral supports were formally offered across K–12 schools: the special education system. According to federal law mandating its existence (Individuals with Disabilities Education Act [IDEA]), the purpose of special education is to

> ensure that all children with disabilities have available to them a free appropriate public education that emphasizes special education and related services designed to meet their unique needs and prepare them for further education, employment, and independent living. (IDEA, 2004)

The phrase "designed to meet their unique needs" demonstrates that differentiated supports are core to special education. Within the special education system, these differentiated supports are identified and addressed through the development of an Individualized Education Program (IEP) for students who meet eligibility criteria for a disability and require specialized instruction to make adequate educational progress. IDEA was instituted in the 1970s because of advocacy from families of children with disabilities, disabled individuals, and their allies. At the time, many children with disabilities were not attending school at all. Advocates argued against the idea that any child was "uneducable," and asserted that what was needed was a more differentiated system that could provide all students with a free and appropriate public education. Today, approximately 15% of students meet special education eligibility criteria (NCES, 2024e). Specially designed instruction is delivered based on a comprehensive evaluation of each student's strengths, needs, and present levels of performance. Annual goals and benchmarks are created by the IEP team, which includes the students' caregivers. This promotes accountability for providing the student with the supports they need to be successful, and to mitigate the impact of the disability on their educational progress.

IDEA has allowed many students to receive the differentiated academic, social, emotional, or behavioral supports they need to be successful in school. But many students who do not have a disability *also* need support to be successful in school, as there are many experiences other than disability that have adverse effects on development. Although special education services are a crucial resource for many students, it is not feasible nor sustainable for special education to be the only mechanism by which students receive differentiated support. MTSS provides targeted support to students for whom school is challenging for a variety of reasons, including but not limited to the effect of a disability on learning. Through targeted intervention, tiered systems of support prevent academic and behavioral challenges from intensifying.

The use of MTSS by schools and districts is highly encouraged and incentivized in the federal Every Student Succeeds Act (ESSA, 2015). ESSA encourages schools and districts to use MTSS to ensure that more students have access to appropriate educational opportunities and incentivizes the use of MTSS through funding opportunities for training and implementation (Schaffer, 2022). Implementation of MTSS differs from school to school, however. Further, the roles of individual educators within these systems can vary greatly depending on a school's organizational structure and community dynamics.

STOP AND REFLECT

1. Think of a time when you had difficulty learning something in school. What support was provided (or could have been provided) to help you learn?
2. Think about students in your current setting. What are some of the reasons that they need extra support?

Components of MTSS

What exactly is MTSS? Regardless of whether a tiered system is designed to provide support for academics, social skills, emotional development, behavior, or physical health, MTSS is characterized by three key components: (1) different interventions for different students, (2) systematic ways of deciding which interventions are appropriate for each student, and (3) systematic ways of monitoring students' progress in response to interventions.

MTSS Component 1: Different Interventions for Different Students

The MTSS framework is designed to facilitate student learning. It operates under the assertion that not all students learn in the same way or need the same types of support for learning. As introduced in Chapter 4, educators may need to differentiate instructional content, processes, products, or learning environments to meet the needs of individual students (Tomlinson, 2014). These changes can be thought of as "interventions": something educators do to try and improve student outcomes. These interventions may include *antecedent* strategies (e.g., planning lessons that are appropriately paced), *teaching* strategies (e.g., using explicit pedagogical approaches), or *consequence* strategies (e.g., strategic, planned responses to behavior; Kilgus et al., 2015). Interventions may target a student's academic, social, emotional, or behavioral outcomes. Typically, RTI models tend to focus on tiered academic supports whereas PBIS models tend to center behavioral interventions. Regardless of the intervention focus, the idea of MTSS is that all available interventions are organized into various "tiers" that represent increasingly resource intensive interventions (Vetter et al., 2024). These tiers are often referred to as Tier 1 (universal), Tier 2 (targeted), and

Tier 3 (intensive). In Figure 7.1 we provide examples of interventions that may occur at each tier.

Tier 1 interventions are provided to all students within a classroom or school and are typically delivered by the general education teacher. In alignment with the principles of Universal Design for Learning, these interventions support students' ability to engage, receive information, and demonstrate learning in multiple ways (Thomas et al., 2023). Examples of Tier 1 interventions include developing and teaching schoolwide behavioral expectations; providing visual cues to support verbal instruction; establishing classroom routines for transitions; providing immediate positive praise or corrective feedback and opportunities to respond; and modeling of expected behaviors by adults.

Level of Intervention	Examples of Academic Interventions	Examples of Behavioral Interventions
Tier 1	• Applying Universal Design for Learning principles (Ralabate, 2011) • Explicit instruction with feedback and guided practice (Hughes, Morris, et al., 2017)	• Schoolwide conflict resolution lessons; restorative circles (Garnett et al., 2020) • Schoolwide SEL curricula; mindfulness practices (Vetter, 2024)
Tier 2	• Small-group literacy lessons focused on reading comprehension, fluency, phonemic awareness, phonics, and/or vocabulary (Porowski, 2024) • Small-group math lessons, such as Number Rockets (Fuchs, 2008) or Pirate Math Equation Quest (Powell, 2020)	• Check in/check out (Maggin et al., 2015) • Small groups focused on coping with trauma (Jaycox et al., 2009) or social pragmatics (Vetter, 2024)
Tier 3	• IEP with individualized content-specific goals, with associated specialized instruction (IDEA, 2004) • Access to a paraeducator to support academic instruction (IDEA, 2004)	• Behavior intervention plan (BIP) developed through functional behavioral analysis (FBA) (Scott et al., 2008) • Cognitive coping training (Beck, 2011) or cognitive-behavioral therapy intervention (Jaycox et al., 2012) delivered by school clinician

FIGURE 7.1. Examples of Tier 1, Tier 2, and Tier 3 interventions.

Tier 2 interventions are offered to a smaller portion of students who demonstrate a need for additional support beyond the Tier 1 interventions that are provided to all students. Tier 2 interventions may be implemented within the general education classroom or in a separate space within the school building, as they are often delivered to small groups of students. Examples of Tier 2 interventions include small-group instruction with a reading interventionist or a social skills group led by a school social worker. Check-in/check-out (Campbell & Anderson, 2013) is also a common Tier 2 intervention in which students begin and end their day with a familiar adult and use a behavior reinforcement sheet throughout the school day to receive regular feedback on their progress toward behavioral goals.

Tier 3 interventions are the most intensive. Although states differ widely in how they conceptualize the relationship between special education and MTSS (Berkeley et al., 2020), special education services are often considered a Tier 3 intervention. However, students do not need to have an IEP or 504 plan to receive Tier 3 MTSS interventions. Tier 3 interventions may include the development of an individualized behavior intervention plan (BIP), specialized instruction with an academic specialist, or counseling with the school psychologist or social worker. Students receiving special education services may also receive these interventions (services) in settings or modalities more typically associated with Tier 2, such as a small group led by a special educator, related services provider, or paraprofessional.

MTSS "tiers" are sometimes referred to as *layers* of support, because students should continue to receive Tier 1 supports even if they receive Tier 2 or Tier 3 supports (Simonsen et al., 2021). To provide an analogy, adding Tier 2 or Tier 3 MTSS supports is like adding layers of clothing when it is cold out: when someone decides that a T-shirt is not warm enough, they add protective layers like a sweatshirt or jacket, but do not take the T-shirt off. Instead, they put the sweatshirt or jacket on top of the layer they are already wearing. When students receive Tier 2 and Tier 3 supports, they also receive Tier 1 supports. In Figure 7.2, we provide a visual example of these three tiers within an MTSS system. Interventions that address students' academic, social, emotional, behavioral, and physical development can be provided in both school and community settings, as seen in the figure.

MTSS Component 2: Systematic Decision-Making Procedures

Having tiered levels of support available begs the question: Which students get access to each tier? A second key component of MTSS is that there are systematic procedures for making decisions about which students would

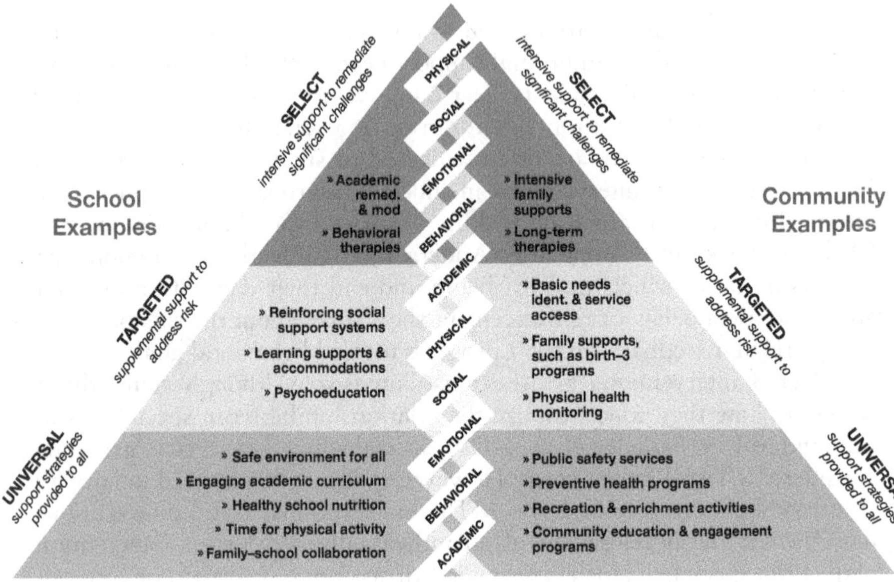

FIGURE 7.2. Integrated MTSS: Whole school, community, and child. Reprinted with permission from the University of Connecticut Collaboratory on School and Child Health.

benefit from which tiers of intervention. Consider a school that has three different fourth-grade classrooms. Each of the three fourth-grade classroom educators can identify students within their own class who would likely benefit from Tier 2 or Tier 3 support. But how do these students' needs compare to those of the larger group of fourth-grade students? To understand the needs of the entire fourth-grade student population and provide equitable access to Tier 2 and Tier 3 supports, there must be a systematic process for data collection and decision making.

MTSS is designed to aid schools in collecting data and using data to distribute resources among students. As described in Chapter 6, universal screening is an important tool for collecting these types of data. Universal screenings provide an initial starting point for recognizing needs across a school building or grade level, including academic, social, emotional, and behavioral needs. In addition, most schools implementing MTSS utilize a referral process by which educators can request preventative services for specific students in their classroom at any time during the school year.

Data collected through screenings and referrals should then be reviewed by an interdisciplinary team. This team might be called an MTSS implementation team, student support team, child study team, or something similar. This team is likely to include a variety of educators (e.g., general educators, special educators, school mental health providers, administrators) who regularly review student data and make decisions about the types of Tier 1, Tier 2, or Tier 3 supports to provide. Generally, all staff members can participate in referring students for additional support, and the MTSS team uses this data to systematically allocate resources. To promote equitable interpretations of MTSS data, it is important that the team establishes a shared vision for expected student outcomes and is composed of staff members with varied roles and areas of expertise. Although family members are not typically part of the MTSS team due to protections on student data, MTSS teams can consider soliciting feedback from families and students as they develop their MTSS system so that it is responsive to the unique goals and needs of the school community.

The goal of MTSS is to distribute available resources in ways that are fair and maximize students' and educators' capacity to be successful. But the equitable distribution of resources within school communities does not happen without strategic and ongoing efforts to do so. Because schools are microcosms of society, they fall into the same patterns of systemic racism and ableism seen in broader society. Without systematic efforts to counter racism and ableism, white and able-bodied students and educators will continue to receive more support than students and educators of color and those with disabilities (DeMatthews, 2020). MTSS can help school communities to collect and use data that highlight and address the impact of ableism and racism in schools. For example, MTSS can help schools understand which interventions best support students with disabilities in accessing fair educational opportunities as well as help ensure that educators' disciplinary decisions are equitable rather than shaped by biases toward or against certain students.

STOP AND REFLECT

1. To what extent does your school's current MTSS promote equity?
2. What facilitates or threatens its success in doing so?

Component 3: Systematic Progress Monitoring and Rearrangement

The third characteristic of MTSS is that there is an established procedure for monitoring students' progress. If a student is receiving additional supports, it is important to make sure that those supports are generating positive outcomes. To do so, educators can use various types of progress monitoring systems to track student growth over time, such as short assessments repeated at regular intervals (e.g., daily, weekly, or monthly) and comparison of student data across assessments. Progress monitoring data shows educators how the student responds to the intervention. In addition, fidelity of implementation data also needs to be collected, which measures how well the intervention itself is being implemented. If, for example, a student is supposed to receive math facts practice five days a week for 10 minutes per day, fidelity of implementation data will indicate whether that is actually happening. If the student is not making progress, and the intervention has not been implemented as intended, different conclusions should be made than if the intervention was implemented as intended (Sanetti & Collier-Meek, 2019). If fidelity of implementation is low, implementer training might be needed, or a more feasible intervention might make sense (e.g., the original one was too time intensive or burdensome to implement). If the intervention is being implemented with fidelity, but the student is not making progress, then a new intervention may be warranted. Interventions can be adjusted responsively, with regard to intensity, type, and modality (August et al., 2018).

MTSS is designed so that students can fluidly move across tiers of support, with data to support this movement (August et al., 2018). In other words, students who receive Tier 2 or Tier 3 services may not necessarily receive them for a whole school year. There is no universal amount of time that any one intervention should be tested before changing interventions; data should be reviewed at regular intervals to determine next steps (Iris Center, 2025). At the time of this writing, MTSS processes varied greatly across schools. Researchers are actively studying the best practices for "decision rules" regarding how to move students across tiers of support and adapt interventions over time (August et al., 2018).

PBIS as a Form of MTSS

To provide an example of these three components of MTSS, we now turn to PBIS, a type of MTSS focused on providing preventative behavioral supports (Horner et al., 2020; Sugai & Horner, 2009). For example, schoolwide implementation of PBIS can reduce office disciplinary referrals, thereby keeping students in the classroom rather than excluding them (e.g., Bradshaw et al., 2012). In PBIS systems, Tier 1 supports provided to all students include transparent and explicit behavioral expectations, instruction of the skills needed to meet these expectations, and educator modeling of these skills (Barrett et al., 2018; Weist et al., 2018). For example, explicit instruction of SEL skills may be considered part of Tier 1 of PBIS (Barrett et al., 2018).

Although *all* students in schools implementing PBIS receive Tier 1 supports, only some students receive Tier 2 and Tier 3 supports. In a PBIS model there are mechanisms through which educators can refer a student for Tier 2 and Tier 3 supports. An interdisciplinary team will then meet to discuss educator concerns and recommend Tier 1, Tier 2, or Tier 3 supports. Tier 1 supports might include strengthening classwide SEL instruction or reviewing classroom routines and expectations after school breaks. Tier 2 supports might include small-group SEL instruction, check-in/check-out systems, or a social skills lunch group. Tier 3 supports might include a functional behavioral analysis and behavior intervention plan or counseling with a school mental health provider. Then, the educators providing these Tier 1, 2, and 3 supports collect progress monitoring data to determine if the intervention is improving student learning or behavior. Data used for progress monitoring may include educator observations, behavioral rating scales, check-in/check-out data collection, or disciplinary data. Finally, the team will reconvene (often after 6–12 weeks of the intervention[s] being in place) to review progress monitoring data and provide recommendations (e.g., adjusting tiered supports, next steps). Through this process of providing responsive, tiered behavioral supports, school teams can prevent behavioral concerns from intensifying.

How Can Tiered, Differentiated Systems Prevent Mental Health Challenges?

MTSS can prevent mental health concerns from intensifying in several ways. First, Tier 1 practices help educators identify students at risk of serious mental health concerns. For example, Tier 1 interventions such as universal screenings can help educators to identify students experiencing suicidal ideation and coordinate support before risks intensify (Goodman-Scott et al., 2022). In addition, targeted supports provided by MTSS in Tiers 2 and 3 can help to support mental health by increasing students' coping skills, self-efficacy, and sense of belonging in school. Finally, when students receive instruction at their level, with appropriate supports, they are more likely to be engaged in learning and willing to take risks. Tiered instructional supports can thereby reduce anxiety about learning tasks.

Likewise, MTSS supports *educator* mental health by increasing role clarity and making the distribution of resources more transparent. Educators' well-being may be threatened both by ambiguity in their roles (i.e., not knowing the boundaries of what is expected of them) and by inequitable distribution of resources across roles (i.e., being asked to take on more work than their colleagues). MTSS can provide educators with clarity on their respective roles related to student needs, while also affirming that all students belong to all staff members. MTSS establishes the norm that all students are all staff members' responsibility, and that all educators are critical to the success of the system.

STOP AND REFLECT

1. What role(s) do you have in delivering tiered supports in your setting?
2. How is your mental health affected by role clarity and work distribution in your setting?

Implementing MTSS to Support School Mental Health

With increased familiarity with the characteristics of MTSS and the impact of tiered systems on school mental health, educators might be wondering: What is *my* role in creating and implementing tiered systems that support school mental health?

First, it is important to recognize that schools vary widely in their implementation of MTSS, so educators' roles will look different across schools. Berkeley and colleagues (2020) found that 39 out of 50 states had a statewide tiered intervention model described on their Department of Education websites, and many offered MTSS training to support implementation. For example, in Massachusetts, a state-funded SEL Academy has provided leaders in over 190 schools with training on how to integrate SEL initiatives, mental health supports, and other student supports in their school using MTSS (Vetter et al., 2024). For any MTSS implementation to be effective, district and school leaders need to be committed to supporting ongoing training and coordination efforts (Freeman et al., 2015). One step that educators might take is exploring the models and training being promoted within their own states and advocating for more training to be brought to their schools.

Second, we encourage educators to consider that tiered systems that improve student and educator mental health are characterized by a shared commitment to cultural reciprocity, and a willingness to frequently reflect on and evolve the system. Expectations of what is "good" or "respectful" behavior in school are shaped by culture, and there are vast cultural differences between students and educators in many schools—including differences in race, ethnicity, class, language, and generation. When tiered systems are designed to reward behaviors seen as good or respectful by educators and administrators, without input from students and families, students with the greatest cultural distance from their educators are more likely to be excluded. When this occurs, MTSS, which aims to increase students' access to appropriate services and support, can reproduce racial inequities in schools rather than disrupt them (Fallon et al., 2023).

Educators might consider advocating for changes that increase the cultural responsiveness of existing systems. As Banks and Obiakor (2015) write, "Classrooms are not culturally neutral terrains, but rather are constructed around a set of norms, values, and expected behaviors that are culturally bound" (p. 84). Ways to integrate cultural considerations into MTSS include (1) identifying and emphasizing the strengths of the school community (not just needs), (2) making space to talk about race and its impact on the school community, and (3) using culturally responsive assessments during data collection and progress monitoring (DeBoer et al., 2022). "Color blind" approaches that minimize cultural differences can distract from addressing the cultural nuances that lead to inequities, whereas acknowledging and addressing cultural differences can help the community to understand their collective strength and see culture as part of the solution rather than a problem (Banks et al., 2015). When implementing tiered supports, whether at Tier 1, 2, or 3, educators should always consider the cultural context in which the intervention is delivered, including the cultures of the school, provider, and student (Malone et al., 2022). Cultural adaptations of interventions, informed by input from members of the school community, may include both changing the content to align with students' customs and language as well as shifting program delivery, such as setting or facilitator (Brown et al., 2018).

Finally, we encourage educators to remember that the outcomes of MTSS are deeply linked to the trust and collaboration of the adults in the school community: unless adults are willing to engage in critical, collaborative reflection about the system itself, it is going to be more challenging for MTSS to improve mental health outcomes for students or educators in the school community. When adults engage in critical collaboration and reflection, MTSS offers school communities a way to establish shared visions for the outcomes they hope to see in their communities and systematic, data-informed processes they can use to move toward these visions (Bohanon & Wu, 2011).

Establishing a vision for success, including what success looks like academically, socially, emotionally, and behaviorally—for both educators and students—can be a source of hope and pride for a school community. As a starting point for vision setting, Bohanon and Wu (2011) offer three questions to guide reflection and goal setting within school teams: "What do we want all students to know and be able to do academically, behaviorally, socially, and emotionally? How will we know whether students are developing the aforementioned skills? How will we respond when students are not developing these skills in all domains?" (p. 38).

STOP AND REFLECT

1. How would you currently answer the questions offered by Bohanon and Wu?
2. Do you think your colleagues share your responses?
3. How might you move toward more consensus on these questions in your setting?

Conclusion

We encourage educators to take some time to build relationships with colleagues in their schools who play a role in tiered systems of support but have different professional roles. For example, it is important for general educators to get to know speech and language pathologists in their setting, and for school social workers to get to know paraeducators. The more relationships that are developed, the better each community member can understand the various types of support available to students. With strong relationships, educators can better collaborate to identify interventions that are most beneficial to students, and determine which professionals are best positioned to provide the intervention. Even though establishing and maintaining MTSS is a complex and ongoing process, efforts to develop and sustain tiered systems of support are an important investment for school mental health.

RELATED RESOURCES

Center on Positive Behavioral Interventions and Supports
www.pbis.org
Provides resources and trainings to support implementation of PBIS.

National Center on Intensive Intervention
https://intensiveintervention.org
Offers evidence and guidance regarding tiered academic and behavioral supports.

Council for Exceptional Children's High Leverage Practices
https://highleveragepractices.org
Provides a comprehensive guide of high leverage, evidence-based practices that can be implemented as part of tiered supports for students with and without disabilities.

CHAPTER 8

Family and Community Partnerships

KEY IDEAS

1. By collaborating with families, educators can more effectively support students' mental health.
2. Cultural reciprocity is key to effective communication and collaboration between educators and families.
3. Educators can help families to prevent student mental health concerns from intensifying by connecting them with resources in the school and community.

Daniela is an eighth grader in Ms. Rayas's class. At the beginning of the school year, Daniela appears to be thriving academically and socially. However, by mid-October, Ms. Rayas notices that Daniela's grades have declined, she is withdrawn in class, and she is less talkative at lunch. Ms. Rayas puts in extra effort to talk with Daniela before and after class, but Daniela is quiet and disengaged in these conversations. For the next couple of weeks, Ms. Rayas tries calling Daniela's mom to check in with her but reaches voicemail each time. Ms. Rayas asks Daniela if there is a better way to connect with her mom, and Daniela says that sometimes her mom doesn't reply because she's self-conscious about her English speaking skills. With this new information, Ms. Rayas uses an online translator to send a simple email to Daniela's mom, explaining that if she is willing to meet, they will have an interpreter available.

Daniela's mom replies and agrees to meet. During the meeting, Ms. Rayas begins by sharing some of Daniela's strengths: she looks out for her peers and has tremendous academic potential. Ms. Rayas then shares her concerns about Daniela's recent changes in affect and declining grades. Daniela's mom, Rosa, explains that Daniela's father is in the U.S. Navy and was recently deployed. Rosa says they are both worried about him and having a tough time adjusting to their new routines. She knows Daniela is also struggling but isn't sure how to help.

Ms. Rayas expresses gratitude to Rosa for sharing what's been going on in their family and acknowledges the difficulty of their family's situation. Ms. Rayas asks Rosa if she might allow Daniela to check in with a school counselor to talk about what has been going on and to establish some in-school supports to help her academically and emotionally. Rosa agrees that this would be helpful. Ms. Rayas also offers to connect Rosa with the school's social worker who can share community resources that are available to support both Rosa and Daniela. Ms. Rayas also takes the opportunity to ask Rosa about her preferences for future communication and establishes that emails or meetings with an interpreter are best. Ms. Rayas ends the meeting by reiterating Daniela's strengths and her desire to see Daniela do well and asking if it's okay to reach out again soon to check in on how Daniela is doing.

School Mental Health beyond School Walls

Much of this book addresses knowledge, skills, and practices that facilitate mental health for members of the school community *within* the school building. For example, in Chapter 2, we explore the important role that school climate plays in mental health outcomes for students and educators. In Chapters 3 (whole-child instruction), 4 (SEL), and 6 (universal screening), we demonstrate the impact of educators' practices on student mental health outcomes. But as the vignette demonstrates, regardless of educators' efforts to support mental health within school, many factors beyond educators' control shape students' mental health.

In Chapter 3, we briefly introduced Bronfenbrenner's (1979) ecological model. We return to that theoretical framework here to consider the many factors that can shape students' mental health over time. Students' mental health is shaped by their biological makeup, their interactions with their family and loved ones, the culture and dynamics of their community (such as their athletic teams, neighbors, religious groups, or online friends), and the environment around them. Because educators' interactions with students at school are affected by all these other layers of influence, it is essential for educators to understand how outside-of-school factors relate to efforts to improve school mental health.

In the case of the vignette, Ms. Rayas has no control over the deployment of Daniela's dad. However, knowledge of what Daniela is experiencing can help Ms. Rayas and her colleagues to support Daniela's educational progress. Without Ms. Rayas's effort to partner with Daniela's family, she would not have understood the factors affecting Daniela's mental health, nor been able to help connect Daniela with supportive resources addressing the root of her current mental health challenges. Likewise, Daniela's mom, Rosa, is better able to understand her daughter's experience and academic progress when she can collaborate with the professionals who spend significant time with her daughter in school.

In some ways, we hesitate to write a separate chapter about family and community partnerships in a book on school mental health, as family and community partnerships are an integral aspect of all topics discussed in this book. For example, emergency response (Chapter 13) depends heavily on coordination and collaboration with community partners. Likewise, the provision of differentiated supports (Chapter 7) depends on the sharing of information about students between school and home. Both families and community members hold integral expertise about students. Their partnership is crucial for the implementation of school-based mental health supports and services. We hope that readers can see the importance of family and community partnerships as a throughline in this book.

However, we chose to dedicate a chapter to family and community partnerships precisely because of the significance of these relationships. Researchers who have designed interventions focused on family-school partnerships have found that increased communication and collaboration is directly related to improved student mental health (Sheridan et al., 2019; Smith et al., 2020). We felt it was crucial to provide educators with a dedicated space and opportunity to reflect on their roles within these relationships.

We begin the chapter by discussing the different meanings of "partnership," and the ways that educators might build relationships with families and community members. Then, focusing on family relationships, we discuss specific strategies for partnering with families about student mental health. We draw on the concept of cultural reciprocity as a key communication framework, considering that conversations about student mental health are often vulnerable, sensitive, and informed by cultural beliefs for all collaborators. Next, we address the important role of educators in connecting families to community-based mental health resources. We conclude with an invitation for educators to engage in resource-mapping within their own communities. Understanding community-based mental health resources can help educators to connect students and their families with the resources they may need—ultimately improving student mental health and success in school.

Throughout this book, we have chosen to use the term *family caregivers* instead of *parents*, except when citing research specifically focused on parents. We use the term *family caregivers* to refer to the people who are responsible for taking care of a child. Family caregivers may include parents, grandparents, aunts, uncles, older siblings, or foster care providers. We use the term *family caregivers* because not all students' parents are able to be active participants in their lives, and because other adults often play crucial roles in raising students.

STOP AND REFLECT

1. This chapter is about family and community partnerships. What does the word *partnership* mean to you?
2. What are some of the best partnerships you've experienced? What made them successful?

Defining Partnership

What does it mean to *partner* with family caregivers? Partnering with family caregivers likely means different things to each educator. Researchers who study family-school partnerships include a wide range of activities under the umbrella of *partnership*, including families' involvement in homework and school-based activities, educators' involvement in supporting home activities, and relationships between families and educators (Smith et al., 2020). The ways that individual educators view family partnerships are often shaped by their own experiences in school, their professional training programs, and the structure and organizational dynamics of their school. For example, some schools offer facilitated opportunities to build relationships with families, such as through conferences, family nights, or cultural events open to the community. Some schools employ family liaisons and interpreters to support educators' abilities to build relationships with families. School leaders may set explicit expectations regarding how often and in what modalities educators are expected to communicate with families. Other schools explicitly or implicitly limit opportunities to build relationships with families through English-only policies, closed buildings, or limited hours that do not align with family's work schedules, for example. Still others fall somewhere in the middle, emphasizing the importance of these relationships while also setting boundaries regarding the availability of educators outside of contractual time. Although some educators may feel fully supported in their efforts to build relationships with families, other educators may feel isolated in their efforts. In this chapter, we discuss strategies that educators can use to partner with families and to navigate these different external norms and expectations regarding this partnership.

Strong relationships between families and educators predict a variety of positive mental health outcomes for students (Sheridan et al., 2019). For example, Wang and Sheikh-Khalil (2014) found that the extent to which parents were involved in their child's schooling was associated with high school students' engagement in school, grade point average, and symptoms of depression. In a review of research on family-school partnerships, Smith and colleagues (2020) found that increasing communication between families and schools was associated with improved academic, behavioral, and mental health outcomes. In fact, without relationships with families, educators may not be able to provide students with access to the supports they need for their mental health. For example, many students' Individualized Education Plans (IEPs) include goals and services designed to support their mental health. If family caregivers do not agree with the IEP and therefore do not sign it, the school cannot provide these services. In some states, family caregivers also need to provide permission before school-based clinicians can provide nonemergency services in small group settings (e.g., counseling, skills groups). When educators and families partner together to build a support plan for the student, each party is more likely to understand the student's needs and thereby develop and agree on an effective plan for meeting those needs.

There are many ways to partner with families to facilitate positive mental health outcomes for students. The foundation of these partnerships is communication between families and educators. Therefore, in the following section, we offer the concept of cultural reciprocity as a key starting point for effective communication and collaboration between educators and families, especially in conversations regarding student mental health.

Cultural Reciprocity Regarding Mental Health

Cultural reciprocity is an important way of framing educator-family-community interactions around student mental health. Yosso (2005) defines culture as "behaviors and values that are learned, shared, and exhibited by a group of people . . . [which are] neither fixed nor static" (p. 75). Culture is much more than race, ethnicity, or nationality. It includes beliefs about the value of education, the purpose of school, the trustworthiness of school professionals, and expectations for students' academic and behavioral development.

Culture also informs how students, educators, and families understand mental health (Caplan, 2019; Jensen & Mendenhall, 2018; Planey et al., 2019). For example, socioeconomic status, or class, may shape family caregivers' beliefs about mental health services. Family caregivers may see mental health supports as a privilege they cannot afford, or unhelpful due to differences in language, class, race, or other identity markers (Wang et al., 2019). Furthermore, there is wide variation in how mental health is defined and described across languages. Therefore, even with translations or interpretation services, communication and interpretation may not always be straightforward across linguistic differences (Acharya et al., 2017).

Interactions are shaped by the culture of an educator as well as the culture of students' families. Culture includes expectations regarding the role of a family caregiver, expectations regarding the extent to which discussions about mental health should be public or private, beliefs regarding the use of medication to treat mental health concerns, and thoughts regarding the root causes of mental health challenges. Often, cultural beliefs and dispositions toward education and mental health also vary among members of the education team or the family caregiving unit. For example, a school psychologist and a special educator may have different cultural beliefs about how to talk about depression, or a mother and father about how to manage their child's behavior at home.

Cultural reciprocity is the idea that these differences are acknowledged and respected during partnership. It means not only seeking to understand others' cultures, but also identifying one's own culture and how it shapes interactions (Kalyanpur & Harry, 2012). It means recognizing more subtle types of difference rather than stereotyping others, and positions both family caregivers and educators as holding power (Kalyanpur & Harry, 2012).

To effectively partner with families, it is crucial that educators reflect on their own beliefs and practices related to mental health. Once an educator recognizes that their own beliefs and practices are cultural, they can begin to recognize and respect the ways that the beliefs and practices of others are also informed by their cultures. This also helps educators to have more empathy for the reasons why families might hold the beliefs and practices that they do and to better integrate families' cultures into their classrooms. For example, educators might reflect upon how their race, ethnicity, age, gender, educational background, disability status, familial roles, religion, socioeconomic status, sexual orientation, national origin, and native language affect their beliefs and practices as an educator.

STOP AND REFLECT

1. Which aspects of your own culture and identity feel most salient to your professional practice?
2. Which aspects of your own culture and identity might have a more subtle but still important influence on your practice?

In addition to the ways that culture impacts perceptions of mental health, educators need to recognize that culture impacts families' beliefs about schools and educational professionals in general. Some family caregivers have positive memories of school and trust educational professionals. Other family caregivers have experienced negative, discriminatory, or even traumatic experiences within school buildings, and feel well-justified apprehension toward educational professionals. Likewise, educators themselves bring their own experiences with school into their professional lives and may use their own family dynamics as blueprints for how they expect families to behave (or not behave) in schools. As educators work to build relationships with families, it is important to recognize the role that each person's educational history and family dynamics may play in shaping interactions.

STOP AND REFLECT

1. Think about your own family's culture regarding school and education professionals as you grew up. How did this culture align with (or diverge from) the expectations of your school and your educators?
2. How did this alignment or divergence impact communication between the school and your home?

As the previously discussed considerations demonstrate, cultural reciprocity is a crucial lens regardless of how much overlap there is between an educator's culture and that of their students' families. Because educators have been deeply socialized into the cultures of their schools and professions, it is easy to lose sight of how foreign the school culture, language (jargon), or processes may feel to families communicating with educators about their child's mental health needs. For some families, mental health challenges are not openly addressed or acknowledged within their culture. Communicating with educators, particularly about their child's mental health, may raise a wide range of emotions for family caregivers, including dread, shame, relief, anxiety, or hope. This can also vary among caregivers within the caregiving unit (e.g., one experiences relief while another experiences shame).

In writing about cultural reciprocity, we recognize that partnership requires mutual effort from all parties involved, and that sometimes, family caregivers or educators engage in the partnership very differently. When there are conflicts in cultural beliefs and practices regarding mental health, both educators and family caregivers play an important role in resolving these conflicts and engaging in a path forward that best serves the student. In the following section, we provide suggestions for educators regarding how they might communicate with families in ways that increase the likelihood of effective family-school partnerships.

Communication with Families about Student Mental Health

Communication between educators and family caregivers is crucial for student outcomes, including both academic and mental health outcomes (Sheridan et al., 2019; Smith et al., 2020). Through communication with family caregivers, educators can better contextualize their interactions with each student. Families can help educators understand the developmental and academic history of the child, the onset of any mental health concerns, the child's strengths and coping strategies, and the supports available to the child within their home and community. These contextual understandings can help educators implement proactive and preventative strategies (such as those discussed in prior chapters) in ways that are differentiated for the student's unique strengths and needs. In addition, communication with families may facilitate earlier sharing of information between the family and school, enabling students to receive important support and intervention sooner.

In the following sections, we invite educators to reflect on various aspects of their own communications with families. We focus on (1) varied communication channels and circumstances; (2) coordinating communication across providers; (3) respecting privacy regarding mental health information; and (4) educators as connectors to community resources.

Varied Communication Channels and Circumstances

Educators might consider how they choose to communicate with family caregivers and the circumstances for which to have that communication. There are a variety of ways educators and families can interface. For example, they may choose an in-person meeting, whether at a scheduled time or through an informal conversation at drop-off or pick-up. Depending on their school's contact norms, they may also communicate with families via email, phone, messaging, or video. Although some schools have policies that promote or prohibit educators' use of certain forms of communication, educators often have some agency in these decisions. Likewise, some schools may expect educators to communicate with families in particular circumstances, such as at the beginning of the school year, at parent-teacher conferences, when students are absent, or in the case of specific behaviors. Other schools may have expectations regarding the frequency of communication, such as having educators send out a weekly newsletter or check in with family caregivers once a quarter.

Although there is no ideal method regarding the frequency or modality of communication between educators and family caregivers, establishing communication methods early in the school year (or in the relationship, if the student joins class during the year or classes rotate throughout the school year) is important. By using a variety of communication channels, educators increase the likelihood that family caregivers will be able to connect with them. It is also important to communicate positive news and student strengths, rather than only concerns. For example, Francis and colleagues (2016) conducted focus groups with families regarding their experiences with educator communication. The researchers found that families appreciated when educators made suggestions rather than telling them how they should parent, as well as when educators positioned the parent as the experts regarding their children. Families also appreciated a range of modalities of communication, but especially positive communication about specific things their child did.

STOP AND REFLECT

1. How do you typically communicate with families? How often and using which modalities?
2. How might you alter or expand your communication modalities to efficiently reach more families?
3. How could you increase your communication about student strengths or growth to families?

The amount of background information that an educator has access to varies widely from student to student. Educators typically have even less knowledge about students' caregivers. Therefore, an important, but sometimes subtle, dynamic to consider when communicating with family caregivers about student mental health is the family member's own prior (or ongoing) experiences with it. When discussing concerns regarding student mental health, it is important to recognize that family caregivers may also be experiencing their own challenges with mental health. In some cases, multiple family members, not only the student, may have endured the same harmful event that resulted in posttraumatic stress disorder (PTSD) for some. Many mental health disorders have biological or genetic components, making it possible that other family members are experiencing similar concerns. Even if family caregivers are not struggling with specific mental health challenges, many caregivers experience fear and worry about their children's safety and well-being, particularly caregivers who live in underresourced neighborhoods.

Therefore, when educators communicate with family caregivers about student mental health, an empathetic and trauma-informed approach to communication with families is beneficial. By *empathetic*, we mean recognizing the distress and concern mental health challenges create for students and their families. By *trauma-informed*, we mean communicating with the knowledge that a large proportion of children and families have experienced potentially traumatic events, and reactions to these events may underlie the behaviors or mental health concerns educators are observing.

In Chapter 11, we provide a detailed overview of trauma and PTSD and approaches to addressing their impact within schools.

Coordinating Communication across Providers

Another aspect of communication that educators may want to consider is how they can support its coordination across providers. Students with mental health challenges may receive services and support from a variety of educational professionals and clinicians. Within schools, there may be multiple school mental health professionals with varying responsibilities and expertise (see Chapter 1), such as a school social worker, school psychologist, and school counselor (Frey et al., 2022). There are sometimes interns and prelicensed professionals working in schools as well. With so many professionals holding different titles and having different types of expertise—or having the same title but whose roles vary from school to school—it can be confusing for educators themselves, never mind to the families who interact with the school. One of the ways that educators can support families is by having a clear understanding of the different mental health professionals' roles within their own school and ensuring that families understand who they are communicating with. Sometimes, one educator is identified as the "point person" or liaison for each student, but this is not always the case. Educators can help to coordinate communication by ensuring that the family is aware of how to contact each member of the team, and what each member's role is pertaining to their child.

Likewise, it is important for educators to recognize that there might be a need to coordinate communication across adults in the student's home and community. When family caregivers are divorced or separated, educators may need to put extra care into ensuring that all family caregivers have access to relevant information. Even when family caregivers are together, they may disagree about how to best support the child. Educators cannot resolve these differences but should ensure that all parties receive relevant communication about the student. This can be particularly tricky when there is shared custody, when a parent is incarcerated, or when a child is in foster care. Educators should communicate with their administrators or front office regarding who should be receiving communication. In the case of restraining orders, for example, some communication may be forbidden. However, educators also must ensure that student privacy is upheld. This brings us to the next section: How do we honor privacy while also fostering collaboration and coordination of services?

Respecting Privacy Regarding Mental Health Information

In addition to considering the frequency and coordination of communication, educators should also consider how they communicate student mental health information to students' family caregivers and other members of the school community. Sometimes, students directly disclose to educators information about their mental health. Other times educators receive information from students via assessments or from other school personnel. Regardless of how educators receive information about a student's mental health, it is important that they treat it with sensitivity and in accordance with the law.

Students' educational records are protected by the Family Educational Rights and Privacy Act (FERPA). This federal law protects students from their educational records being disclosed without parental consent and protects parents' rights to access their child's educational records and to request amendments to them (U.S. Department of Education, 2019). When a student turns age 18 or attends a postsecondary institution, these rights transfer to the student (U.S. Department of Education, 2019). Likewise, the Individuals with Disabilities Education Act (2004) also protects students' educational records (such as their IEPs). Therefore, educators must always ensure that they have parental consent before they share any student information with any adult who does not have a "legitimate educational interest" that requires access to the information. Student records can only be viewed by those who provide services to the child within the school, unless parental consent is granted—except in cases of a health or safety emergency (U.S. Department of Education, 2019). In cases where an educator is hoping to collaborate with an external provider (e.g., the student's therapist), written permission should be sought from family caregivers. Administrators or school mental health professionals often have standard release forms that can be shared with family caregivers for their signature after having a conversation seeking this permission.

Another important consideration is ensuring that students and families are aware that educators are mandated reporters. Being a mandated reporter means that educators are required to report suspected sexual misconduct, abuse, or neglect to local child protective services (U.S. Department of Education, 2025). It is important for educators to review the policies in their own state and district and know their own role in the reporting process within their school. They should also ensure that families are aware of this role, as role transparency is an important component of family-educator trust.

Last, it is also important to be transparent with both students and families that educators do not have clinical training. Families may ask questions that require responses from trained mental health professionals. In these cases, educators should acknowledge the limitations of their own training and offer to connect students or families with the relevant clinician. Table 8.1 includes several tips and strategies for communicating with families. In the following section, we describe the important role educators can play in connecting families with community mental health resources.

TABLE 8.1. Communication Tips and Strategies

Strategy	Reflection questions
Explore expectations regarding modality and circumstances and invite family caregivers to give input on their preferred modality	*How do you know what types of communication work best for your students' families?*
Set and communicate personal boundaries and goals for communication, such as only replying to texts or calls at certain hours or responding to emails within a certain timeframe	*What boundaries do you currently have regarding communication with families? How might you communicate them to families?*
Reach out with strengths-based communication on a regular basis	*What family caregivers have you recently contacted with praise for their child? How could you establish a routine of reaching out to families with positive information?*
Envision communication from the lens of a family caregiver, and consider what emotions they might feel during communication	*How might the family caregiver interpret this email or text? What could be done to make it clearer or less emotionally charged?*
Reduce or define educational jargon or school lingo	*Would someone who doesn't work in a school understand this abbreviation or technical term? What language in this message could be simplified or explained?*
Run it by a colleague	*Does my colleague interpret this the same way I do? Do they have any ideas for how to make it more effective?*
Make it actionable	*Is there a clear action step or ask that I am presenting to the family caregiver?*
Acknowledge what you do not know	*Have I acknowledged the limits of my own experience, and offered to connect the family with someone who might have more expertise?*
Affirm family's expertise about their child	*Have I validated the family's expertise about their child? Have I communicated openness to their expertise or alternative perspectives?*

Educators as Connectors to Community Resources

As described in the previous section, educators are not trained as mental health clinicians. However, educators play an important role in identifying students' strengths and needs across tiered levels of support (see Chapter 7) and in connecting families with the resources they may need. Some of these resources and supports may be directly related to mental health, such as community-based mental health clinicians or providers who conduct mental health assessments. Other resources and supports may address mental health indirectly, such as organizations that help families to meet their basic needs (e.g., food banks, medical clinics, housing, and legal assistance). Educators can play a crucial role in school mental health by serving as a connector between families and resources in their broader community.

Although it is impossible (and inappropriate) for educators to try and meet all their students' mental health needs themselves, they can play a crucial role by familiarizing themselves with community resources and connecting families to these opportunities. When educators are aware of the continuum of mental health supports both within and outside of the school, they are better able to suggest appropriate resources to families in need of various types of support. In Table 8.2, we provide an exercise for educators to map the resources available in the surrounding community. Educators can choose how broadly to define *community*, but resources should generally be within transportation distance for most families in the school. We also encourage educators to connect with colleagues (e.g., school administrators, school mental health professionals, family liaisons) to see if this type of mapping has been done for their school and if it is okay to share this information with families. Some schools may choose to share with all families in the community whereas others may share with specific families asking for additional resources.

After completing this resource map, educators are better prepared to connect families with the resources needed to support their children's mental health. Educators may also become more aware of their students' lives outside of the classroom. In fact, communication with families plays an instrumental role in helping educators to better understand the dynamics of the community that shape their students' experiences in their classes. It may be a useful exercise for educators to develop an initial list of resources, and then ask students, families, and colleagues for input on additional resources within the community. The map can become a living document to share within their class and with other families who may benefit from it in the future. Once educators have mapped out available resources, the next step is to begin building relationships with some of the people or organizations associated with these resources. It is also important for educators

TABLE 8.2. Mapping Community Resources

Category	Examples	Using Google and your social network, jot down notes about available resources in your school's community
Community mental health	• Community mental health providers • Group counseling, behavioral health interventions • Applied behavior analysis providers • Assistive technology • Transition services, occupational therapy, physical therapy, speech and language pathologists • Parent and family advocates • Local mental health advocacy groups	
Cultural pride and social opportunities	• After-school programming (YMCA, Boys and Girls Club, etc.) • Free youth activities • Community centers • Local community establishments—diners, bodegas, dance and concert halls, churches, etc.	
Food	• Food banks, food pantries • Community meals, soup kitchens, delivered meals • Supplemental Nutrition Assistance Program (SNAP), Special Supplemental Nutrition Program for Women, Infants, and Children (WIC)	
Health services	• Community health centers and clinics • Substance and addiction support clinics and services • Local parks and recreation department events and classes • Local youth sports leagues • Access to public tracks, fields, courts, gyms • Laundromats and pharmacies • Low-cost exercise and yoga classes	
Safety	• Emergency preparedness training or consultation • Public works, fire department, police department, EMTs, etc. • Housing assistance, furniture banks, etc.	

to recognize that each school has a very different relationship with its surrounding community.

STOP AND REFLECT

1. What is your school's relationship to the surrounding community?
2. What new resources did you learn about in your school's community? How might these support the families of students with whom you work?

Conclusion

Family caregivers and community members are essential to school mental health efforts. In this chapter, we have provided educators with opportunities to reflect on proactive communication and relationship-building strategies that can help them understand their students' mental health experiences and collaborate with families to keep challenges from intensifying or going unnoticed. We also invited educators to reflect on the idea of cultural reciprocity, the role of culture in how families approach schools generally, and mental health specifically. Finally, we provided an opportunity to consider ways that educators can serve as connectors to mental health resources in the school and community. Partnerships with families and communities are an essential resource for improving students' mental health.

RELATED RESOURCES

National Association for Family, School, and Community Engagement
https://nafsce.org/page/resources
Offers a range of resources for educators seeking to engage with families in their school communities.

Center for Family Engagement at the National Parent Teacher Association
www.pta.org/the-center-for-family-engagement/resources
Provides research briefs and resources explaining best practices in strengthening relationships between educators and families.

Wheel of Social Identities Exercise
https://sites.lsa.umich.edu/equitable-teaching/social-identity-wheel
Developed by the University of Michigan, this tool supports educators in reflecting on their own identities, which can strengthen their cultural reciprocity when working with families.

CHAPTER 9

Strategic Use of Technology

KEY IDEAS

1. Technology can be both a resource and a threat to student and educator mental health.
2. When used strategically, technology can be a helpful tool for the prevention of mental health challenges.
3. Students benefit from policies, direct instruction, and modeling in how to use technology in ways that support their mental health and prevent its negative effects.

Erica and Maria are both in the seventh grade. They share a bus, a homeroom, and all their classes. Their families have known each other for years. They were close friends in elementary school but have drifted apart in the past few years. One day at lunch, a monitor, Ms. Johnson, notices a cluster of students gathered around Maria, who is showing them something on her phone. The kids are snickering, and it is clear that they are trying to hide the contents from adults in the lunchroom.

Ms. Johnson walks over and asks what's going on. Maria quickly puts her phone away, and the other students go back to eating their lunches. Ms. Johnson mentions the incident to the students' guidance counselor, Ms. Diaz, after lunch. Later, Ms. Diaz pulls the students aside individually to get more information about what was happening. One student finally shares that they were watching a video that a peer had posted of herself on social media. Ms. Diaz later sees Erica crying. Based on prior incidents, she has a good guess about who the student in the video was.

Technology Within and Beyond School Walls

The word *technology* likely suggests a wide variety of products, devices, and processes for educators. It may also evoke a range of emotions. Throughout one's career as an educator, the role of technology will evolve. At the time of this writing, technological innovations in schools include personalized learning, gamification, machine learning, augmented reality, artificial intelligence, and immersive virtual environments (Spector, 2024; Van Mechelen et al., 2023). Technology will continue to develop and change students' and educators' experiences in schools at a rapid pace. Considering this ongoing and swift innovation in technology, educators, researchers, families, and policymakers are giving increased attention to the positive and negative effects of technology on mental health.

Technology has changed how students learn within the classroom, and has softened the boundaries between school, community, and home. A stark example of this was the shift in many school districts to online learning during the COVID-19 pandemic: in the spring of 2020, 77% of public schools provided instruction online (NCES, 2022). By September 2021, 96% of school districts reported providing tablets or other digital devices to students who needed access (NCES, 2022). Although most schools have returned to in-person learning, they continue to increasingly rely on technology. For example, after developing systems for online learning during the pandemic, some districts are now implementing "remote learning days" in the case of weather emergencies (Wagner, 2025).

Technology has brought the classroom out of the school building and into students' and educators' homes. At the same time, as illustrated in the vignette, technology has also brought students' experiences in their homes and communities *into* the classroom. For example, remote instruction during the COVID-19 pandemic provided educators with insights into students' homes and family life in ways they may not have witnessed previously. Day to day, students' experiences on social media often impact peer dynamics within the school building, necessitating educator involvement and intervention to maintain positive classroom and school climates. These softened boundaries raise important questions about educators' responsibilities regarding the impact of technology on students' mental health. Some of these questions have been addressed through the legal system or through school-level policies (Prothero, 2024), but many of the questions raised by emerging technology are so novel that they have yet to be addressed through formal systems or policies.

The relationship between technology and mental health looks different for each student and educator. This can be based on factors such as each individual's orientation toward technology, technology use, and developmental stage, for example. Before diving into this chapter, we invite readers to take a few minutes to reflect on their beliefs about the role of technology on their own mental health and that of their students.

STOP AND REFLECT

1. When you think of the word *technology*, what devices, programs, or applications come to mind?
2. Which of these has had the biggest impact (positive or negative) on your own mental health?
3. Which of these do you think has the biggest impact on the mental health of your students and their families?

Although this chapter addresses the impact of some specific types of technologies on school mental health, we recognize that its role is ever evolving. Therefore, we have two overarching goals in this chapter. First, we provide examples of how technology can serve as both a resource and a threat to the mental health of school community members. Then, we provide educators with ideas for using technology to promote mental health and prevent intensification of mental health concerns within their school communities.

Technology as a Facilitator and Threat to School Mental Health

In the following sections we describe three ways in which technology can both facilitate and threaten mental health in schools. First, technology increases the availability of mental health information (*facilitator*), but it also increases community members' access to misinformation (*threat*). Second, technology increases opportunities for school community members to be included and feel a sense of belonging (*facilitator*), but it also increases the potential of being excluded or bullied (*threat*). Finally, technology increases community members' access to practices and resources to support their well-being (*facilitator*), but excessive technology use can also reduce their engagement in other activities that are essential for well-being (*threat*). We discuss each of these considerations in the following subsections.

Increased Availability of Mental Health Information—and Misinformation

Technology has made information about mental health conditions significantly more accessible, thereby increasing opportunities for school community members to build their mental health literacy. *Mental health literacy* is a term used to describe "knowledge and beliefs about mental disorders which aid their recognition, management, or promotion" (Jorm, 2000, p. 396). One way that technology can support mental health is by expanding access to mental health trainings (e.g., via webinars, live chats, or online support groups). Online and virtual learning opportunities allow school community members to explore mental health topics in new ways. For example, Long and colleagues (2018) describe how participating in virtual mental health scenario simulations shifted educators' attitudes related to recognizing and responding to student mental health concerns. Parents and family caregivers can also access webinars and trainings regarding mental health online (Jones et al., 2013). For all community members, mental health campaigns on social media may also help to increase literacy around specific challenges and resources. Some social media influencers have built their entire brands based on their own experiences of mental health, sharing their personal stories and providing information to others about warning signs. Some mental health professionals also engage with social media platforms as influencers themselves (Pretorius et al., 2022).

For many adolescents, barriers to seeking mental health support may include limited knowledge, social stigma or embarrassment, trust, and financial costs (Radez et al., 2021). However, exposure to discourse about mental health and personal mental health testimonies via social media may help to destigmatize the process of identification and assessment of mental health concerns. In fact, 72% of educators in a 2024 *Education Week* survey reported that social media use helped students to acknowledge mental health concerns more easily (Klein, 2024). For some young adults with mental health challenges, opportunities to share their stories online are an important way of accessing community (Naslund et al., 2016). Researchers have also used various technology-based interventions to improve help-seeking behaviors (Johnson et al., 2022).

STOP AND REFLECT

1. How have you used technology to learn about mental health?
2. Can you think of any celebrities who shared their mental health experiences via technology (e.g., social media, podcasts, interviews)? How did this contribute to increased awareness about mental health?

Technology has helped to destigmatize conversations around mental health and provide crucial learning opportunities regarding it. However, the negative side of this increased access to mental health information is that technology also increases school community members' access to mental health *mis*information. Much of the information available on social media is not supported by scientific evidence and runs counter to the advice of mental health professionals with years of training and expertise (Starvaggi et al., 2024). In addition, social media users may define mental health conditions much differently than mental health professionals, leading to discrepancies between professional diagnoses and individuals' descriptions of their own experiences or self-diagnosis (Haltigan et al., 2023).

Mental health is personal, and it is important that individuals have agency throughout the assessment and treatment processes. It is essential for students to self-advocate and engage in the complex process of identity development and self-exploration. However, differences in language use and conceptualizations of mental health challenges can cause confusion for school teams and clinicians as they work to name and address concerns.

Furthermore, given increased access to discourse regarding mental health, some students and other school community members may attempt to address their mental health challenges independently, rather than seeking professional care and support. For example, in 2023, a survey conducted by the Education Week Research Center showed that more than half (55%) of high school students said that they had self-diagnosed a mental health problem using social media at least once (Klein, 2024). Some of the risks of relying on social media and other technologies to self-diagnose are misidentification of mental health concerns and trying to address these concerns using practices that are not evidence-based (Salter et al., 2025).

Increased Opportunities to Be Included—and Excluded

Technology can also help individuals feel included and engaged in the community. For example, technology extends educators' opportunities to give and receive social support beyond face-to-face interactions, such as via text messages or emails. Research demonstrates that educators who experience higher levels of social support experience lower levels of burnout (Fiorilli et al., 2019). Technology makes it possible for educators to receive social support virtually, such as via virtual mentoring opportunities or online educator support groups. For example, the Happy Teacher Revolution holds free, quarterly, online support groups for educators to address the role of emotions in their work, and trains educators to lead support groups within their own schools (*Happyteacherrevolution.com*). Likewise, technology offers opportunities to access support from licensed clinicians through virtual therapy options. Given their busy personal and professional schedules, educators may not be able to attend in-person therapy appointments, but online therapy allows educators to receive this form of support.

Relationships are crucial for mental health. Technology allows educators to connect with students and families more frequently and in more flexible ways, such as through virtual learning opportunities, email, messaging apps, and phone calls. The use of hybrid and virtual learning spaces may allow students who are not able to join in-person to still engage and be included in school. Technology also provides family caregivers with opportunities for caregiving training, support groups, and affinity groups that they might not be able to access in person. Through technology, families have increased access to school meetings and community events. For example, family caregivers with busy work schedules may not be able to come to the building for an in-person meeting or event but may be able to join remotely via phone or a video platform. These opportunities for virtual collaboration can help to build relationships between families and educators, which are especially important for students with mental health challenges (see Chapter 8). Furthermore, for students with identified mental health concerns, the use of technologies such as integrated data systems, phones, and data tracking software can help the many members of care teams to collaborate and support students' mental health (Lyon et al., 2016).

However, technology can also threaten community members' inclusion in the school community in multiple ways. First, technology is not equally accessible to all students. For example, students' socioeconomic backgrounds and/or disability identities may shape their access (or lack thereof) to technology. In cases of lack of access, this "digital exclusion" can have negative consequences for students' educational opportunities (Passey et al., 2024). Technology may also make extremist ideologies and influences more accessible to students, increasing the risk of their engagement with harmful external communities that detract attention from their life at school (Morris, 2016). Even when students are not consuming overtly harmful media, their use of technology can isolate them from peers. For example, both students and educators can easily slip into the habit of scrolling through content on their phones or interacting with artificial intelligence (AI) chatbots during lunch or other breaks, rather than building relationships with their peers. In a study of Danish high school students' use of AI chatbots, Herbener and Danholdt (2025) found that students who engaged with chatbots as "friends" were significantly lonelier and reported lower social support than their peers.

Perhaps the most concerning threat of technology on mental health is the role of technology in bullying and other forms of social exclusion among school-aged youth. According to NCES (2024d), about one out of five adolescents reported being bullied during school. Of these, 22% reported being bullied online or via text. Compared with in-person bullying, cyberbullying can be more persistent—as technology is continually available—and more permanent—as public messages or images posted online can be hard to contain or erase (U.S. Department of Health and Human Services, 2025). However, less than half of students who are bullied report it to an adult at school (NCES, 2024d). Being bullied has negative impacts on students' educational experiences and mental health (Arseneault et al., 2010), and technology makes it more possible.

Access to (and Distraction from) Practices That Promote Well-Being

Technology can promote mental health by helping to facilitate school community members' use of well-being strategies. For example, new wearable technologies (e.g., watches, rings) can track biodata, such as heart rate, and signal wearers to breathe or rest when their heart rate is elevated (Hickey et al., 2021). Other apps and websites provide short movement breaks (e.g., GoNoodle) or mindfulness sessions (Headspace; Smiling Mind). These technologies can help students and educators become more aware of the connections between their emotions and their bodies. Other technologies help users track their emotions and mental health. For example, some apps allow school community members to log their daily emotions and track patterns over time (e.g., *HowWeFeel.org*). In addition, apps and online tools that support executive functioning, such as calendars, timers, and goal-setting apps, can help address anxiety and other mental health concerns associated with executive functioning challenges. Many websites and apps that provide such resources are freely available and only take a few minutes to use.

However, technology can also serve as a distraction from pursuits that promote well-being, such as physical activity (Chiang et al., 2024), a healthy diet (O'Neil et al., 2014), and free play (Whitebread, 2017). Technology can be addictive, making it hard to engage in other important (albeit less stimulating) activities that support mental health. In a 2023, Gallup survey researchers reported that teens spent an average of 4.8 hours per day on social media (Rothwell, 2023). Social media can cause an individual's brain to release high levels of dopamine, making it hard to "sign off" and making in-person interactions feel less stimulating by comparison (Goldman, 2021).

Numerous studies document the potential cost of social media use on students' mental health (Keles et al., 2020; Seabrook et al., 2016; Vuorre et al., 2021). For example, Barry and colleagues (2017) found that the number of social media accounts and the frequency with which adolescents checked them correlated with higher levels of inattention, hyperactivity, impulsivity, anxiety, depression, and loneliness. However, researchers also note that more research is needed to understand the associations between social media use and mental health: Does social media cause poor mental health, or are students with poor mental health seeking out social media more frequently? More longitudinal studies are needed to explore these questions. Although the exact mechanisms of social media's impact have yet to be determined, there is strong evidence that excessive use has negative implications for students' and educators' mental health.

STOP AND REFLECT

1. What positive and negative effects of technology have you seen on students' mental health? How about on your own?
2. What is one step you can take to improve the role of technology in your mental health?

Strategies to Reduce Technological Threats on Mental Health

As demonstrated in the previous sections, technology has the potential to both facilitate and threaten students' and educators' mental health. In the following sections, we describe three strategies that educators can use to reduce technological threats on mental health. First, we discuss the value of participating in the development and implementation of school policies regarding technology use. Second, we describe the importance of providing direct instruction and guidance on technology use to students. Finally, we ask educators to consider ways that they themselves might model healthy boundaries with technology for their students.

Developing and Revising Policies Around Technology Use

Participating in school- and classroom-level policy development regarding technology use is an important way for educators to support school mental health. As technologies continue to evolve, school communities must grapple with their implications for students, educators, and families. School-level technology policies may include expectations and procedures related to (1) cell phone usage in the building, (2) responses to cyberbullying, (3) educator communication (e.g., use of texts, walkie-talkies, or emails to collaborate); and (4) emergency communication procedures (see Chapter 13).

At the time of this writing, schools varied greatly in their policies across all these areas. One of the most significant policy challenges revolves around students' use of cell phones in schools. In a nationally representative survey conducted by Common Sense Media in 2021, 43% of 8- to 12-year-olds had a smart phone as did 88% of 13- to 18-year-olds (Rideout et al., 2022). In a 2024 nationally representative survey of school leaders, 86% of public elementary schools reported having policies prohibiting students from using cell phones during class, whereas 55% of secondary schools reported having such policies (NCES, 2025). Of schools that did not prohibit cell phone use during class, some had policies allowing educators to decide, some allowed students to always use their phones, and some had no policy around cell phones at all (NCES, 2025). As of June of 2026, at least 38 states and Washington, DC, had laws requiring districts to address cell phone use through bans or restrictions (Prothero et al., 2026). Educators largely support cell phone use restrictions: in a 2024 poll of nearly 3,000 teachers, the National Education Association found that 90% of teachers supported prohibiting cell phones and personal devices during instruction and 83% supported prohibiting them for the entire school day (Walker, 2025). But for many family caregivers and students, restricted access to cell phones threatens their sense of security, as they worry about communication with loved ones during a school emergency.

Clear and accessible policies around technology use can support both educator and student mental health by providing transparent and consistent expectations about technology use, which can reduce decision fatigue and anxiety regarding behavioral responses for both educators and students. Educator-facing technology policies, such as norms around their own phone use, speed of email response, and social media engagement, can also support educators' mental health by making implicit professional norms more explicit. These policies may also help to reduce the burden of decision making on individual educators when difficult technology situations arise. By taking time to understand and discuss current technology policies within their schools, educators can help shape the conversation about future policies and build collective buy-in for the development of policies that support the school community.

Educators may also consider how they might design and implement classroom-level policies or procedures regarding technology in ways that can support mental health. For example, having a classwide discussion at the beginning and middle of the year about cell phone usage can help educators address sources of technology-related student anxiety underlying their usage. Another helpful practice is teaching and reteaching procedures for addressing forgotten, broken, or battery-depleted devices to reduce stress levels in the face of students' inevitable (and ongoing) issues with tablets, iPads, and other in-class technologies. At both the school and classroom level, soliciting community input into policies and practices, and providing opportunities to collectively revisit and revise these policies and practices, is likely to increase buy-in, trust, and appropriate use of technology within the classroom and beyond.

Providing Direct Instruction and Guidance Regarding Technology

In addition to creating policies and practices around technology use, a second proactive measure that educators can take to address potential threats of technology is to provide direct instruction to students about technology use. Such instruction may include strategies for identifying and navigating misinformation, information about disconnection and addiction, strategies for using technology in inclusive ways, how to respond to online bullying, and literacy around artificial intelligence.

STOP AND REFLECT

1. What do you think educators' roles are in supporting students with technology?
2. How directly do you teach students skills pertaining to technology use in your classroom or setting?

Given the nuances and complexities of technology, teaching students *everything* they need to know about safe and productive technology use may feel daunting. Rather than taking on responsibility for addressing all topics pertaining to technology, we invite educators to begin by picking one or two topics that feel particularly salient to their classroom communities and embedding short activities or lessons regarding those topics into their existing instructional plans. Next, we highlight a few topics that may be beneficial for educators to integrate within existing instructional activities in their classrooms.

Navigating Misinformation

Technology gives students increased access to information. With this, they also have increased access to misinformation, including misinformation about mental health. One of the key skills that students need is the ability to sift through the different claims that they encounter online and understand what types of evidence are being used to support them. *Influencers* abound on social media. They received this label for a reason: their stories and actions are appealing to students, and their beliefs about mental health—while not always evidence-based—are impactful. Educators might consider providing explicit questions for students to ask of sources they encounter online, such as *Who is profiting from this information? Why do I believe this source? How does giving this source my attention positively impact my life and my community?* Educators can help combat misinformation by building media literacy and helping students to develop critical evaluation skills. The News Literacy Project, Common Sense Media, and MediaSmarts all offer resources to guide educators' lesson planning (Levitt & Grubaugh, 2024).

Using Social Media to Include Rather Than Exclude

Another important area of direct instruction pertains to social media use. Educators might consider facilitating classroom discussions about the ways that social media can be used to include or exclude community members.

For example, educators might share how social media has provided an important platform for disability rights advocates (Sannon et al., 2023), while also sharing data regarding the disproportionate frequency of cyberbullying experienced by students with disabilities (PACER Center, 2020). Providing opportunities for students to facilitate discussions with their peers in this area may be particularly powerful, as adolescents seek validation and advice from their classmates.

Interacting with New Technologies

As new technologies emerge and evolve, it is important for educators to provide direct instruction to students regarding (1) what these technologies are, (2) who benefits from their use, and (3) the risks involved with their use. When students are equipped with knowledge regarding technology, they can make better choices regarding their interactions with it. As new technologies emerge, we encourage educators to discuss them with their students, and to help students acknowledge the benefits and drawbacks of new technologies as they enter their lives.

Modeling Technological Boundaries That Support Mental Health

Our last recommendation to educators concerned about the role of technology in school mental health is to consider the ways in which they model their own technology use for their students. Modeling is an important instructional skill: by "thinking aloud" or providing a step-by-step example during an activity, educators allow students to understand how to engage with a new idea or skill (McLeskey et al., 2017). Modeling is often used in the context of teaching academic skills, such as talking aloud as one solves a math problem or demonstrating how to mix chemicals in a lab before asking students to do so. However, educators also model social and emotional skills for students. For example, during a challenging interaction, an educator might take a few deep breaths and say to students, "I'm feeling a little overwhelmed, so I'm going to take a few deep breaths to help me calm down." This helps students to learn skills they can use when they are feeling overwhelmed.

Modeling technology use is another way educators can help students develop skills to maintain their mental health. Depending on their students' developmental level, educators might share how they navigate their own boundaries with social media and how they decide what to pay attention to. Sharing these lessons with students can help educators remain accountable and help students by having a model. For example, consuming media results in frequent exposure to tragedies, which can take an emotional toll on educators. Therefore, educators may set boundaries around their own media consumption to protect their mental health. It is likely that these boundaries may shift over time and need to be reevaluated every so often. Sharing this process with students can further build their skills to navigate and adapt to shifting technology and mental health needs. This educator modeling reinforces that having a strategic approach to consumption of technology can promote mental health across the life course.

Conclusion

As illustrated in the previous sections, there are many ways that technology can be used to promote mental health in schools. But technology can also pose serious risks to the mental health of students and educators. Careful consideration of the benefits and drawbacks of technology can help educators use it as a resource rather than a threat to mental health. When used strategically, technology can be an important tool for the promotion of mental health and prevention of mental health challenges. As new technologies emerge, continual reflection and discussion will be needed to allow students and educators to respond and adjust when technology does not promote their mental health.

RELATED RESOURCES

News Literacy Project
https://newslit.org
Offers lesson plans for educators to help students navigate sources of information.

American Academy of Pediatrics: Center of Excellence on Social Media and Youth Mental Health
www.aap.org/en/patient-care/media-and-children/center-of-excellence-on-social-media-and-youth-mental-health
Provides research and resources on the role of social media in youth mental health.

Media Smarts
https://mediasmarts.ca/teacher-resources
Includes lesson plans and resources for educators to help students navigate media and technology.

SECTION III

RESPONDING TO SPECIFIC MENTAL HEALTH CONCERNS

Introduction to Section III

Now that we have covered school mental health promotion and prevention, we turn to responding to specific mental health concerns. In this third and final section, we aim to equip educators with an understanding of specific mental health conditions that affect students, and strategies they can use to promote learning and success with these students in school. We expect that response strategies will be most useful with individuals who are demonstrating mental health challenges or have been diagnosed with a mental health disorder, but this does not prevent educators from using the strategies more broadly.

We fully recognize that most educators are not mental health professionals and therefore are not trained or responsible for clinical mental health interventions. Instead, throughout this section, we focus on strategies that can support the learning for students with mental health conditions in the classroom, and alert educators to signs of distress that may warrant consultation with or referral to a mental health provider. Educators are uniquely positioned to notice signs of mental health conditions because of their relationships with students, the amount of time they spend with them, and their knowledge of developmental norms for the students with whom they work (Whitcomb, 2017). Educators are an important source of referral to mental health services for students (Green et al., 2022); the importance of this role cannot be overstated.

Because there are several common mental health conditions that present in schools, we have grouped them into three chapters: Anxiety and Depression (Chapter 10); Trauma, Posttraumatic Stress Disorder, and Secondary Traumatic Stress (Chapter 11); and Other Behavioral Conditions (Chapter 12). We draw upon the American Psychiatric Association's (2022) *Diagnostic and Statistical Manual of Mental Disorders, Fifth Edition, Text Revision* (DSM-5-TR) to describe symptoms of various mental health conditions. We acknowledge that this manual is regularly updated based on updated research and conceptualizations of mental health and distress. Furthermore, classification criteria have changed over time and will continue to evolve (First et al., 2022). Because of educators' nonclinical roles, we share general information about mental health symptomology to help educators understand what students might be experiencing, and how it might present in the classroom. We discourage educators from trying to diagnose students, themselves, or others in their lives and instead refer them to trained mental health professionals (e.g., psychologists, social workers, doctors) about any concerns.

Definitions and manifestations of distress can also differ cross-culturally. Therefore, students experiencing mental health distress may present with symptoms that differ from the DSM-5-TR criteria. For example, *ataque de nervios* is considered to be a cultural idiom of distress affecting individuals of Latino heritage. *Ataque de nervios*, which translates to "attack of the nerves," can include trembling, convulsions, uncontrollable screaming, feelings of impending loss of control, shortness of breath, shaking of arms and legs, and aggression (Koydemir & Essau, 2018). Although sharing similarities with anxiety and panic attacks, *ataque de nervios* has unique features not captured in the DSM-5-TR definition of panic attacks or anxiety. There are several additional examples of cultural idioms of distress like *ataque de nervios*. Therefore, it is important to recognize and respond to students' subjective experiences of distress. That is, even if it would not be distressing to others, if it is distressing to the student, it may be a cause for concern.

In each of the next three chapters we will follow the same general chapter structure. We will first introduce the range of mental health disorders to be covered in the chapter. Then, for each condition, we will describe its symptoms and how it may present in the classroom (e.g., behavioral manifestations of anxiety). We will then articulate the strategies and goals of evidence-based interventions that students may access in clinical care. Although educators are not expected or advised to deliver these interventions, we share this information to increase their knowledge of the skills their students might be working to develop in other settings. Finally, for each condition, we will offer evidence-informed strategies to support students in the classroom. After these three chapters, we conclude with a chapter on responding to emergencies, which prepares educators with strategies and resources for responding to emergencies in their settings. In Figure III.1, we summarize the chapters included in this section.

In Chapter 10, we focus on anxiety and depression. We review the symptoms that students may experience and how they may affect learning and classroom behavior. We also briefly explain evidence-based treatments for these conditions to increase educators' understandings of the skills their students might be working on. We dedicate the majority of the chapter to sharing strategies educators might use in their settings to support students experiencing anxiety or depression. In doing so, we hope to increase educators' knowledge and self-efficacy with which to support the learning and mental health of their students suffering from anxiety or depression.

In Chapter 11, we discuss trauma, posttraumatic stress disorder, and secondary traumatic stress. The chapter begins by explaining the types of

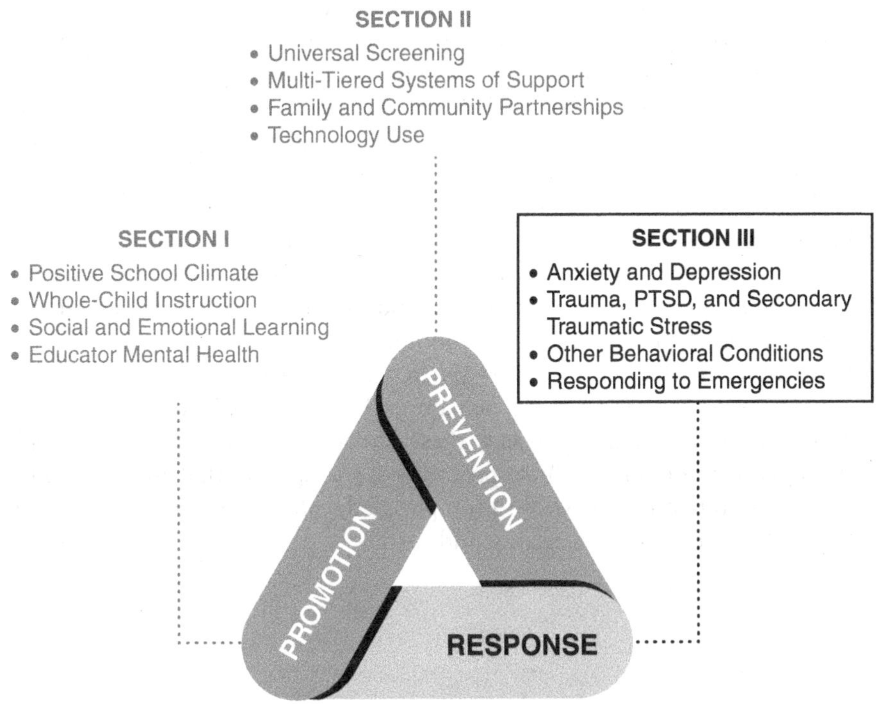

FIGURE III.1. Section III: Response.

events that can be traumatic for students. We describe the effects of trauma on learning and behavior in the classroom and strategies educators can use to promote learning for students exposed to trauma. Symptoms related to one potential condition resulting from trauma, posttraumatic stress disorder (PTSD), are detailed. We then turn our attention to the mental health of educators working with students exposed to trauma. We define secondary traumatic stress and share strategies for preventing or mitigating its potential effects on educator mental health. We conclude with considerations related to student and educator experiences of loss and grief.

In Chapter 12, we discuss other behavioral disorders, including attention-deficit/hyperactivity disorder (ADHD), oppositional defiant disorder, intermittent explosive disorder, conduct disorder, and substance use disorders. For each disorder, we review its symptoms and how they may present in the classroom. We then briefly describe evidence-based treatments for these conditions to increase educators' understandings of the skills their students might be working on outside of the classroom (e.g., in school- or community-based therapy). We then detail supports educators can provide in the classroom to bolster the learning of students with these mental health disorders. In doing so, we hope to increase educators' knowledge, empathy, and self-efficacy with which to work with these students.

Finally, Chapter 13 discusses responding to emergencies. In this chapter, we explore educators' roles in responding to school-based emergencies. This work often begins prior to an emergency happening through emergency planning and preparation. We specifically address system-wide emergency operations planning (EOP) processes and inclusive, trauma-informed drills. We then turn to two strategies that educators can use to support individual students experiencing a crisis: *threat assessment* and *de-escalation*. Finally, we describe short- and long-term strategies that educators can use when responding to community-wide emergencies. Because we know that this chapter may carry particularly heavy emotional weight, we begin with an invitation to participate in three brief breathing exercises—and we encourage readers to seek these out at any point. As we have done throughout the book, each chapter includes a vignette that illustrates key points and reflection questions prompting educators to pause and consider applications in their own setting and work.

CHAPTER 10

Anxiety and Depression

KEY IDEAS

1. Symptoms of anxiety and depression affect a substantial number of children and adolescents.
2. Anxiety and depression can impact learning and classroom behavior in a variety of ways.
3. There are many strategies that educators can use to support students experiencing anxiety or depression.

> Kesha recently moved after her family's home was flooded during a hurricane. Kesha is experiencing anxiety about going to lunch in her new school's cafeteria. She fears not having anyone to sit with, is overwhelmed by its size and noise, and worries she won't know how to follow the routines (e.g., in which line to get lunch, when to throw away her trash). The thought of going to the cafeteria overwhelms her with feelings of fear and distress. In her first few days at school, Kesha hides in the school bathroom to avoid going to the cafeteria.

Anxiety and depression are two serious conditions in childhood and adolescence. Because many of the symptoms and behavioral manifestations of these disorders happen internally (within an individual), they are sometimes referred to as *internalizing disorders* (Achenbach, 1978; Liu et al., 2011). As of 2019, close to 10% of children and adolescents ages 3–17 had been diagnosed with an anxiety disorder (Bitsko et al., 2022). Nearly 5% of the same population had been diagnosed with depression.

This chapter has two primary sections. The first half of the chapter focuses on anxiety whereas the second half addresses depression. Within each section we follow a similar format. We first review the symptoms of each of these conditions and how they may affect learning and classroom behavior. Then, we briefly explain evidence-based treatments for these conditions to increase educators' understanding of the skills students might be working on, and how they might reinforce these skills in the classroom. Finally, we share strategies educators can use in the classroom or school environment to support the learning of students with each of these conditions. In doing so, we hope to increase educators' knowledge and self-efficacy with which to support the learning and mental health of their students experiencing anxiety or depression.

Symptoms and Treatment of Anxiety Disorders

Anxiety is an emotion characterized by feelings of tension (American Psychological Association, 2018a). It often includes worried thoughts and physical changes such as increased blood pressure. Low to moderate levels of anxiety can improve performance and are a typical part of learning and development (Ray et al., 2016). In small doses, anxiety increases one's attention, arousal, focus, and motivation to perform well. For example, a deadline can motivate individuals to work more quickly. A challenging puzzle can sharpen one's attention and focus. Students experiencing an anxiety disorder, however, have frequent and high levels of anxiety. Untreated, it interferes with their ability to attend and focus and makes it difficult to perform well. High levels of anxiety are likely to interfere with daily activities, interactions, and educational progress. When these symptoms are frequent, intense, and impairing daily functioning, a clinical diagnosis may be warranted.

Anxiety can manifest in the classroom in various ways. Students experiencing an anxiety disorder may withdraw from classroom activities because they are afraid to make a mistake or to be judged by peers. They may seek constant approval or reassurance, cling to adults or peers, or try to control other aspects of their life that feel less threatening (e.g., overplanning; Ray et al., 2016). Table 10.1 shows some common fears and manifestations of anxiety in childhood and adolescence. Whereas some manifestations are common and consistent from early childhood through adolescence (e.g., difficulty sleeping), others shift or emerge over the developmental period.

There are several types of anxiety disorders: separation anxiety (e.g., fear of separation from a caregiver), specific phobias (e.g., fear of dogs, spiders, storms), social anxiety, and generalized anxiety. Each type has a varied focus of the anxiety. Regardless of the type, however, without treatment, anxiety is unlikely to subside or go into remission. In this chapter, we focus on social and generalized anxiety disorders due to their broader scope.

Social anxiety disorder can have significant effects on learning and school behavior (Ray et al., 2016). Students with social anxiety disorder experience intense fear or distress related to social situations in which they might be scrutinized (e.g., sharing classwork, leading a team; American Psychiatric Association, 2022). This anxiety can result in crying, tantruming, freezing, shrinking, or failing to speak. Students with social anxiety disorder may work hard to avoid anxiety-provoking situations. When confronted with such a situation, they will exhibit significant distress (e.g., sweating, crying, fleeing). These students will experience significant impairment in their daily functioning and intense distress in social situations.

TABLE 10.1. Common Fears and Manifestations of Anxiety across Developmental Stages

Stage	Common fears	Common manifestations of anxiety
Early childhood	• Monsters or fictional characters • The dark • Separation from caregivers	• Difficulty sleeping • Frequent stomachaches or headaches not explained by another medical cause • Clinging to caregivers, extreme shyness • Tantrums, refusal
Middle childhood	• Potential danger (e.g., car accident, robbery, death) • Grades and achievement	• Difficulty sleeping • Frequent stomachaches or headaches not explained by another medical cause • Frequent worrying, asking "what if" questions • Difficulty concentrating • Avoidance (e.g., school refusal, new activities or people) • Perfectionism
Adolescence	• Grades and achievement • Peer approval • Increased responsibility and independence	• Difficulty sleeping • Frequent stomachaches or headaches not explained by another medical cause • Frequent worrying about routine parts of life • Difficulty concentrating • Avoidance (e.g., school refusal, new activities or people) • Sensitivity to feedback, highly self-conscious • Perfectionism

Note. Content based on Galanti (2024).

Students with untreated generalized anxiety disorder experience excessive and numerous worries on most days, which they find difficult to control (American Psychiatric Association, 2022). They may also experience physical symptoms such as trembling, sweating, or nausea. They may also exhibit perfectionistic tendencies, a constant need for reassurance, or high levels of conformity (Ray et al., 2016). The frequency and intensity of these worries is disruptive to their functioning.

Although many students do not receive formal services, anxiety is treatable. The most common treatments for anxiety in older children and adolescents include cognitive behavioral therapy (CBT), behavioral interventions, and medication (Ray et al., 2016). Although these treatments are implemented by trained clinicians, it can be helpful for educators to understand the goals of treatment. One common goal of treatment is decreasing the frequency and intensity of worries so that children and adolescents are able to navigate their days with less interference from worried thoughts. It also aims to increase awareness of emotional states and reactivity so children and adolescents can recognize distress earlier and apply coping skills. Related, treatment is designed to increase self-regulation skills for responding to anxiety-provoking thoughts or situations. Finally, treatment focuses on increasing tolerance for negative emotional experiences so that negative experiences become less distressing and the fear response is more consistent with actual levels of threat. These treatments are generally delivered individually, although some group or family treatment models are also available.

CBT is a well-established treatment for childhood and adolescent anxiety (e.g., James et al., 2020; Wang et al., 2017). CBT teaches children and adolescents that their thoughts, actions, and feelings are all interconnected, and that changing one of these can change the others. To treat anxiety, CBT often teaches children and adolescents to identify thoughts and situations that invoke fear. A clinician providing CBT treatment helps a student to recognize how adjusting their thoughts or behaviors can reduce anxiety symptoms. For example, a CBT lesson might teach the skill of thought stopping, in which a command such as "No" or "Stop" is used when one's thoughts become unhelpful. It may also encourage engaging in particular activities that are calming or energizing and then to reflect on how those activities affected one's thoughts and emotions. Because CBT requires self-reflection, understanding cause and effect, and perspective taking, it is generally not recommended for children under 8 years old.

Behavioral therapy is similar to CBT but focuses only on behavioral strategies. In the treatment of anxiety, behavioral therapy can include social skills training and exposure sessions to build children and adolescents' tolerance for negative emotional experiences (Ray et al., 2016). Treatment for younger children can achieve similar treatment goals through parent–child interventions, parent training, or child-centered play therapy.

Finally, some students benefit from medication for anxiety. The most commonly prescribed medications to treat anxiety disorders (with the exception of specific phobias) are selective serotonin reuptake inhibitors (SSRIs) and serotonin–noradrenaline reuptake inhibitors (SNRIs; Locher et al., 2017; Walter et al., 2020). These medications can help to reduce feelings of worry, fear, and panic. However, they can have some adverse side effects (e.g., gastrointestinal problems, insomnia, headaches) that tend to be temporary but should be monitored by doctors and families (Craske et al., 2017).

Classroom Supports for Students with Anxiety Disorders

Although the treatment approaches previously discussed require clinical training and expertise, there are also many strategies educators can use in the classroom to support students experiencing anxiety in their day-to-day classroom experiences. When a student is experiencing anxiety, their worry and preoccupation can hinder their thinking, concentration, and ability to focus on the task at hand. They may also fear making a mistake more than peers not experiencing anxiety, which may make it seem like they are disengaged or unwilling to participate. Common classroom triggers for students experiencing anxiety include sharing aloud in a small or large group, and long or complex assignments. Rather than avoiding these triggers entirely, educators can proactively support students in navigating these tasks. Next, we offer several strategies for proactively supporting students who are experiencing anxiety in the classroom. In Figure 10.1 we offer additional targeted strategies for two common manifestations of anxiety in the classroom: difficulty sharing ideas aloud and becoming overwhelmed by longer or independent tasks. Then, we discuss two strategies in greater detail: facilitating graduated exposure and teaching self-monitoring.

Consider the following proactive strategies for supporting students who are experiencing anxiety in the classroom:

1. Use predictable structures and routines so students can anticipate what is coming next. Try to alert them to any changes in routine before they happen.
2. Reduce the number of options given to students. This can help with decision making while still allowing for student choice and autonomy.
3. Model and verbally acknowledge that mistakes are a normal part of learning.
4. Provide frequent feedback to encourage continued effort (e.g., encouragement for completing a section of work).

If students experience anxiety related to sharing their ideas:

1. Offer think–pair–shares to allow students to organize their thoughts individually first.
2. Collaborate with the student to develop a cue that they are ready to respond.
3. Give student advance notice of what you would like them to share (e.g., during group work say, "This is excellent! When I ask the class how they solved this problem, I'd love to have you share what you wrote for #2" *or* "At Morning Meeting today, I'm going to ask you to share today's date—let's practice together right now").
4. Offer alternative presentation options (e.g., videos, one-on-one with the teacher, various presentation modalities).
5. Allow students to choose group roles based on personal strengths (e.g., leader, notetaker, presenter).

If students become overwhelmed with longer tasks or independent work:

1. Model positive self-talk (e.g., "I can do this!"; "I'm doing my best.").
2. Break assignments into smaller parts (e.g., only present one page of a packet at a time).
3. Teach organizational and self-monitoring strategies. For example, teach students to create a list of the small tasks needed to complete an assignment, and to check off each completed task to celebrate the accomplishment and orient to the next small task.

FIGURE 10.1. Additional targeted supports for students experiencing anxiety.

5. When delivering feedback, use "and" instead of "but" ("You worked really hard on this *and* only need to add a couple of things").
6. Lead classwide stress reduction exercises (e.g., deep breathing, stretching) and offer stress reduction tools (e.g., fidgets, soft music).
7. Model calm responses to stressful situations.
8. Collaborate on attainable goals with the student (e.g., volunteer one time per class).
9. Consider how you might facilitate graduated exposure opportunities to help students overcome their fears (explained in greater detail next).

We will now discuss two strategies for supporting students with anxiety in greater detail: facilitating graduated exposure and teaching self-monitoring.

Facilitating Graduated Exposure

Anxiety causes students (and adults) to experience an exaggerated level of threat and fear about particular situations (American Psychiatric Association, 2022). For example, public speaking is a common source of anxiety.

Individuals might sweat, feel nauseous, or freeze prior to, or during, a public speaking engagement. However, avoidance reinforces anxiety (Ray et al., 2016; Dymond, 2019). Until someone experiences some success with the feared experience, they are likely to continue to be afraid of it, and this level of fear may continue to increase. When students are experiencing intense anxiety about something they need to do at school, graduated exposure can help. Graduated (or graded) exposure refers to small and planful steps taken to work toward facing the feared experience (Kazdin & Weisz, 1998; Seligman & Ollendick, 2011). Let's return to Kesha, who was first introduced at the beginning of this chapter. Recall that she was hiding in the school bathroom to avoid going to the cafeteria for lunch. She feared not having anyone to sit with, not knowing the cafeteria routines, and is overwhelmed by its size and noise level.

> A few days into school, Mrs. Williams, Kesha's homeroom teacher, finds Kesha lingering in the bathroom. She prompts Kesha to go to the cafeteria, but Kesha becomes visibly distressed (e.g., loses all color from her face, freezes, and becomes tearful). Not sure what to do, Mrs. Williams invites Kesha to eat lunch in her classroom.

What could Mrs. Williams do next? First, she might consult with an administrator or school mental health professional. A strategy they or Mrs. Williams might use is supporting Kesha through graduated exposure to build her confidence and tolerance for the cafeteria. Working collaboratively with Kesha, they could (1) establish a goal and (2) brainstorm small steps that gradually build up to achieving that goal. The plan should begin with what Kesha can currently do comfortably. An example of what this might look like is provided in Figure 10.2.

As can be seen in this example, various parts of the feared experience (e.g., navigating lunch routines, identifying someone to sit with) can be worked on in different steps to reduce the level of fear invoked. For

Goal: Attend lunch in the cafeteria	
5. Attend lunch in the cafeteria 4. Go to cafeteria early with peer to get lunch and eat in cafeteria 3. Go to cafeteria early with a peer to get lunch and eat in counselor's office 2. Eat lunch in classroom with teacher and peer 1. Eat lunch in classroom with teacher	↑ Increasingly difficult, beginning with what the student can do now. Move to the next step once the student is able to do the current step comfortably.

FIGURE 10.2. Example of graduated exposure to build student success toward a goal.

example, in Steps 2 and 3, selecting a peer to eat with in the classroom and then the counselor's office (a less familiar environment to build tolerance for a different setting) may help Kesha to overcome the fear of not having anyone to sit with. In Steps 3 and 4, being allowed to go to the cafeteria early reduces the fear of becoming overwhelmed by the various lines and allows Kesha to be supported by her peer and the cafeteria staff to get her lunch. Graduated exposure works best when each step introduces a tolerable level of distress and the student is allowed to become comfortable with the step before moving on. For example, it may take one or more days to complete each of these steps. If the student starts to show signs of extreme distress, it is a sign the steps are progressing too quickly or there is too big of a jump in the level of perceived threat. In this case, returning to the previous step, adding supports (e.g., staff joining in the cafeteria to provide guidance on routines), or adding intermediate steps (e.g., eating with a peer at a table in the hallway outside of the cafeteria) can be helpful. Note that it is advised to remain on the same step after absences, weekends, or school vacations to ensure the step has remained tolerable or comfortable before moving to the next one.

Educators might consider using graduated exposure to face their own fears as well. For example, if calling caregivers to share concerns, asking colleagues to share resources, or approaching an administrator for support feels overwhelming or impossible, an educator could build a hierarchy of steps that helps to build their tolerance for the discomfort invoked by these situations. Ultimately, graduated exposure offers an opportunity to build one's professional skills by increasing comfort with collaboration or self-advocacy, for example.

STOP AND REFLECT

1. Is there a professional skill you would like to develop but are afraid of trying? What five to seven small steps could help you to gradually build your tolerance, comfort, and confidence with the skill?
2. What feared experiences have you observed in your students (e.g., public speaking, taking standardized tests)? How could you break these skills into small component parts to provide graduated exposure to the feared experience?

Teaching Self-Monitoring

Although helpful on its own, graduated exposure can be strengthened by incorporating a self-monitoring component. When using self-monitoring with graduated exposure, a student reports their level of anxiety prior to engaging in the activity (e.g., on a 1 to 5 scale) and then after engaging in the activity (on the same scale). An example is shown in Figure 10.3. Often,

Goal: Attend lunch in the cafeteria	**Fear Scale** 1 = not scary at all 2 = a little scary 3 = somewhat scary 4 = very scary 5 = terrifying

Start of plan—September 10: How scary does attending lunch in the cafeteria feel? 5

End of plan—September 27: How scary does attending lunch in the cafeteria feel? 2

Date	Action	Before: How scary does this feel?	After: How scary was it?
September 27	Attend lunch in the cafeteria	2	2
September 26	Attend lunch in the cafeteria	3	2
September 25	Attend lunch in the cafeteria	3	2
September 24	Attend lunch in the cafeteria	4	3
September 23	Go to cafeteria early with peer to get lunch and eat in cafeteria	2	2
September 20	Go to cafeteria early with peer to get lunch and eat in cafeteria	3	2
September 19	Go to cafeteria early with peer to get lunch and eat in cafeteria	4	3
September 18	Go to cafeteria early with peer to get lunch and eat in cafeteria	4	3
September 17	Go to cafeteria early with a peer to get lunch and eat in counselor's office	3	1
September 16	Go to cafeteria early with a peer to get lunch and eat in counselor's office	3	2
September 13	Go to cafeteria early with a peer to get lunch and eat in counselor's office	4	2
September 12	Eat lunch in classroom with teacher and peer	2	1
September 11	Eat lunch in classroom with teacher and peer	3	2
September 10	Eat lunch in classroom with teacher	2	1

FIGURE 10.3. Graduated exposure with student self-monitoring.

the actual event is less frightening than what the student thought it was going to be. Over time, the student's perceived fear will begin to decrease as they recognize the actual experience has not been as bad as they thought it would be, and they build their tolerance for it. In Figure 10.3 we show examples of this on September 12 and 23. Kesha is repeating the same step, but her "before" rating of how frightening the situation feels is lower. This shows that Kesha is experiencing less fear about the situation. This can also be a sign that the student is ready to move to the next step in the plan.

STOP AND REFLECT

1. Consider a student who is experiencing debilitating symptoms related to presenting in front of the class. At the mention of an upcoming assignment, the student is consumed by fear. When trying to talk to you about the assignment, they tremble, sweat, and become tearful.
2. What are some alternative options you could offer this student for the assignment?
3. If seeking to help the student overcome this fear, what are five to seven steps you and the student could use to gradually expose the student to the feared experience?

Now that we have shared the symptoms, treatment, and strategies for supporting students with anxiety, we turn to another internalizing disorder: depression.

Symptoms and Treatment of Depression

Although prevalence rates suggest that approximately 5% of children and adolescents (ages 3–17) in the United States have been diagnosed with depression (Bitsko et al., 2022), adolescents report much higher rates of depressive symptoms. For example, in 2023, 40% of U.S. adolescents said that they had experienced persistent feelings of sadness or hopelessness over the past month (CDC, 2024a). Rates were even higher among females, American Indian, Latino, multiracial, and LGBQ+ students. These rates steadily climbed between 2011 and 2021 (CDC, 2024c), peaking at 42% in 2021. Prevalence rates in 2023 suggest some improvement as COVID-19 restrictions were lifted but still signify high and concerning levels of sadness and hopelessness in adolescents.

Most children and adolescents experience brief, but sometimes intense, sadness (Zalaquett & Chatters-Smith, 2016). Most will also likely experience changes in appetite or sleep patterns. Shifts in activity level, focus, and self-esteem are also common. These developmentally normative shifts in mood typically pass with time and can be distinguished from depression based on their intensity, duration, and degree of interference with daily functioning.

Depression is an episodic condition that occurs on a continuum ranging from mild to severe (American Psychiatric Association, 2022). An episodic condition is one that ebbs and flows. There will be periods—or episodes—of symptoms, and other times when symptoms are in remission (i.e., they go away for some time). Because of this, symptoms are generally measured over the past two weeks. Once a child or adolescent has experienced an episode of depression, they are at greater risk for additional future episodes, making treatment important (Zalaquett & Chatters-Smith, 2016).

Untreated, depression causes persistent feelings of sadness, irritability, emptiness, or hopelessness. It also includes changes in cognition and physical behavior that can interfere significantly with daily functioning and routines. Students experiencing depression are likely to demonstrate diminished interest or pleasure in daily activities or excessive feelings of guilt or worthlessness. These students might ask to quit a previously preferred activity because it is no longer enjoyable to them. Students experiencing depression may also express negative statements about themselves, voice feelings of guilt or worthlessness, or experience suicidal ideation. Cognitively, students with depression may experience difficulty concentrating. They may appear to be preoccupied or absent. Physical symptoms can include significant changes in appetite, weight, and sleeping habits. Students may appear to be in slow motion as they move around the classroom and school, or increasingly restless, unable to settle their bodies.

Persistent feelings of sadness may also present as enduring irritability, including frequent or prolonged anger (American Psychiatric Association, 2022). Unlike moodiness—which tends to subside in the presence of preferred activities (e.g., time with friends, greeting a pet)—depression tends to cause more sustained and pervasive sadness or irritability that is harder to redirect (Zalaquett & Chatters-Smith, 2016).

In addition to the impact on daily functioning and routines, depression increases the risk for suicidal ideation and attempts (Hua et al., 2023; U.S. Preventative Services Task Force, 2022). Rates of suicidal ideation, plans, and attempts are staggering among U.S. adolescents. In 2023, 20% of U.S. adolescents reported seriously considering suicide (CDC, 2024a). Sixteen percent of adolescents reported making a suicide plan, and 10% attempted suicide (CDC, 2024a). These rates were even higher for LGBQ+ students. If educators have concerns about a student experiencing depression or suicidal ideation, it is crucial that they consult with a school mental health professional or administrator. School mental health professionals are trained in conducting risk assessments to determine next steps and to implement a safety plan (see Chapter 13 for more information on risk assessment).

Rumination—the repeated and prolonged replaying of negative events, emotions, or thoughts about oneself in one's head—can be a key feature of depression (Watkins, 2008). It can compound feelings of sadness, despair, shame, or isolation (Watkins & Roberts, 2020). Rumination can make it challenging for students to focus on the present moment, attend to instruction, problem-solve, or actively engage in classroom activities. It also can contribute to the maintenance of mental health disorders and interfere with treatment (Watkins & Roberts, 2020).

Depression is treatable. The evidence base for treatments of child and adolescent depression is less developed than that of adults (Zalaquett & Chatters-Smith, 2016) but is rapidly growing. The most common treatments for depression in preadolescents (generally ages 10+) and adolescents include CBT, behavioral therapy, interpersonal psychotherapy, and medication.

CBT that is used to treat depression aims to increase children and adolescents' awareness and skills with which to reduce their symptoms of depression. Behavioral components of CBT focus on teaching coping skills, interpersonal skills, social problem solving, and participation in enjoyable activities (Kazdin & Weisz, 1998). Cognitive aspects of CBT focus on teaching children and adolescents to identify and challenge unhelpful thinking patterns. Children and adolescents might be taught to recognize distorted thinking (e.g., "I always mess up!) and to more accurately appraise situations ("I messed up."). They may also be taught to use more balanced self-talk ("This is hard" instead of "I'm so dumb"). We will return to this topic later in the chapter.

Behavioral therapy focuses less on the cognitive aspects of depression and instead on the consequences of actions. Children and adolescents participating in behavioral therapy to treat depression might be taught strategies such as self-monitoring, self-reinforcement, and activity scheduling to improve their mood. Students may be encouraged to recognize the consequences of their actions (e.g., staying in bed all day makes me feel worse) and to engage in actions that help them to achieve their goals (e.g., getting out of bed to feel better). Behavioral therapy may also target social skills through role-playing, modeling, and assertiveness training (Zalaquett & Chatters-Smith, 2016).

Finally, students engaged in interpersonal psychotherapy learn about depression, the effects of depression on their relationships, and skills to apply to future depressive episodes. Because interpersonal psychotherapy has a particular focus on the effects of depression on one's relationships, it can be particularly helpful in cases of interpersonal challenges or disputes, grief, or role transition (Mufson et al., 2004). Interpersonal psychotherapy is generally a time-limited intervention consisting of up to 20 weekly 1-hour sessions (Zalaquett & Chatters-Smith, 2016).

Similar to anxiety, medication can also be used to treat depression. SSRIs are considered a first-line treatment for moderate to severe depression (Cheung et al., 2018; Locher et al., 2017). Because there is less evidence about their use, SNRIs are suggested as second- or third-line treatment options for moderate to severe depression. These medications are used to improve mood and reduce distress caused by depression. Side effects can include nausea, headaches, or increased suicidality, and therefore should be closely monitored by doctors and families.

Classroom Supports for Students with Depression

Although educators are not credentialed to provide the clinical treatments previously discussed, there are many practical strategies and supports that can be provided in the classroom to assist students experiencing depression. We provide a list of proactive strategies here, and then discuss two others in greater detail: teaching positive self-talk and reframing cognitive distortions.

Consider the following strategies for proactively supporting students experiencing depression.

1. Facilitate opportunities for goal setting and self-monitoring progress. This can help to motivate students, encourage future orientation, and maintain students' focus on a goal.
2. Consider providing accommodations or modifications to support fluctuations in mood or concentration (e.g., reduced length of assignments, extensions).
3. Allow for short breaks throughout the day to reduce overwhelm.
4. Consider pairing students as they complete assignments or prepare for an exam. This can reduce the task demand on each student, and the collaborative support can help a student experiencing depression to stay focused and complete the task.
5. Add physical movement breaks, which can reduce mild depression symptoms and energize students.
6. Ensure that students are engaged with peers and not isolated. Isolation can fuel rumination and negative thinking.
7. Infuse brief mindfulness or emotion regulation strategies into the day. For example, during transitions, prompt students to take three deep breaths or to listen carefully to the sounds outside of

the classroom (facilitates present moment attention by engaging senses).

Teaching Positive Self-Talk

Self-talk refers to internal dialogue in which a person silently or quietly speaks to themselves (American Psychiatric Association, 2023). Self-talk can be used when talking oneself through a complex task, repeating a mantra, or having an automatic reaction to a situation. Self-talk is often labeled as negative or positive. Negative self-talk generally confirms or reinforces negative thoughts or attitudes, whereas positive self-talk is more constructive. Examples are shown in Table 10.2. Self-talk affects how individuals interpret and approach situations, including challenging academic or social tasks. When presented with a challenging writing task, a student who immediately thinks, "There's no way I can do this!" is going to have a harder time initiating the task than a student who immediately thinks, "I'll do my best." Despite being a silent and automatic process, self-talk can have a significant impact on emotions and behaviors.

Students can be taught to recognize their self-talk and to adjust it. For example, Zones of Regulation, a SEL program developed by Leah Kuypers (2011), teaches students that they have an "inner coach" and an "inner critic," with the inner coach providing positive, reassuring messages, and the inner critic providing negative, self-defeating messages. Similar to strategies used in teaching a growth mindset (i.e., a learner's belief that their abilities can be improved through effort, learning, and persistence; Dweck, 2008), educators can teach students about self-talk and provide examples and opportunities for students to practice narrating these internal messages. In cases where educators hear students using negative self-talk, they might point it out or provide a more positively framed alternative. Educators might also consider displaying positive statements, having classroom sayings or mantras (e.g., "We can do hard things"), and modeling their own self-talk in the face of challenging situations (e.g., "Wow, this is tough. I'll give it my best try.").

TABLE 10.2. Examples of Negative and Positive Self-Talk

Examples of negative self-talk	Examples of positive self-talk
"I can't do this."	"I'll give it my best try."
"Everyone hates me."	"I'll find my people."
"This is too hard."	"Mistakes help me learn."
"I'll never be good at this."	"I can try something new."
"This is impossible."	"I haven't learned how to do this yet."

Reframing Cognitive Distortions

Both anxiety and depression can distort students' (and adults') thinking. With anxiety, the perceived level of threat is much higher than what it is in reality. With depression, thoughts of worthlessness and guilt are out of proportion with current circumstances and are persistent and pervasive. In Table 10.3, we list common thought distortions that educators might recognize and redirect in their students or themselves. Thought distortions refer to faulty or inaccurate thinking, perceptions, or beliefs (Burns, 1999). These thoughts often include absolutes, such as *always* or *never*, and generally do not take nuance or context into consideration. Although there can be overly positive distortions (e.g., in the case of narcissism; Steiner et al., 2021), thought distortions are more commonly negative and self-critical.

It is expected that the majority of people will experience some of these thought distortions intermittently across time and scenarios (Burns, 1999). However, thought patterns of those experiencing anxiety or depression may be overrun by these types of cognitions, and these types of thought distortions may fuel or reinforce symptoms of anxiety or depression. Although educators are not expected to treat the anxiety or depression of their students (or anyone else for that matter), knowledge of these thought patterns can help them to understand what their students are experiencing, empathize with their distress, and potentially redirect (or "reframe") some of their thinking.

STOP AND REFLECT

1. Can you recognize any of these patterns in your own thinking? The next time it happens, just notice the thought pattern. Then, consider how you might redirect or reframe the thought.
2. Can you think of a student that regularly made statements such as those in Table 10.3? How might you respond to statements like these when you hear them in your setting?

Reframing is a term used in psychology to describe the process of reconceptualizing a problem to see it from a different perspective (American Psychological Association, 2018b). For example, a student might say to their teacher, "My mom never shows up to school events." This is an example of overgeneralization, where the absence of the student's mom at one event is being overgeneralized to all events. Let's first pay attention to what is likely fueling this statement. The student likely feels sad, left out, or jealous seeing other parents attending the event. The teacher might begin by validating those feelings: "I know it's hard when your mom can't make it to an event, and other students have grownups here." Next, the teacher might reframe the cognitive distortion: "Your mom is working hard, and

TABLE 10.3. Examples of Cognitive Distortions

Cognitive distortion	Description	Example
Black-and-white thinking	Viewing something as either-or, without considering the full range of possible evaluations	• "I never get picked to help." • "I always mess this up."
Mind reading	Assuming that others are thinking negatively about oneself	• "She doesn't like what I'm wearing." • "They don't want me to be in their group."
Fortune telling	Predicting the future without taking realistic stock of the likelihood of something happening	• "I am going to fail this test." • "No one is going to sit with me at lunch"
Personalization or blame	Assuming that one is the cause of a negative event, ignoring other factors; or blaming others and ignoring one's contributions to the issue	• "This is all my fault." • "He always gets me in trouble."
"Should" and "must" statements	Thinking that things must or should be a certain way	• "I should join more clubs so I get into college." • "I should be able to do this."
Overgeneralization	Assuming that the occurrence of one negative event means that additional bad things will happen	• "I'll never win." • "I can't count on anyone!"
Catastrophizing	Making negative predictions about the future based on little or no evidence	• "My mom is late. She's never going to come." • "My friends aren't here. They ditched me."
Labeling	Classifying oneself negatively after an undesired event	• "I'm so stupid." • "I'm the dumbest person alive."
Disqualifying the positive	Ignoring or dismissing positive things that have happened	• "Oh, that doesn't count. I just got lucky." • "They didn't mean that. They were just being nice."

Note. Based on Burns (1999).

her work schedule makes it difficult for her to come to school events during the day. I saw you both at Math Night last month—she looked so happy to be here with you." Here, the teacher has validated the student's feelings and then reframed the conversation about their mom's attendance at school events to include a more factual representation of the situation. This can help to adjust the student's thinking and may gradually encourage them to consider more nuanced explanations of what is upsetting them.

Let's consider another example. Frustrated, a student says, "I'm so stupid. I'm awful at math." Refer back to Table 10.3. What type(s) of thought distortion is present here? This example has two—labeling ("I'm so stupid.") and black-and-white thinking ("I'm awful at math."). Again, let's pay attention to what is likely fueling this statement. The student is likely feeling frustrated, overwhelmed, or embarrassed by the difficulty they are having. Educators can begin by validating these feelings: "You sound frustrated." Then, they might reframe for the student, saying: "Fractions have been pretty tricky for you. But you did excellent with our place value unit last month. I know if you keep at it, fractions will get easier." Notice here that the educator did not say, "Don't be silly. You're great at math." When a student knows that they are struggling, this type of statement may be seen as ingenuine or placating. Educators also run the risk of invalidating the student's emotions (frustration, overwhelm, embarrassment) or discrediting their experience (having a tough time with the math assignment). Therefore, educators are more likely to shift the student's thinking if the reframed statements they offer are authentic, genuine, and factual. In Table 10.4, we offer three additional examples. Consider how you might reframe each of these student statements to reengage students in their learning.

TABLE 10.4. Reframing Practice

Student statement	Type of cognitive distortion	Potential reframing	Double check
"There's no use. I'll never be able to keep up."			☐ Authentic ☐ Genuine ☐ Factual
"No one likes me here anyway."			☐ Authentic ☐ Genuine ☐ Factual
"I'm a terrible person."			☐ Authentic ☐ Genuine ☐ Factual

As we conclude this chapter, we invite you to stop and reflect on some steps you might take in the next week.

STOP AND REFLECT

1. Are there specific students you are concerned about? What will your next steps be?
2. Are there proactive strategies you can use in your setting to help one or more students?
3. What one or two recommendations from this chapter can you try out over the next week?

Conclusion

In this chapter, we discussed anxiety and depression and their effects on children and adolescents in the classroom. We shared several strategies for supporting students with each of these disorders in the classroom, including graduated exposure, self-monitoring, teaching positive self-talk, and reframing cognitive distortions. In the next chapter, we turn our focus to trauma, posttraumatic stress disorder, and secondary traumatic stress.

RELATED RESOURCES

Child Mind Institute
https://childmind.org/topics/resources-for-teachers
Offers guidance for working with children and adolescents with anxiety or depression, among other mental health conditions.

American Academy of Pediatrics—Supporting Students with Anxiety in School
www.aap.org/en/patient-care/school-health/mental-health-in-schools/supporting-students-with-anxiety-in-school
Differentiates between healthy anxiety and anxiety disorders, explains symptoms of different types of anxiety, and offers suggestions for supporting students with anxiety at school.

Mental Health America
https://mhanational.org/mental-health-learning-hub
Provides concise descriptions of the causes, symptoms, and treatments of many mental health disorders, including anxiety and depression.

CHAPTER 11

Trauma, Posttraumatic Stress Disorder, and Secondary Traumatic Stress

KEY IDEAS

1. Many students experience potentially traumatic events. Some of these students endure ongoing traumatic stress that impacts their learning and classroom behavior.
2. There are many strategies that educators can use to support students experiencing ongoing traumatic stress.
3. Knowing about students' experiences of trauma can cause secondary traumatic stress in educators, but there are strategies that educators can use to prevent or mitigate its effects.

Thomas and Jake were recently in a serious automobile accident with their teammate from another town. Thomas and Jake sustained injuries but have been released from the hospital and have returned to school. Their teammate, Liam, who was driving the vehicle, did not survive. In Thomas and Jake's return to school, their coach has noticed stark differences in how they seem to be processing the event. Thomas appears sad at times, but has resumed participating in class activities, attending practice, and socializing with friends. Jake has been much more withdrawn. He is frequently absent, often asks to be excused from class, has withdrawn from his friends, and rarely attends practice.

Defining Trauma

Trauma is experienced when an event (or series of events) overwhelms an individual's capacity to cope (Herman, 1997). Generally, traumatic events generate feelings of fear, terror, and powerlessness (Herman, 1997). They may also compromise feelings of safety, agency, dignity, or belonging (McGlynn-Wright & Briner, 2021). As evidenced by the vignette, however, individuals exposed to the same event may not respond to it in the same way. Trauma is defined by a person's *response* rather than the event itself (SAMHSA, 2014a). There are a number of factors that can influence how a student (or adult) responds to a potentially traumatic event, including personal (e.g., age, preexisting mental health concerns), social (e.g., level of family and community support before, during, and after the event), and contextual factors (e.g., severity and chronicity of the event, additional stressors; Chafouleas et al., 2019; Harvey, 1996). It is important to not assume that a student exposed to a specific event has experienced trauma; instead, one should monitor for signs of traumatic stress to determine next steps.

In this chapter, we first discuss the types of events that can be traumatic for students. We then describe the effects of trauma on learning and behavior in the classroom, along with strategies educators can use to promote healing and learning for students exposed to trauma. We detail symptoms related to one potential condition resulting from trauma: posttraumatic stress disorder (PTSD). We then turn our attention to the mental health of educators working with students exposed to trauma. We define secondary traumatic stress and share strategies for preventing or mitigating its effects on educator mental health. We conclude with considerations related to student and educator experiences of grief.

Although trauma can occur at any age, young children are particularly vulnerable to the negative effects of trauma due to their biological need for attachment and the rapid brain development happening during this period (Perry & Pollard, 1998; Shonkoff et al., 2012). Early social interactions—whether they are consistent and predictable or chaotic and unpredictable—shape and organize the neural pathways of a child's brain (Perry, 2008; Perry & Pollard, 1998; Perry et al., 1995; Shonkoff et al., 2012). When children's early experiences are traumatic, they may become hypervigilant, often scanning for danger to protect themselves. As a result, they may experience an immediate "fight, flee, or freeze" response at any sign of threat, whether real or perceived (Perry, 2009; Perry & Pollard, 1998; Shonkoff et al., 2012). Fighting refers to physically or verbally lashing out in an effort to protect oneself. Fleeing refers to escaping the threatening environment (e.g., running away). Freezing refers to shutting down (e.g., reduced movement, speech) in an effort to protect oneself. Each of these responses are adaptive—the young child's body is trying to protect itself from any further harm. However, this overutilization of the stress response early in life not only taxes the system but can also cause other areas and functions of the brain to be underused and therefore underdeveloped (Davis et al., 2015).

Substantial research has been conducted on *adverse childhood experiences* (ACEs; Felitti et al., 1998): events during childhood that are potentially traumatic. When the term ACEs was first introduced, it focused primarily on events within a child's household: psychological, physical, or sexual abuse; neglect; domestic violence; or substance use, mental illness, or incarceration of a member of the household (Felitti et al., 1998). In general, adults who experienced multiple ACEs as children have substantially poorer mental and physical health in adulthood than adults who have not experienced multiple ACEs during childhood (Felitti et al., 1998; Hughes, Bellis, et al., 2017). The conceptualization of ACEs has since been expanded to include community and collective violence (e.g., bullying, gang violence, war), immigration and migration experiences, parental separation or divorce, discrimination, and natural and manmade disasters (Bernard, 2020; Garner et al., 2021; WHO, 2018). There has been increased acknowledgment of the potentially traumatic nature of racism and discrimination (American Psychological Association, 2017). Black youth, for example, endure an average of five experiences of racial discrimination each day (English et al., 2020), and these experiences have been linked to negative mental and physical health outcomes for Black youth (Cave et al., 2020; Priest et al., 2013). As evidenced from the example of racial trauma, potentially traumatic events are not always finite events; instead, they can be ongoing in nature.

Educators and schools have the potential to cause, compound, or heal experiences of trauma. Consider again that trauma can be experienced when an individual is overwhelmed by feelings of fear, terror, and powerlessness. When during the school day or in a school building might this occur? Unfortunately, there are several examples present in schools. Students may experience trauma in response to bullying or other acts of physical or relational violence (Idsoe et al., 2012; National Academies of Sciences, Engineering, and Medicine, 2016). Exclusionary and punitive discipline practices (e.g., suspension, expulsion) may also cause trauma for students (Cribb Fabersunne et al., 2023). Finally, implicit or explicit attacks on one's identity can be traumatic (Allwood et al., 2022). In schools, this might include harassment based on one's gender identity; policing of the language, hair styles, or clothing one wears; or a lack of representation of one's identity in the curriculum. Each of these experiences can cause students to feel powerless, or stripped of safety, agency, dignity, or belonging. It is important that educators and schools recognize their influential role in students' lives. Educators have tremendous potential to be supportive and caring adults in students' lives in ways that buffer students from the negative effects of trauma (Hong, Kim, et al., 2024; Moore & Ramirez, 2016; Murphey & Sacks, 2019). Educators and schools, however, can also advertently or inadvertently contribute harm to students' lives (e.g., Wolf & Kupchick, 2016), and thus, it is important to reflect upon if and how this might be happening.

STOP AND REFLECT

1. What are some examples of practices in your setting with the potential to promote student safety, agency, dignity, and belonging? How might you strengthen the use of these practices?
2. What are some examples of practices in your setting that have the potential to cause students to feel fearful or powerless? How might you limit the use of these practices?

Trauma does not guarantee negative outcomes for students (Garner et al., 2021; Sherin & Nemeroff, 2011). Students experiencing trauma are often resourceful in adapting to a world that has not been kind to them. Some students may even experience posttraumatic growth, including positive mental, emotional, or psychological growth after a traumatic event (Tedeschi & Calhoun, 1995; Tedeschi et al., 2018). Examples of posttraumatic growth include increased self-awareness, self-confidence, appreciation for self or others, or a greater appreciation for life (Tedeschi & Calhoun, 1995). If these positive changes occur, they are experienced in addition to the negative effects of trauma (Meyerson et al., 2011). Recall that, by definition, trauma also includes negative impacts on daily functioning (SAMHSA, 2014a).

Symptoms of Trauma

Trauma can have several negative effects on student learning and behavior in the classroom. Most notably, the stress response system of students experiencing chronic or ongoing trauma may over- or underreact to potential threats in the environment. In optimal conditions, the human stress response system uses current and prior information and available resources to judge the severity of any threat (Lazarus & Folkman, 1984). In the case of threat, it activates the autonomic nervous system, helping individuals to "fight, flee, or freeze" to protect themselves from danger (Perry et al., 1995). However, for students chronically exposed to trauma, it becomes adaptive to constantly scan the environment for danger and to respond to any indication of potential danger. In these cases, students are more likely to "fight, flee, or freeze" in response to small signs of danger or even neutral stimuli (Perry, 1995; Perry & Pollard, 1998). Students may have an exaggerated startle response, responding to any loud noises, slight touches, or perceived slights. They may also constantly scan adults' faces for signs of danger and interpret neutral facial expressions as signs of anger or frustration. This has been adaptive in other circumstances; their safety and well-being have been jeopardized. Scanning for any sign of danger is the body's way of trying to protect itself.

In addition to a compromised stress response system, students exposed to trauma may exhibit other learning and behavioral difficulties in the classroom. These can include challenges with attention (Perfect et al., 2016), language (Perfect et al., 2016), memory (Cross et al., 2017; Perfect et al., 2016), and cognitive flexibility (Cross et al., 2017). Students' ability to regulate emotions (Cross et al., 2017), build and maintain relationships, and maintain self-esteem can also be affected by trauma (e.g., Cicchetti & Doyle, 2016; Harter, 1998; Kim, Lee, et al., 2022; Riggs, 2010; Tricket et al., 2011). Importantly, not all students exposed to trauma will experience these negative effects. However, familiarity with these common effects can provide insight into students' challenges in the classroom and help educators to identify appropriate supports when the concerns surface.

Educators might see challenges with attention in the classroom because students exposed to trauma are worried about things outside of the current lesson (e.g., safety of a parent; Craig, 2016). Due to a heightened stress response system, students may also be scanning for danger rather than attending to classroom instruction. This constant scanning for danger can also affect students' memory. If the brain is scanning for danger, there is less available working memory to process instructional content and verbal information (Pickens & Tschopp, 2017). Trauma can also have enduring effects on students' visual, verbal, spatial, and working memory (Perfect et al., 2016). In addition, it is common for educators to witness difficulties with communication in students exposed to trauma. As previously discussed, because the brain is trying to prevent further harm, it may interpret neutral body language or tone of voice as threatening (Pickens & Tschopp, 2017). Furthermore, the part of the brain responsible for language production, Broca's area, is highly sensitive to stress hormones (Kolassa & Elbert, 2007). Therefore, when a child is highly stressed (which happens more frequently for students exposed to trauma), they may remain speechless or silent because they are not able to produce the speech needed to respond.

Students exposed to trauma may also display challenges with emotional and behavioral regulation, self-esteem, and social skills. Challenges with emotional and behavioral regulation can be caused by the student's heightened stress response system. Because this system interprets information as more stressful than it would appear to a typical stress response system (Perry & Pollard, 1998), it is quick to jump into "fight, flee, or freeze," aiming to protect the student. However, when the body moves into a "fight, flee, or freeze" state, the area of the brain responsible for higher order thinking, including emotional and behavioral regulation, becomes less available (Siegel & Bryson, 2012). In these moments, which can occur frequently for those exposed to trauma, students have less access to the areas of the brain that assist with emotional and behavioral regulation. Educators may find that students exposed to trauma have difficulty with cognitive flexibility or viewing a situation from multiple perspectives. In general, students under high levels of stress need to brainstorm solutions quickly—they do not have time to weigh multiple options or perspectives for their potential benefits (Craig, 2016). Thus, although children who have experienced trauma are very resourceful in solving problems, it may be less relevant to them to explore multiple options before choosing a path forward. In Table 11.1, we list several strategies educators can use to compensate for and build these skills in their students.

Students exposed to trauma may also exhibit difficulties with self-esteem. Traumatic experiences can make children and adolescents feel deficient and flawed (Pickens & Tschopp, 2017). Trauma often involves students being hurt by others (e.g., abuse, neglect, interpersonal violence). Students may interpret these actions as an indicator of their self-worth, resulting in negative long-term effects on their self-esteem (Alexander, 2019).

Last, students exposed to trauma may have difficulty building or maintaining relationships. In some cases, students have learned that adults can be unreliable or dangerous. They may avoid relationships to protect themselves from further pain (Pickens & Tschopp, 2017). Trauma can halt brain development at the age at which it was experienced until it is addressed (Perry, 2020). Therefore, students may lack developmentally appropriate social skills for engaging with their peers (Pickens & Tschopp, 2017).

Classroom Supports for Students Experiencing Traumatic Stress

Table 11.1 includes several strategies educators might use to support students displaying various areas of challenge associated with exposure to trauma. In addition, educators can work to reduce potential triggers in the

TABLE 11.1. Common Areas of Challenge and Potential Classroom Supports for Students Experiencing Traumatic Stress

Areas of challenge	Potential supports
Attention	• Use multisensory instruction (e.g., pair verbal directions with visual cues, pictures, or gestures; Alexander, 2019). • Embed opportunities to actively engage with the content (e.g., collaborative work, creating a product; McLeskey et al., 2017). • Provide scaffolding for planning and problem solving (e.g., graphic organizers, explicit instruction, peer or adult support; McLeskey et al., 2017).
Cognitive flexibility	• Across content areas (e.g., math, social relationships), allow students to share multiple ways of solving problems. Emphasize the value in these varied approaches, the unique benefits of each approach, and the shared outcome that they all achieve (McLeskey et al., 2017). • When the class encounters a problem (e.g., something is missing), brainstorm multiple ways to solve it and then decide on the approach to try first. • Use literature as an opportunity to teach perspective taking (e.g., considering a plot or conflict from different characters' perspectives; Alexander, 2019; Burdick & Corr, 2021). • Limit the use of sarcasm as students often misinterpret or are confused by these statements. • Offer your perspective on situations ("It seems to me that . . .) and invite students to share their perspectives to illustrate a variety of perspectives (Alexander, 2019).
Language	• Pair language about your emotions with nonverbal cues (e.g., in addition to a big smile or high five, say "I'm so proud of you!"; Liu et al., 2019). • Begin scaffolding when you see facial expressions that indicate panic (e.g., the "deer in headlights look") to prevent further shutting down. • Reduce verbal demands if you can see that the student is in a heightened state of arousal (Dorado et al., 2016).
Memory	• Use cues or visuals to help with retrieval from memory (Pearson & Wilbiks, 2021). • Use instructional scaffolding techniques such as word banks, number lines, and other references free up working memory for critical thinking (McLeskey et al., 2017). • Reduce cognitive load through explicit instruction (Hughes, Morris, et al., 2017) • Teach metacognitive strategies for memory—such as rehearsal strategies—which can help with encoding material into long-term memory (de Boer et al., 2018).

(continued)

TABLE 11.1. *(continued)*

Areas of challenge	Potential supports
Emotional and behavioral regulation	• In moments of dysregulation, "bottom-up" sensorimotor strategies can help calm a student's sensory system. Try deep breathing, tapping, or humming next to the student to see if they will join you (Perry, 2009). • If the student's dysregulation caused harm or disruption that needs to be repaired, support the student in restoring the relationships that were impacted (e.g., through shared conversations that identify the harm, consider other's perspectives, and develop a plan for repairing the relationship; Romero et al., 2019). • Take time to reflect on your own emotional regulation strategies, as educators' emotions impact students, and educators' displays of emotional regulation can serve as important models for students (Frenzel et al., 2021).
Self-esteem	• Provide specific praise indicating what students do well (McLeskey et al., 2017). • Invite students to take caregiving roles (e.g., taking care of a plant, class pet) and classroom jobs (Romero et al., 2019). • Provide choice. This builds students' confidence in their abilities to influence what happens to them (Sciaraffa et al., 2018). • Pair high expectations for performance and behavior with scaffolds and accommodations that allow students to be successful (McLeskey et al., 2017).
Building and sustaining relationships	• Demonstrate curiosity, warmth, acceptance, and empathy toward students (Burdick & Corr, 2021). • Aim for a 5:1 ratio of positive to negative interactions (Duong et al., 2019). • Learn about student interests and hobbies; ask about these with no other agenda (Burdick & Corr, 2021; Romero et al., 2019). • Deliver predictable, consistent, and nonpunitive responses to student behavior (Pickens & Tschopp, 2017). • Support students' connections with peers by scaffolding social interactions and giving them opportunities to demonstrate their strengths (Sciaraffa et al., 2018). • Speak positively about students in ways that are not directly contingent on academics or behavior (Mikami et al., 2013). This may improve peers' perceptions of their classmates (Hughes & Im, 2016).

Note. Adapted from Koslouski et al. (2023), Understanding and responding to the effects of trauma in the classroom: A primer for educators. *Social and Emotional Learning: Research, Practice, and Policy, 1,* 100004. Copyright © 2023 Elsevier. Adapted with permission.

classroom. Because of their resemblance to features of the original traumatic event, triggers can activate the stress response system of students who have previously been exposed to trauma and invoke a "fight, flee, or freeze" response. Trauma is often stored as sensory memories, and having similar sensory experiences (e.g., sounds, smells, images) in the present can activate the traumatic memory (Perry & Pollard, 1998). A common sensory feature of traumatic experiences can be loud noises (yelling, fighting, slamming doors, sirens, alarms; Alexander, 2019; Perry & Pollard, 1998; Pickens & Tschopp, 2017). Hearing these noises in the school setting can cause students to reexperience the feelings (e.g., fear, terror) associated with the original traumatic event. Smells can also generate particularly strong memories (Toffolo et al., 2012). If, for example, the aroma of citrus or cleaning supplies was present at the original event, these smells in the classroom may trigger memories or feelings associated with the original event. Physical touch can also be triggering in cases where the student has experienced physical or sexual abuse, for example. Emotions can also be associated with the original event and cause negative reactions in the classroom. If, for example, a student felt ashamed, embarrassed, or helpless during the original event, experiencing these feelings in the classroom (e.g., not knowing an answer, making a mistake) may cause the student to act out or shut down (Alexander, 2019). Finally, anniversaries or certain times of year (e.g., holidays associated with negative experiences) can bring back memories associated with the original event (Alexander, 2019; Pickens & Tschopp, 2017; Sciaraffa et al., 2018).

Educators will not be able to avoid all of these potential triggers in the classroom. Instead, it is valuable to recognize the range of classroom experiences that might trigger students' memories of past traumatic events, and to recognize that sudden changes in behavior (e.g., acting out, shutting down) might be in response to undisclosed triggers. Importantly, even when students cannot remember the traumatic experience(s), or experienced it as an infant or toddler, their body will have stored sensory memories of it (Perry & Pollard, 1998). Similar sensory experiences, such as fighting, screaming, or sirens, can elicit the feelings of fear and terror that were originally experienced (Crespo & Fernández-Lansac, 2016; Perry & Pollard, 1998). Students may not recognize the connection between the traumatic event and present moment but will respond strongly to these triggers. In addition to building their own awareness, educators can work to minimize the effects of these triggers in the school setting. For example, educators can pay attention to student responses to physical proximity and touch, provide warnings before transitions and loud noises, and avoid raised voices to reduce the occurrence and impact of these potential triggers.

Symptoms and Treatment of PTSD

> Jake has not been able to stop thinking about the car accident, even in the middle of class. The moments leading up to the accident keep replaying in his head. Each time, he begins sweating, his heart races, and he jumps when the car gets struck. On the occasional nights that Jake is able to sleep, he wakes up sweating and terrified from nightmares about the accident. He is afraid to get in a car and hasn't been able to drive by the location of the accident. Jake wishes he had been the one to die and feels intense guilt that Liam passed away. Jake has found it challenging to attend school—he cannot concentrate on his schoolwork and doesn't understand how other students can be laughing or smiling. Most often, he just wants to be alone but finds he cannot escape the horrific flashbacks.

Jake is likely experiencing symptoms of PTSD, which affects approximately 5% of children and adolescents by the age of 18 (Merikangas et al., 2010). As evidenced by Thomas in this chapter's vignette, not all students exposed to trauma will experience PTSD or sustained mental health impairment. It is important to know, however, that PTSD is not the only mental health condition that can result from experiences of trauma. Because children and adolescents can have varied responses to trauma, and symptoms overlap across conditions, anxiety, depression, attention-deficit/hyperactivity disorder (ADHD), and oppositional defiant disorder (ODD) can also emerge as a result of a traumatic event (Perry, 2008; Perry & Pollard, 1998). This chapter focuses on PTSD but also see Chapter 10 for more information about anxiety and depression, and Chapter 12 for more information about ADHD and ODD.

PTSD has two sets of criteria: one for children ages 6 and below, and one for children and adults ages 7 and above (American Psychiatric Association, 2022). We first introduce the criteria for older children and adults and then describe key differences in the criteria for younger children. Regardless of age, a diagnosis of PTSD is only warranted after an individual's exposure to actual or threatened death, serious injury, or sexual violence (American Psychiatric Association, 2022). The trauma exposure can be direct (experiencing it), witnessing it live, or learning about the traumatic experience of a close family member or friend. In addition to exposure, an individual experiencing PTSD will have intense psychological distress or physiological reactions (e.g., racing heart, sweating, fainting) when exposed to reminders of the trauma. They will also experience involuntary flashbacks or nightmares about the trauma. They may experience excessive guilt about the event, persistent negative thoughts about themselves and the world, and feel isolated from others. Lastly, individuals experiencing PTSD will often have difficulty sleeping and concentrating and may display hypervigilant or irritable behaviors.

STOP AND REFLECT

1. Refer back to the vignette. What details suggest that Jake might be experiencing PTSD?
2. What details from the vignette suggest that Thomas is likely not experiencing PTSD?

There are some key developmental differences in how PTSD may manifest in children ages 6 and younger (American Psychiatric Association, 2022). In young children, psychological distress might be displayed as unprovoked outbursts with high levels of anger and irritability (e.g., extreme temper tantrums). Intrusive memories and flashbacks may be expressed through play rather than words. Young children experiencing PTSD might display increased fear, confusion, or sadness. They may withdraw from social situations, and like older children, adolescents, and adults, may experience difficulty with sleep and concentration.

PTSD is not diagnosed until symptoms have persisted for at least 1 month (American Psychiatric Association, 2022). It is expected that individuals exposed to trauma may experience these symptoms in the immediate aftermath of the event (SAMHSA, 2014b). Generally, these will subside and a PTSD diagnosis is not warranted. When these symptoms persist for at least a month, and cause significant impairment in daily functioning (e.g., relationships, home, school), a PTSD diagnosis may be warranted.

PTSD is most commonly treated using cognitive-behavioral therapy (CBT), and often with trauma-focused CBT. Trauma-focused CBT teaches children and adolescents anxiety management techniques (e.g., deep breathing, muscle relaxation) to help them cope with reminders of the traumatic event (Cohen & Mannarino, 2015). Once these strategies have been mastered, counseling often involves reconstructing a narrative of the trauma, and work to reframe any overgeneralizations (e.g., all cars are dangerous) or cognitive distortions that have arisen from the traumatic experience. As needed, gradual exposure to feared situations may also be incorporated into therapy. In younger children not yet developmentally ready for CBT, play therapy can be used to help them heal from the experience (Humble et al., 2018). In Figure 11.1, we offer an important note about student trauma disclosure.

Symptoms of Secondary Traumatic Stress

The gravity of a traumatic event can also be felt and experienced by individuals not directly exposed to it. This is most common in helping professionals including educators, psychologists, social workers, counselors,

Note to the Reader: Although a common part of counseling in the aftermath of trauma includes reconstructing a narrative of the traumatic event, it is not advised that educators without mental health licensure lead students in this activity. If a student talks to you about a potentially traumatic event, we suggest restating what they have shared rather than asking questions that seek new information. Generally, students will share as much as they are ready to process, and your presence and attention are all that are needed. Introducing questions can bring up parts of the experience the student did not intend to share and can cause psychological or physiological distress. An important exception to this recommendation is asking the student if they feel safe. In the United States, educators are mandated reporters. This means you do need to follow your school's procedures to report signs of potential child neglect, abuse, or endangerment.

FIGURE 11.1. A note about student trauma disclosure.

and medical personnel. Secondary traumatic stress has been described as "the stress resulting from helping or wanting to help a traumatized or suffering person" (Figley, 1995, p. 7). The terms *compassion fatigue* (Figley, 2002) and *vicarious trauma* (McCann & Pearlman, 1990) are also used to describe secondary exposure to trauma. Secondary traumatic stress can affect educators when they learn about the trauma experiences of their students. Symptoms of secondary traumatic stress can mirror PTSD and manifest across cognitive, physical, emotional, interpersonal, or professional domains of an educator's life (see Table 11.2). Secondary traumatic stress can cause difficulties in one's personal and family life, and professional disengagement. It may also cause declining work performance, and eventually, leaving the profession (Lawson et al., 2019).

> Mr. Phillips, Thomas's and Jake's coach, has found himself overwhelmed with worry about Jake. Mr. Phillips is having trouble sleeping and has little interest or energy for teaching. Mr. Phillips has been unusually impatient with his own children and frustrated by the pettiness of his colleagues.

The onset of secondary traumatic stress is often sudden and in response to an educator becoming aware of a particular event or set of circumstances in a student's life (Stamm, 2002). Without intervention, secondary traumatic stress can cause significant impairment in educators' personal and professional lives (Hydon et al., 2015). The negative effects of secondary traumatic stress can be prevented or remediated through shared conversations about it and various self-care techniques (Caringi et al., 2015). Professional support may also help educators experiencing secondary traumatic stress.

TABLE 11.2. Symptoms of Secondary Traumatic Stress

Domain	Symptoms of secondary traumatic stress
Physical	• Low energy, feeling fatigued in the classroom • Upset stomach or nausea • Breathing challenges • Difficulty sleeping
Emotional	• Feeling numb or detached from students • Feeling anxious • Feeling guilty about not doing enough for students or caregivers • Feeling powerless or hopeless that students will succeed • Feeling sad or depressed • Feeling overwhelmed
Behavioral	• Altering routines at home or school • Changes in eating habits • Withdrawing from colleagues • Sleep disturbances or nightmares • Addiction • Self-injury or suicidal ideation
Cognitive	• Diminished concentration affecting the ability to teach • Difficulty with decision making • Decreased self-esteem • Self-doubt • Blaming others for student challenges • Hypervigilance • Experiencing traumatic imagery
Interpersonal	• Physically and emotionally withdrawing from colleagues or family • Decreased interest in intimacy or physical touch • Isolation from family, friends, and support systems • Becoming impatient or intolerant with others • Mistrust or projection of blame on school leadership
Spiritual	• Questioning the meaning of life • Lost sense of purpose in life • Lacking self-satisfaction • Becoming angry with a Higher Power • Questioning religious or spiritual beliefs
Professional	• Demonstrating little effort toward teaching • Low performance of tasks and responsibilities • Low morale, which affects relationships with colleagues

Note. Adapted from Hydon et al. (2015).

STOP AND REFLECT

1. Refer to Table 11.2. What symptoms of secondary traumatic stress does Mr. Phillips seem to be experiencing?
2. What actions might you take to support a colleague if you notice they are experiencing potential symptoms of secondary traumatic stress?

Supporting Your Own Mental Health While Working with Students Exposed to Trauma

In addition to recognizing the signs of secondary traumatic stress, there are additional steps educators can take to maintain their mental health and well-being while engaging with students who have experienced trauma. Here, we focus on four strategies: (1) conceptualizing student behavior challenges as signs of distress, (2) identifying personal triggers, (3) balancing personal and professional responsibilities, and (4) advocating for a manageable workload.

Conceptualizing Student Behavior Challenges as Signs of Distress

Behavior is a form of communication (Minahan & Rappaport, 2012). Students clap their hands to express excitement, smile to communicate happiness, and cry to show sadness. In the same way, withdrawn, disruptive, or aggressive behaviors communicate emotional experiences or distress. Withdrawn behaviors may communicate exhaustion, defeat, or a lack of trust toward the world. Although disruptive or aggressive behaviors are sometimes perceived as indicators of disrespect or hostility, they may signal unmet physical needs, such as sensory overload or hunger. They may also indicate unmet emotional needs, such as a student lacking a sense of belonging or connection. Finally, disruptive and aggressive behaviors can be the result of underdeveloped skills, such as emotion regulation, impulse control, or social skills.

When students display withdrawn, disruptive, or aggressive behaviors, educators can consider asking themselves, "What is this student trying to communicate?" Most often, it is some form of distress. Perhaps the task demand, environmental conditions, or interpersonal dynamics are not working for them. The student may perceive the task demand as too challenging, become overwhelmed by noise in the environment, or uncomfortable working with a new service provider. After determining what the student might be trying to communicate, educators can consider how to support that need. When educators are able to shift their focus about student behavior from frustration or anger to curiosity about what the student is trying to communicate, they are better positioned to provide responsive supports (Koslouski et al., 2023). Furthermore, educators are less likely to take students' behavior personally, which can help to protect their mental health.

Identifying Personal Triggers

Whether or not they have previously reflected upon it, there are often specific behaviors that are particularly upsetting to educators. When these behaviors occur, educators might feel blood rush to their face, their body temperature rise, or their jaw clench. These are signs that regulating one's emotions might be more challenging (Alexander, 2019). For some educators, a student mocking them might be particularly upsetting. For others, it might be a student ripping up materials that they spent a lot of time creating. Still others might have a strong visceral reaction when a student antagonizes a peer.

Educators can carefully plan for their responses if they are able to proactively identify student behaviors that are particularly challenging for them (Alexander, 2019; Koslouski et al., 2023). Self-awareness of these challenging behaviors can also help educators to validate their own experiences and recover more quickly. Once educators have identified the student behavior(s) that are particularly upsetting to them, they can consider how they generally react, both physiologically (e.g., sweating, heart racing) and behaviorally (e.g., raised voice, deep breath). Educators may notice that they find it challenging to think clearly when consumed by their body's physiological responses to these moments.

By proactively identifying these behaviors, however, educators can consider how they would like to respond to this student behavior in the future. Educators might consider taking a few deep breaths before interacting with the student to help regulate their emotions. They might also consider using a mantra to ground themselves (e.g., "The only behavior I can control is my own."). If possible, educators might switch places with a colleague in these moments (e.g., having a co-teacher step in while they move to another area in the classroom). Consider, for example, an educator who is particularly upset by a student mocking them. The educator might develop a uniform response for when this happens (e.g., saying "No thank you" to the student and walking away). Having a preplanned response can help them to respond in a way that is consistent with their goals and values and to be less flustered in the moment when this behavior occurs.

Most educators will have at least one student behavior that is particularly upsetting to them. Sharing this behavior with trusted colleagues can help educators to proactively plan their responses and to receive validation and feedback from their colleagues. Proactively recognizing the behavior that upsets them most not only increases self-awareness but also can decrease its impact on educators' emotions and mental health.

STOP AND REFLECT

1. What student behaviors do you find particularly upsetting?
2. How do you typically respond to these behaviors, both physiologically (e.g., sweating, increased heart rate) or behaviorally (e.g., raised voice, walking away)?
3. How would you like to respond to these behaviors in the future?

Balancing Personal and Professional Responsibilities

Working with students exposed to trauma can be demanding. Educators may find themselves not only responding to the behavioral and cognitive effects of trauma in the classroom but also thinking about these students long after the school day has ended. Recognizing one's own limits, taking time to rest and replenish, and engaging in self-care are key to maintaining one's mental health and well-being when regularly exposed to the suffering of others, such as working with students exposed to trauma (e.g., Alexander, 2019). Drawing on current frameworks of well-being (e.g., Brown & Applegate, 2012; Robertson & Microys, 2001; Roscoe, 2009), educators might consider six different types of self-care: physical, social, emotional, intellectual, financial, and spiritual. *Physical self-care* includes staying hydrated, eating nutritious meals, exercising, and scheduling preventative medical appointments. *Social self-care* relates to having trusted others, a sense of belonging within a group or organization, and satisfying social interactions. *Emotional self-care* includes the ability to regulate emotions, a sense of control and adaptability in life, and the presence of fun and laughter in one's life. *Intellectual self-care* refers to engaging in work that is stimulating and rewarding, participating in professional learning, and experiencing satisfaction with one's job and hobbies. *Financial self-care* includes living within one's means, saving for unforeseen circumstances, and spending and saving in accordance with one's values. *Spiritual self-care* refers to having a sense of meaning and purpose, engaging in regular reflection and growth, and feeling peaceful. Roscoe (2009) explains that these types of well-being are thought to be synergistic, with holistic improvements supporting overall well-being. Engaging in various types of self-care, recognizing one's own limits, and taking time to rest and replenish allows educators to be more effective across their roles and responsibilities, including supporting students exposed to trauma.

STOP AND REFLECT

1. Revisit the various types of self-care previously discussed. Which areas do you attend to most strongly? Can you identify areas for improvement in your self-care practices?
2. Can you identify one change to implement over the next week that is designed to strengthen an area of self-care?

The types of self-care that benefit each person can differ. In addition, the extent to which school cultures encourage and support self-care varies. It is important to remember that self-care practices may vary substantially across educators within a school, and to practice flexibility with oneself and colleagues in this area.

Advocating for a Manageable Workload

In addition to seeking balance in their own life, advocating for a manageable workload can help educators balance personal and professional responsibilities. Excessive workloads can contribute to educators' emotional exhaustion and desire to leave the profession (Bettini et al., 2017). Educators might suggest institutional audits of their workloads, including an examination of class and caseload sizes, contractual time for completing job responsibilities (e.g., instructional planning, administrative paperwork), and relevant professional learning experiences (Stark et al., 2022). To maintain a healthy workforce, administrators and school boards also need to take responsibility for creating conditions in which educators are able to sustain and thrive professionally. Supporting educator mental health and well-being requires both individual and systemic efforts.

Supporting Students and Educators Navigating Loss and Grief

Before closing out this chapter, we conclude with a discussion of loss and grief as it relates to both students and educators. Although not inherently traumatic, the death of a family member or friend can be unexpected or life altering. As such, we share some considerations around grief to alert educators to how students and colleagues might respond to loss and how they can provide support.

Loss and grief are universal human experiences that can happen at unpredictable times (e.g., in the case of an accident or sudden death), prematurely (e.g., a child dying before their parent), or after an extended illness. When discussing grief, we are referring to the emotions experienced in response to a loss, most commonly a close family member, friend, or pet (see Figure 11.2 for a note about grieved expectations). Because loss can be life-altering, especially in the case of the death of a caregiver or sibling, it is important that educators be informed about grief and its effects on learning.

Grief is neither linear nor timebound. There are also common responses to grief in childhood and adolescence that can be helpful for educators to understand. Although individuals may experience stages of grief, such as denial, anger, bargaining, depression, and acceptance (Kübler-Ross, 1969), these stages are not universal nor always sequential in nature. Transitions and milestones can also resurface feelings of loss and grief. For example, as a high school student approaches graduation, they may feel sadness that their parent who passed away when they were a young child will not be at graduation.

Young children may have difficulty understanding the permanent nature of death and ask the same questions repeatedly as they process it (Dougy Center, 2023). They may also express their feelings or concerns through play. Children may oscillate between periods of strong reactions to the loss (e.g., crying, anger) and periods of acting as though nothing happened. They may have difficulty sleeping or worry about themselves or others dying. Young children may also worry that their wishes, thoughts, or actions caused the death. As much as possible, predictability and structure help children who are grieving to feel a sense of control amid the uncertainty and upheaval in their lives. Offering choice ("Would you like to work at the table or on the carpet?") whenever possible can help children to feel some control in their lives. Children will also likely need flexibility in expectations, as they may have greater difficulty regulating their emotions, following routines, and using previously learned skills (e.g., temporary regression is common in young children).

Note to the Reader: In this chapter, we focus on grief in response to the loss of a close family member, friend, or pet. Grief can also be experienced in relation to an unrealized expectation or vision for one's life. For example, caregivers may experience grief after receiving a diagnosis for their child that will affect their independence across the lifespan. Caregivers may need time to mourn the unrealized vision and dreams they had for their child's life. By understanding that others (and ourselves) may be grieving unrealized expectations, we can exhibit greater understanding and empathy in our interactions.

FIGURE 11.2. A note about grieved expectations.

For older children and adolescents, the permanence of the death will be clearer, and they may contemplate the long-term effects of the loss on their life (Dougy Center, 2023). Like younger children, older children may worry that their thoughts, wishes, or actions caused the death. Some grieving students may show perfectionistic tendencies. Older children and adolescents are likely to experience difficulties sleeping and concentrating. They may also be experiencing substantial changes in routines and responsibilities (e.g., in the case of the death of a parent or sibling). Predictability and structure can help students to feel some sense of control, but flexibility may be needed with assignment deadlines, class attendance, and emotional support (e.g., space to express anger, sadness, frustration, jealousy, exhaustion as needed).

Finally, many educators will have their own experiences of grief. Attending to professional responsibilities amid this grief can elicit a range of emotions (e.g., exhaustion, anger, comfort, relief). Like students who are grieving, educators who are grieving may benefit from structure paired with flexibility. We encourage educators to offer themselves or their colleagues patience, flexibility, and compassion. Again, although loss and grief are not inherently traumatic, the importance of social support and educator understanding in the face of life-altering loss cause us to discuss grief in this chapter.

STOP AND REFLECT

1. What grief reactions have you observed in students or others in your life?
2. When you are experiencing grief, what supports are most helpful to you? How might you let others know that these supports are helpful to you?
3. How might you support colleagues experiencing grief?

Conclusion

In this chapter, we defined trauma and how it affects learning and behavior in the classroom. We shared several strategies for supporting students exposed to trauma and discussed secondary traumatic stress as it relates to educators' work with students. We concluded with considerations related to student and educator experiences of grief. In the next chapter, we transition to supporting students with other behavioral conditions, including attention deficit/hyperactivity disorder (ADHD), oppositional defiant disorder, intermittent explosive disorder, conduct disorder, and substance use disorders.

RELATED RESOURCES

National Child Traumatic Stress Network (NCTSN)
https://nctsn.org
Includes concise resources on different types of trauma, trauma-informed care, and secondary traumatic stress. Resources can be filtered to list those specifically relevant to school personnel.

Trauma and Learning Policy Initiative (TLPI)
https://traumasensitiveschools.org
Offers videos, free downloadable books, and related resources about the impact of trauma on student learning and creating a trauma-sensitive school.

Dougy Center
www.dougy.org
Provides grief resources for school personnel, children, adolescents, and family caregivers. Includes resources for various types of loss, including after an accident, long-term illness, suicide, or violent death.

CHAPTER 12

Other Behavioral Conditions

KEY IDEAS

1. Behavioral conditions—such as attention-deficit/hyperactivity disorder (ADHD), oppositional defiant disorder, intermittent explosive disorder, conduct disorder, and substance use disorders—affect a number of children and adolescents.
2. These conditions can impact learning and classroom behavior in a variety of ways.
3. There are many strategies that educators can use to support students experiencing these behavioral conditions.

Mr. Lee is beside himself. Despite his best efforts, his second block math lessons are not going to plan. Students are not grasping the content. Some students are becoming overwhelmed or frustrated, while others are deliberately ignoring his instructions and disrupting the class. Mr. Lee is not sure where to begin. Generally, he believes that effective instruction engages students and reduces disruptive behavior, but he feels that he has not been able to provide effective instruction with this class. He has begun dreading second block and knows this is likely affecting the effort he is putting into his instruction as well as his relationships with students.

Mr. Lee decides to take a step back. He takes out his second block class list and begins recording notes next to each student's name.

- Annie—grasping the content, annoyed by her classmates' behavior;
- James—flighty, often arriving late to class, struggles to keep up despite wanting to please, does better in a small group;
- Savannah—difficult, defiant, hard to reach;

- Matthew—can't sit still, always moving, wants to learn;
- Will—eager, motivated, seems to be teaching himself.

As Mr. Lee continues this activity, he notices two things. First, there are several students that are generally on-task and invested in their own learning. Second, several students are displaying similar distracted behaviors. For the most part, Mr. Lee perceives that these students want to do well but have trouble sitting still, organizing themselves, and staying on task. Mr. Lee starts to wonder how he might alter his instruction to more effectively teach these students.

Some of the behaviors Mr. Lee is noticing are symptoms of externalizing disorders, conditions that affect the learning and behavior of many children and adolescents. In contrast to internalizing disorders, in which behaviors are directed inward (see Chapter 10), externalizing disorders include behavior that is directed outward toward the environment (e.g., aggression, impulsivity; Achenbach, 1978; Liu et al., 2011). Close to 10% of children and adolescents ages 3–17 have been diagnosed with attention-deficit/hyperactivity disorder (ADHD; Bitsko et al., 2022). Approximately 1–5% of children and adolescents exhibit more intense externalizing disorders, such as oppositional defiant disorder, intermittent explosive disorder, or conduct disorder. A final segment of externalizing disorders that we will cover—substance use disorders—affect 1–3% of adolescents, meaning that educators will likely work with students with a range of externalizing disorders over the course of their careers.

This chapter has three primary sections. The first section focuses on ADHD. The second section focuses on oppositional defiant disorder, intermittent explosive disorder, and conduct disorder. The third section focuses on substance use and substance use disorders. Within each section, we follow a similar format. We first review the symptoms of each of these conditions and how they may present in the classroom. Then, we briefly explain evidence-based treatments for each condition to increase educators' understandings of the skills their students might be working on outside of the classroom (e.g., in school- or community-based therapy). Finally, we share strategies educators can use in the classroom or school environment to support the learning of students with each of these externalizing disorders. In doing so, we hope to increase educators' knowledge, empathy, and self-efficacy with which to work with these students.

Symptoms and Treatment of ADHD

ADHD is a neurodevelopmental disorder characterized by a persistent pattern of inattention, hyperactivity, or impulsivity across settings (American

Psychiatric Association, 2022). The term *neurodevelopmental* means that the disorder generally begins in early childhood as the body's nervous system is developing, though it may not be recognized until later in development, if at all. In its current conceptualization, ADHD can be diagnosed with a primarily inattentive presentation, primarily hyperactive/impulsive presentation, or a combined presentation. Like other mental health disorders, many of the symptoms of ADHD are commonplace and experienced by people without ADHD. For example, most individuals experience moments of distraction at various times. However, it is the frequency, intensity, and severity of symptoms that suggest an ADHD diagnosis may be warranted (Kushner, 2016).

In order for ADHD to be clinically diagnosed, symptoms need to be present for at least six months, incongruent with developmental norms (e.g., toddlers are not expected to sustain attention to tasks for extended periods of time), and interfering with daily functioning (American Psychiatric Association, 2022). ADHD persists through adulthood but requires an onset of symptoms prior to age 12. It is more commonly diagnosed in males. Females tend to exhibit more inattentive than hyperactive symptoms, and it is thought that these symptoms might be more frequently overlooked (Kushner, 2016).

Although children and adolescents with a combined presentation display symptoms of both inattention and hyperactivity, some students primarily display only inattention or hyperactivity. Across presentations, the symptoms are neurologically based and not intentional on the part of the student. Children and adolescents displaying inattention often have difficulty sustaining attention to tasks (e.g., have difficulty getting started, get distracted while working), appear to be daydreaming, and misplace materials (American Psychiatric Association, 2022). They generally have difficulty organizing themselves (e.g., poor time management, messy workspace) and may make mistakes because they have not attended to detail. Children and adolescents displaying impulsivity or hyperactivity appear to always be "on the go," fidget, or leave their seat or space at unexpected times (American Psychiatric Association, 2022). They may also interrupt others and have difficulty waiting their turn.

ADHD can be challenging in the classroom due to expectations to sit for extended periods of time, attend to cognitively demanding activities, and show restraint in small and large groups (e.g., waiting for teacher's attention). In addition, the symptoms of ADHD can make it difficult for students to attend to instruction, which can result in reduced academic achievement, especially if ADHD remains untreated (Arnold et al., 2020).

Treatments for ADHD primarily include psychotherapy, behavioral approaches, and medication (Faraone et al., 2024; Kushner, 2016). Behavioral approaches aim to increase students' skills with which to manage the symptoms of ADHD themselves. Targeted skills include self-regulation, organization, executive functioning, and social skills. For example, depending on a student's developmental level, executive functioning skills might include teaching time management, organizing one's workspace, note taking, or study skills. Targeted social skills might include listening, respecting boundaries, teamwork, and empathy (Kushner, 2016). Depending on student, family, and provider preferences, medication can also be prescribed to help students manage the symptoms of ADHD. These medications can help to increase attention and focus while reducing impulsivity. However, they can cause side effects that require close monitoring (Faraone et al., 2024).

Classroom Supports for Students with ADHD

Students with ADHD often display challenges with executive functioning, such as planning and completing multistep tasks, organizing materials, maintaining focus, and monitoring progress toward goals. Although executive functioning skills do not fully develop in any student until adulthood (Arain et al., 2013), students with ADHD demonstrate greater challenges building these skills. In general, executive functioning demands and expectations increase as students mature. For example, adolescents are expected to display greater organizational and attentional abilities than younger children. There are several proactive strategies educators can use in their classrooms to support students with ADHD. In Figure 12.1, we group supports into those related to structuring the physical environment, providing praise and reinforcement, and offering executive functioning scaffolds. It is important to collaborate with students, families, and colleagues to identify which supports might be most helpful. Students, families, and previous teachers can provide insight about when the student is most successful, offering directions for potential supports.

STOP AND REFLECT

1. It is important to remember that ADHD is a neurodevelopmental disorder and does not reflect willful behavior on the part of the student. Consider your own responses to students' impulsiveness, disorganization, or hyperactivity.
2. Do you frequently become frustrated or impatient with students with ADHD?
3. What actions might you take to remind yourself that these behaviors are not intentional?

Let's return to Mr. Lee and his second block math class. What supports might Mr. Lee consider implementing to increase student learning and

Structure the physical environment
1. **Minimize distractions.** As much as possible, seat students with ADHD away from high traffic areas in the classroom and away from the door. Clear students' desks or work areas of distractions. Reduce distracting classroom displays. 2. **Offer flexible seating.** Students with ADHD can have trouble sitting still. Options to stand, sit on the floor, or change seats can be helpful. 3. **Allow tactile fidget objects.** Fidgeting helps some students to concentrate. Consider allowing fidgets that are not distracting to other students (e.g., quiet, discreet). Also note that fidgets do not always need to be manipulated in students' hands. For example, tapping one's foot or sitting on a tactile cushion can also be helpful. 4. **Post routines and instructions for student reference.** Students with ADHD often forget or have trouble keeping track of multistep instructions. Posting routines and instructions provides a visual reminder of what is expected and what is coming next.
Provide praise and reinforcement
1. **Provide frequent and specific behavioral praise.** Students with ADHD are often being redirected for behaviors that they have difficulty controlling. This can reduce students' self-esteem (Harpin et al., 2016). Frequent and specific praise can help to build students' self-esteem, reinforce learning and behavior, and allow peers to see students in a positive light. 2. **Offer opportunities for leadership and success.** Because students with ADHD are often being redirected, they and their peers may develop negative conceptions of their behavior. Opportunities for leadership and success in the classroom can counter these conceptions. Examples include leading the class in a movement break; inviting students to share a favorite hobby, interest, or collection with their peers; or showcasing completed projects that demonstrate students' hard work and success. 3. **Promote an atmosphere of acceptance.** Communicating that all students are working on something helps students to understand that they and their peers each have strengths and areas for growth. This can help all students—including those with ADHD—to feel more secure in their own areas for growth, and to display greater empathy and acceptance toward their peers. 4. **Provide quiet redirection.** When possible, provide feedback in a 1:1 setting. You might also create a nonverbal signal with each student to let them know they need to adjust their behavior. These simple strategies can reduce embarrassment and promote your relationship with the student (e.g., serving as a coach rather than a disciplinarian).

(continued)

FIGURE 12.1. Proactive strategies for supporting students with ADHD in the classroom.

Offer executive functioning scaffolds

1. **Follow a consistent routine.** This helps students to anticipate what will happen even when they become distracted or miss some instruction.
2. **Teach students to use checklists and graphic organizers.** Students with ADHD may forget the steps of completing a task or overlook key components. Checklists reduce the need to remember multistep processes and allow students to monitor their progress toward completion. Checklists can be used for routines (e.g., packing up) or academic tasks (e.g., solving a word problem). Graphic organizers reduce the burden on students to remember the various components of a task and help them to organize their thoughts. Example graphic organizers include Venn diagrams, concept maps, and place value charts.
3. **Chunk multi-step assignments.** Lengthy assignments can be overwhelming for students with ADHD. Chunking assignments into smaller sections can help students to identify all of the component parts needed to complete an assignment, feel that they can meet the expectations, and experience incremental success toward task completion.
4. **Support time management.** Due to challenges with executive functioning and maintaining focus, students with ADHD may have difficulty anticipating how much time a task will take, and then completing it on that schedule. Consider allocating a certain amount of time to each part of an assignment (or collaborating with students to determine those estimates) and then providing students with a timer to monitor their progress. You may also consider offering extended time for completing tests or assignments due to these challenges.
5. **Offer organizational tools.** Consider teaching students to use color-coded folders, binders, or homework assignment books to keep their assignments and materials organized. Regularly review how to use these tools and provide time for students to use them (e.g., writing in homework assignment book, placing work in appropriate folders).
6. **Frequent check-ins.** Use quick check-ins to confirm that students with ADHD understand the instructions and are making progress. Physical proximity to an educator or on-task peer can also help students with ADHD to stay focused.

FIGURE 12.1. *(continued)*

engagement? You might recall that he noted that some students seemed to have difficulty sitting still (fidgeting), organizing themselves, and grasping the content. Mr. Lee might first consider what routines and organizational strategies he has in place. Do students engage in a "do now" or take out their homework when they arrive to class? Are there extra pencils and paper available for students who need them? Immediately engaging students in a routine when they arrive to class might allow them opportunities to immediately be successful and help Mr. Lee to build positive behavioral momentum in his classroom.

Next, how might Mr. Lee scaffold his instruction to help students who are having difficulty focusing? Would checklists or graphic organizers help students to stay organized and complete increasingly complex math problems? Could working in small groups help to offer variety in the pace of class and peer support that more productively engages students?

STOP AND REFLECT

1. Which of your students seem to exhibit attentional challenges?
2. When do you see them being most successful?
3. What types of tasks are most challenging for them?
4. How might you provide supports to reduce these challenges?

Next, we transition to other types of externalizing mental health disorders: disruptive, impulse-control, and conduct disorders.

Symptoms and Treatment of Disruptive, Impulse-Control, and Conduct Disorders

Recall Mr. Lee's mention of Savannah. She did not seem distracted in the classroom but was instead defiant and disinterested. What might be going on here? How might Mr. Lee support Savannah?

The vast majority of children and adolescents display moments of disruptive or impulsive behavior. Yet a small proportion display frequent and intense behaviors that violate the rights of others (e.g., aggression, property destruction) or cause significant conflict with societal norms or authority figures (Lenz & Lancaster, 2016). In this chapter, we focus specifically on oppositional defiant disorder, intermittent explosive disorder, and conduct disorder, as these can be diagnosed in children and adolescents. A fourth related disorder, antisocial personality disorder, is quite rare and cannot be diagnosed until an individual is 18 years of age. It is important to note that the definitions of these disorders continue to be updated and may continue to be revised over time.

Oppositional defiant disorder, intermittent explosive disorder, and conduct disorder exist on a spectrum, with symptom severity and functional impairment becoming more intense with each subsequent disorder (see Figure 12.2). To warrant a diagnosis, behaviors need to be substantially different from what is expected for a child or adolescent's age and gender, and within their culture (Lenz & Lancaster, 2016).

	Oppositional defiant disorder	Intermittent explosive disorder	Conduct disorder
Behavioral presentation	Frequent angry or irritable mood, argumentative behavior, or vindictiveness Loses temper, argues with adults, defies rules and commands, deliberately annoys others, blames others for mistakes	Repeated verbal or physical outbursts that are grossly out of proportion with the current stressor Outbursts are not planned and not used to achieve a desired object	Repetitive and severe rule violations Initiates fights, displays physical cruelty toward people or animals, may use weapons to harm others, deliberately destroys or steals property
Notes related to diagnosis	Behavior can be isolated to one setting, but cannot only be present with a sibling	Only diagnosed in ages 6 and above.	

FIGURE 12.2. Overview of oppositional defiant disorder, intermittent explosive disorder, and conduct disorder.

Symptoms and Treatment of Oppositional Defiant Disorder

Oppositional defiant disorder affects approximately 3–5% of the population and is most commonly diagnosed before the age of 8 (Hawes et al., 2023). Children and adolescents with oppositional defiant disorder frequently display an angry or irritable mood, argumentative behavior, or vindictiveness for a period of at least 6 months (American Psychiatric Association, 2022). They frequently lose their temper, are easily annoyed, and are often angry or resentful. In the classroom, these students may argue with adults, intentionally defy rules or commands, deliberately annoy others, or blame others for their mistakes or behavior. It is important to note that if the behaviors are only directed toward siblings, a diagnosis of oppositional defiant disorder is not appropriate. Unlike ADHD, symptoms do not need to cut across settings. Although less common, symptoms of oppositional defiant disorder can be concentrated to a specific setting (e.g., home, school; American Psychiatric Association, 2022). For children under the age of 5 years, symptoms must be present most days, whereas for school-age children and adolescents, the behavior must occur at least once per week. Like other psychiatric disorders, these symptoms cause significant distress for the individual or those in their immediate social context (e.g., family, educators, classmates) and have negative impacts on the individual's functioning.

Although some cases of oppositional defiant disorder can remit without treatment, several evidence-based individual and family treatments are recommended and demonstrate promising results (Hawes et al., 2023). Parent–child or family-based therapy is often recommended. These types of therapy teach caregivers positive and negative reinforcement techniques and aim to strengthen the caregiver-child relationship. Individual therapies with the child or adolescent most frequently work on building problem-solving skills, distress tolerance, social skills, and prosocial behaviors (Lenz & Lancaster, 2016).

Symptoms and Treatment of Intermittent Explosive Disorder

It is estimated that intermittent explosive disorder occurs in approximately 3–4% of the U.S. population at some point in their lives (Coccaro & McCloskey, 2019). Intermittent explosive disorder is characterized by repeated behavioral outbursts that include verbal or physical aggression and are grossly out of proportion with the current stressor. These outbursts are not premeditated and are not used to achieve a desired object. In the classroom or school environment, educators may see verbal or physical tirades that do or do not cause injury to others. Property destruction is also common during these episodes and can range from ripping paper to destroying furniture or technological equipment.

Recognizing the normative nature of tantrums or behavioral outbursts in toddlers and preschoolers, intermittent explosive disorder is only diagnosed in individuals ages 6 and up. Intermittent explosive disorder most commonly begins in adolescence and persists throughout adulthood and may precede other comorbid psychiatric diagnoses (Coccaro & McCloskey, 2019). Medical conditions and other psychiatric disorders (e.g., disruptive mood dysregulation disorder, substance use disorder) need to be ruled out before a diagnosis of intermittent explosive disorder can be made.

There are not yet treatments specifically designed for intermittent explosive disorder (Lenz & Lancaster, 2016). Reducing aggression is a primary goal of treatment, and it is thought that a combination of medication and psychotherapy is best for achieving this goal. Currently, cognitive-behavioral therapy (CBT) and play therapy are the most commonly used therapy modalities for treating intermittent explosive disorder in children, adolescents, and adults (Lenz & Lancaster, 2016).

Symptoms and Treatment of Conduct Disorder

The most severe of these three disorders, conduct disorder affects approximately 3% of school-age children and adolescents (Fairchild et al., 2019). It is twice as common in males than females. Conduct disorder is characterized by repetitive and severe rule violations. Educators may witness children or adolescents with conduct disorder frequently initiating fights, bullying or intimidating others, and displaying physical cruelty toward people or animals (American Psychiatric Association, 2022). They may also use a weapon to cause harm to others, deliberately destroy property, or steal items of significant value. It is not uncommon for these students to run away from home or skip school. To warrant a diagnosis, it is expected that at least three serious rule violations have occurred in the past year, and at least one of those has occurred in the past six months (American Psychiatric Association, 2022).

Conduct disorder is most commonly treated using parent-based or family-based interventions (Fairchild et al., 2019; Lenz & Lancaster, 2016), which may be combined with medication, especially in the case of comorbid diagnoses (e.g., ADHD; Fairchild et al., 2019). Goals of treatment include increasing prosocial behaviors, strengthening family dynamics, and teaching coping and communication skills.

Classroom Supports for Students with Oppositional Defiant Disorder, Intermittent Explosive Disorder, or Conduct Disorder

Students with oppositional defiant disorder, intermittent explosive disorder, and conduct disorder have difficulty regulating their emotions, complying with rules or commands, and may exhibit disruptive behavior in the classroom. They generally like to be in control, and educators may often find themselves in power struggles with them. These students often get stuck on a thought, believing that there is only one way to solve a problem (inflexible thinking; Minahan & Rappaport, 2012). Although behavior can escalate quickly in students with these disorders, there are often a small set of warning signs that signal that oppositional, disruptive, or explosive conduct is going to take place. Warning signs can include increased volume (e.g., talking louder), grunting, clenched fists or jaw, rocking back and forth, pacing, or breathing heavily (Minahan & Rappaport, 2012). Once a student's specific warning signs are identified, educators can respond in these moments by offering a break or an emotion regulation strategy to try to prevent further escalation. In Chapter 13, we discuss de-escalation strategies that may be helpful in these instances. Teachers, school mental health professionals, and administrators will also likely want to develop a safety plan so that all staff know how to respond in the case of dangerous behavior.

The Behavior Code (Minahan & Rappaport, 2012) and *Behavior Code Companion* (Minahan, 2014) offer several strategies for increasing prosocial behavior and learning with students with oppositional or explosive behavior. Working to build and maintain a positive relationship with these students is the most beneficial step educators can take. When students perceive that educators like and care about them, they are more likely to comply with instructions and engage in the classroom. Educators can demonstrate their care for students through positive attention and noncontingent reinforcement. For example, educators can show genuine interest in who the student is, take time to learn about their interests, and communicate their investment in helping the student to succeed in school. Educators can also consider how to display empathy and understanding when the student is having a difficult time, whether that is refusing to comply, displaying disruptive behavior, or exhibiting other challenging behaviors.

Another helpful tip is that these students often engage in two types of repetitive questioning: information seeking and challenging (Minahan & Rappaport, 2012). Examples of information-seeking questions are "When is lunch?" or "Why do I have to do this?" It is best to simply answer these questions because, otherwise, the student will continue to repeat them. Answering these questions may help the student to move on. Confrontational questions challenge the educator's instructions or authority. In these cases, the student is not seeking information but is instead purposefully challenging the educator. When this happens, it is best to set a limit and redirect the student (Minahan & Rappaport, 2012).

Because oppositional defiant disorder, intermittent explosive disorder, and conduct disorder involve frequent defiance, in Figure 12.3, we offer several proactive strategies for increasing student compliance with classroom routines and instructions. As illustrated by these strategies, small shifts in educators' language and actions can sometimes increase students' willingness to follow instructions.

> Let's return to Mr. Lee and Savannah. Savannah refuses to engage in class and is generally disruptive and oppositional when Mr. Lee tries to engage with her. He initially resorted to allowing her to do what she wanted to allow him to attend to the other students. With other students now more engaged, how might Mr. Lee work to reengage Savannah?
>
> Mr. Lee decides first to focus on building a stronger relationship with Savannah. He indirectly complements her artwork while speaking to the class (e.g., "Perhaps you are a talented artist like Savannah or a talented athlete like Jameson") and asks for her help with classroom routines. He then begins to communicate that he cares about her learning and believes she can be a top math student. He sets a goal for himself of embedding at least one choice into each class assignment and monitoring how she responds. For example, on some days, he allows students to choose to work independently or in small groups. On another occasion he gives students a longer assignment and tells them to choose 5 of the 10 questions to complete. Although there are

Embed choice. There are many ways to embed student choice, allowing students to experience an element of control. For example, you can allow students to choose where to work, with whom to work, when to complete a task, the materials they will use, and when to finish.
Avoid yes-or-no questions. Adults often phrase commands as questions (e.g., "Can we clean up now?") or add "okay?" to the end of their statements ("Let's clean up now, okay?"). This phrasing allows students to say no, which can initiate a power struggle. Unless "yes" or "no" responses are acceptable, do your best to avoid yes-or-no questions.
Use declarative language. Adults often use authoritative statements to give students instructions (e.g., "Pass in your work." "Write your name on your paper."). Students who are oppositional or defiant may resist these types of statements. Consider using declarative language instead, in which you verbalize what you are noticing. Rather than saying "Raise your hand," you might say, "I'm having a tough time hearing with multiple students talking at once." Instead of "Please pick up that paper," try, "Oh, that paper just fell."
Give demands privately and then move away. Private demands can help to reduce oppositional moments with students. Moving away after sharing the instruction gives the student time to process the information, allows them to respond on their own terms, and reduces opportunities for confrontation. For example, you might put a note on the student's desk that says, "Please choose a book from the front table" and then walk away. Alternatively, you might quietly say to a student, "I need help finding a spot for these materials," leaving the materials and walking away. Nonverbal commands can also fulfill a similar goal of keeping the command discrete and reducing opportunities for confrontation. Walking away after sharing the instruction or redirecting your attention elsewhere communicates your belief that the student will follow through with the request, and reduces the public nature of their compliance.
Preview demands with the student. Because students with defiant behaviors like to be in control, knowing expectations ahead of time can help them to feel a sense of control. You might share with the student, "After lunch, we will be going to an assembly in the auditorium" or "When Mrs. Isabella arrives, you can grab your snack and go with her."
Provide rationale first. Adults often state a command, and then provide the rationale. "Please clean up. It is time to go to Music." Consider flipping this statement to provide the rationale first: "It is time to go to Music. Please clean up." Because the student's first instinct might be to object, this gives the student a moment to consider the rationale before hearing the command.
Offer extended time to comply. To embed choice and offer some control, you might offer students extended time to comply. For example, "Please put your work on my desk before you leave for next period" or "Before going home today, please find a time to plug in your device to charge." This allows the student to have some control over the timeline for their compliance and makes the command feel less abrupt.

FIGURE 12.3. Proactive strategies for increasing student compliance with classroom routines and instructions. Based on Minahan and Rappaport (2012).

certainly still times of noncompliance, Mr. Lee begins to have some success engaging Savannah. He makes sure to return completed work to her with written praise and works to keep his instruction and redirection indirect and declarative. He has learned who she enjoys working with in the classroom, as well as some of her interests and talents, which he uses to engage her.

In working with these challenging behaviors, it is crucial for educators to monitor how their own emotions, mental health, and well-being are impacted. Responding to disruptive or defiant behavior can be exhausting and overwhelming. This becomes even more intensified when student learning is regularly interrupted, or student and staff safety is jeopardized. Educators can work to build a repertoire of strategies for regulating their own emotions, taking breaks, and keeping themselves and students safe in these instances. In moments of student noncompliance, educators might switch with another adult or tell the student they will circle back in a few minutes. Both of these strategies can encourage student compliance in addition to giving educators some space from the situation. In cases of severe disruption or aggression, educators will likely need colleagues to help them manage the situation, and potentially to process after the immediate emergency has subsided.

STOP AND REFLECT

1. Looking at Figure 12.3, can you identify strategies you have used successfully in the past or might try in the future? Why were they successful or why do you anticipate they will be successful?
2. How do you regulate your own emotions when engaged in this work? What additional supports would be helpful to you?

Next, we transition to a different set of externalizing disorders: substance use disorders.

Symptoms and Treatment of Substance Use Disorders

Adolescent substance use exists on a continuum, beginning with prescribed medication to address health conditions, to experimentation with unprescribed substances, regular use, and more problematic use. Substance use disorders refer to problematic use: continued substance use despite negative effects on one's daily life and relationships. The most commonly used unprescribed substances by adolescents are alcohol, nicotine vaping, and cannabis (Miech et al., 2023). Unprescribed substance use is relatively common in U.S. adolescents. For example, in 2022, 1 in 12 young people ages 12–20 reported binge drinking (five or more alcoholic beverages on one occasion for males; four or more alcoholic beverages on one occasion for females) over a four-week period (SAMHSA, 2022a). In general, the percentage of adolescents reporting substance use increases between eighth and twelfth grade. For example, in 2023, 15% of eighth graders, 31% of tenth graders, and 46% of twelfth graders reported using alcohol in the past year. Approximately one in four twelfth graders reported nicotine vaping in the past year, and 30% reported cannabis use in the past year (Miech et al., 2023). Illicit drug use other than marijuana (e.g., cocaine, heroin, misuse of prescription medication) is less common: approximately 8% of twelfth graders report illicit drug use in the past year. Adolescent use of illicit drugs has remained fairly stable over the past 15 years (Miech et al., 2023), but there has been a dramatic rise in adolescent overdose deaths, causing substantial concern (Friedman et al., 2022; National Institute on Drug Abuse, 2023). This rise has been attributed to adolescent fentanyl use.

Despite fairly common adolescent use or experimentation with alcohol and drugs, much smaller percentages of adolescents have a substance use disorder. Substance use disorders are characterized by dependence on a substance with negative consequences in one's daily life and relationships. There are many types of substance use disorders, including alcohol use disorder, cannabis use disorder, and opioid use disorder. It is estimated that 1.6% of U.S. adolescents (407,000 adolescents ages 12–17) have an alcohol use disorder and approximately 3.2% of U.S. adolescents (788,000 adolescents) have an illicit drug use disorder (Bitsko et al., 2022). Children or adolescents with substance use disorders have difficulty controlling their substance use, may increase their use over time, engage in risky behavior (e.g., driving under the influence), and be unable to stop using the substance despite their best efforts. They are likely to experience problems in their relationships and fail to fulfill responsibilities (e.g., missing work or school). Students may come to school under the influence of a substance (e.g., drunk, high) or experience withdrawal symptoms in the classroom (e.g., sweating or shaking in the case of alcohol withdrawal; American Psychiatric Association, 2022).

Common psychotherapy techniques for treating substance use disorders include motivational interviewing (increasing the adolescent's commitment to change), cognitive-behavioral therapy (recognizing and changing learned associations), and contingency management (reinforcing abstinence or reduced substance use; Volkow & Blanco, 2023). Treatment aims often include reduced substance use or abstinence and alternative coping strategies. Mutual help organizations (e.g., Alcoholics Anonymous, Narcotics Anonymous) are also available and show promising results on reducing adolescent substance use (Kelly et al., 2008; Kelly & Urbanoski,

2012). In the case of alcohol, opioid, or nicotine use disorders, medication has also been approved to help with substance dependence and withdrawal symptoms (e.g., Volko & Blanco, 2023). Unfortunately, adolescent substance use disorders are often chronic, persisting into adulthood with periods of remission and relapse (McCabe et al., 2022; Volko & Blanco, 2023).

Classroom Supports for Students with Substance Use Disorders

Important areas of focus for supporting students with substance use disorders (or suspected substance use disorders) in the classroom include displaying compassion and understanding and referring students to appropriate supports. Many adolescents report using substances to cope with stress; negative experiences; or symptoms of depression, anxiety, pain, or inattention (Connolly et al., 2024; Dow & Kelly, 2013). Some youth report using substances because of perceived or actual peer pressure (Watts et al., 2024), to bring about a positive state (Dow & Kelly, 2013), or to experiment (Connolly et al., 2024). Importantly, adolescents are exposed to frequent portrayals of substance use (tobacco, alcohol, e-cigarette, marijuana) in the media, which has been shown to increase adolescent substance use (Jackson et al., 2018). Last, a subset of adolescents with substance use disorder were prescribed medications (e.g., opioids) and became dependent on the substance, resulting in a substance use disorder (Hadland et al., 2021; Schroeder et al., 2019). It is important that educators do their best not to judge students for substance misuse, and display empathy toward the extreme challenges students with these disorders are facing.

Adolescents express not always knowing who to reach out to when they need help with a substance use disorder (Youth Wellness Hubs Ontario, 2022). They fear being judged, facing disciplinary consequences, or the information reaching others (e.g., parents) without their knowledge. To support students' mental health, educators can be transparent with students about who in the school building is available to support; normalize the idea that the vast majority of students are likely to struggle with social, emotional, or mental health challenges at some point and that support can help; and be transparent about their responsibilities to disclose certain information to other adults (e.g., safety concerns).

It is also important to become familiar with school procedures for supporting students who appear to be intoxicated or under the influence of substances. Educators should inquire about the resources or referral processes available in their school for students with suspected substance use disorders (or concerning levels of substance use). For example, educators might speak with a school mental health professional in their school to consider next steps in having a conversation with the student, their family, and potential community support services (e.g., pediatrician, behavioral health services, support groups). Some schools also have Student Assistance Programs, modeled from Employee Assistance Programs, that provide supports to students experiencing substance use or misuse or other mental health concerns (SAMHSA, 2019b).

Although we primarily focus on supporting students with existing substance use disorders, there are also steps educators can take to help reduce the likelihood of students developing substance use disorders. Several health education resources exist (e.g., SAMHSA, 2022b; U.S. Department of Justice, 2019). These resources aim to provide students with factual information about the effects of substance use on their brain, development, and behavior; build students' relationships and emotion coping skills so they have strategies for dealing with challenging emotions; educate students about the influences of marketing and media on adolescents; and help students to develop strategies for responding to peer pressure.

STOP AND REFLECT

1. What implicit and explicit messages do your students receive about substance use? Consider their observations of substance use, potential peer or family influences, marketing influences, and media.
2. What developmentally appropriate activities might you embed into existing instruction for your students to learn about substance use, misuse, or healthy coping mechanisms?

Conclusion

In this chapter we discussed ADHD, oppositional defiant disorder, intermittent explosive disorder, conduct disorder, and substance use disorders. We shared the symptoms of each condition as well as strategies for supporting students with each of these disorders in the classroom. As we conclude this chapter on other behavioral disorders, how are you feeling? If sad or overwhelmed, take a few moments to recenter yourself. The symptoms and effects of mental health conditions can be exhausting and demoralizing for students, families, and educators. Consider one next step you can take to support a student, family, or colleague. Over time, consider how you might organize your actions to support a specific student with complex needs or to implement classwide practices to support common needs. Refer back to this book and other resources as needs arise, and when possible, collaborate with colleagues and families to brainstorm additional ideas.

Collaboration may lead to more insightful and creative solutions, optimize student outcomes by providing consistent messaging and supports across settings, and reduce feelings of overwhelm for any one educator. Next, we turn to our final chapter: responding to emergencies.

RELATED RESOURCES

National Center on Intensive Intervention
https://intensiveintervention.org
Provides tools to identify the antecedents and consequences of student behavior as well as guidance on intensive behavioral interventions.

IRIS Center
https://iris.peabody.vanderbilt.edu
Offers short, interactive learning modules on a range of topics, including addressing challenging behaviors, behavior intervention plans, and functional behavioral assessments.

Substance Abuse and Mental Health Services Administration (SAMHSA)
www.samhsa.gov/mental-health/children-and-families
Includes resources on mental health and substance use in adolescents and young adults as well as resources for substance use prevention in schools.

CHAPTER 13

Responding to Emergencies

KEY IDEAS

1. Many different types of emergencies have the potential to impact school community members' mental health.
2. Inclusive, trauma-informed, and collaborative preparation can reduce the risk of negative mental health impacts resulting from emergencies.
3. There are many strategies and frameworks that can help educators navigate their roles and responsibilities in the aftermath of individual or community emergencies.

Over the weekend, Principal Kim's school experiences a crisis: the school's beloved music teacher, Mr. Williams, had a medical emergency and passed away unexpectedly. Principal Kim has notified the school's staff and families of his death, and the news is quickly spreading throughout the community.

Given the potential mental health impact of this sudden loss, Principal Kim is working to develop a crisis response plan for Monday morning when students return to the building. She works with district leadership to arrange for mental health professionals to be available in the school. In addition, she offers an optional, virtual staff meeting on Sunday night for staff to come together and discuss the loss and plan for Monday.

What Is an Emergency?

The word *emergency* may bring different experiences to mind. Due to identity, context, media exposure, and prior experiences, educators have varied levels of worry and fear about various types of potential emergencies. By *Merriam Webster's* definition, an emergency is "an unforeseen combination of circumstances, or the resulting state, that calls for immediate action."

Some emergencies, such as the death of a community member, natural disasters, gun or bomb threats, or the spread of infectious diseases, may impact the entire school community. Others may impact a smaller group of students and educators within a school. For example, physical violence or bullying on school grounds (such as a fight between two students), individual medical events (such as a seizure or anaphylactic reaction), or mental health crises during the school day may not impact the entire community but instead create an emergency for a subset of the school population. The intensity of the emergency's impact will vary among those involved in the event—for example, if a classmate has a seizure in class, the impact of witnessing this event will differ based on students' and teachers' own medical histories and physical and social proximity to the affected student. In Table 13.1 we provide a list of scenarios that could be considered emergency situations.

STOP AND REFLECT

1. Review the potential emergencies listed in Table 13.1. Which of these emergencies do you think about the most? Which do you think about the least?
2. For which of these emergencies does your school have response plans or drills?

In this chapter, we explore educators' roles in responding to school-based emergencies. This work often begins prior to an emergency event through emergency planning and preparation. We specifically address

TABLE 13.1. Types of Emergencies

Type of threat	Examples
Natural threats	Earthquake, tornado, lightning, severe wind, hurricane, flood, fire, extreme temperatures, landslide or mudslide, tsunami, dust storm, volcanic eruption, winter precipitation or snowstorm, dangerous animal
Biological threats	Infectious diseases, contaminated food outbreak, water contamination, toxic materials (asbestos, mold, etc.), hazardous materials (gas leaks, sewage breaks, radiological releases)
Human threats	Medical emergency, active shooter, physical violence or fighting, bomb threat, cyberattack, suicide or self-harm, missing child

Note. Adapted from *Examples of Threats and Hazards Table* developed by the Readiness and Emergency Management for Schools Technical Assistance Center (2022).

system-wide emergency operations planning (EOP) processes and inclusive, trauma-informed drills. We then turn to two strategies that educators can use to respond to individual students experiencing a crisis: *threat assessment* and *de-escalation*. Finally, we describe short- and long-term strategies that educators can use when responding to community-wide emergencies. Because we know that this chapter may carry particularly heavy emotional weight, we begin with an invitation to participate in three brief breathing exercises—and we encourage readers to return to these at any point (see Figure 13.1).

Educators' Roles in Emergency Planning and Preparation

Not only can emergencies have a direct impact on mental health, but concern regarding the *risk* of an emergency occurring can also have detrimental mental health effects. Consider, for example, that while the likelihood of gun violence occurring at any given school is extremely low (Lei & McKenzie, 2023), fear of an active shooter is one of the top reasons why so many teachers worry about their physical safety while at work (Doan et al., 2023). School community members are often exposed through media channels to emergencies that have taken place in *other* schools. Consequently, they may feel fear and sadness about the impact of shootings, even if they have not directly experienced an active shooter situation themselves.

Emergency Operations Planning Processes

Educators can support school mental health by becoming familiar with the EOP process within their school. As of the 2021–2022 school year, more than 90% of public schools had a written *emergency operations plan* for the following crises: active shooter, natural disaster, suicide threat or

1. **Box Breath:** Inhale for four seconds, exhale for four seconds. Repeat four times.
2. **Belly and Heart Breath:** Place one hand on your belly and the other on your heart. As you breathe in and out, imagine your breath traveling from your head to your toes.
3. **Pursed Lips Breath:** Inhale gently. Then, purse your lips and exhale as if using a straw.

FIGURE 13.1. Breathing invitations.

intent, pandemic disease, and bomb threat or incident (NCES, 2024c). The proactive and collaborative development of an emergency operations plan helps school community members understand expected roles, responsibilities, and procedures when a dangerous situation occurs. For example, emergency operations plans may include arrangements for internal and external communication systems, coordination with local law enforcement and medical providers, and decision-making protocols. Aspiranti and colleagues (2024) offer the Comprehensive Crisis Plan Checklist (CCPC-2) to help schools explore the extent to which they are prepared for responding to various types of crises. The checklist is available for free at *www.kathleenaspiranti.com/crisis-plan-checklist.*

For effective emergency response, the strength of partnerships and ease of data communication across parties is essential (CDC, 2024b). As part of these relationships, school districts often have memorandums of understanding with their local police departments. Such documents describe the roles and responsibilities of the school and the law enforcement agency, and the types of information that will be shared between them (Department of Justice, 2023). They may also outline the roles of the police, other first responders, and mental health professionals. Careful consideration of what defines a *crisis* or *emergency* (and what does not) can help clarify when and how the police should be involved. Educators can play an important role in emergency preparation by familiarizing themselves with these memorandums. Emergency operations plans and other planning documents (such as memorandums of agreement) should be frequently revisited and revised based on the needs and resources of the community. In some schools, educators may have the opportunity to directly participate in the development of an emergency operations plan through participation on an EOP committee or by providing feedback solicited by the administration.

STOP AND REFLECT

1. Does your setting have an emergency operations plan? What types of emergencies does it prepare for?
2. What are your expected roles and responsibilities if various emergencies occur?

Emergency Operations Plans That Include Emergency Drills: Inclusive, Trauma-Informed Implementation

As part of their emergency response plans, most schools and districts require at least some emergency drills to take place during the academic year. During the 2023–2024 school year, over 90% of public schools had lockdown drills and practiced shelter in place and evacuation procedures (NCES, 2024c). Such drills are intended to increase safety and reduce negative impacts (e.g., loss, trauma) in the event of an actual emergency. Drills themselves, however, can be distressing for students and educators (Everytown for Gun Safety, 2024). Educators can take steps to implement emergency drills in trauma-informed ways that support school community members' mental health.

It is important to consider the extent to which drills are inclusive and accessible to all students and educators within a school building. Consider that over 10% of K–12 students' first language was not English (NCES, 2024a). Imagine not being able to understand the language fluently, and suddenly having your English-speaking teacher lead you out of the classroom or have you sit against a classroom wall. In this situation, it might be difficult to know whether you are experiencing a drill or an actual emergency—and then when you try to communicate to get clarity, the teacher reminds you to be quiet! Likewise, approximately 15% of students have an identified disability (NCES, 2024e). Imagine having a sensory processing need and being asked to sit quietly against a wall or hearing a fire alarm blare while strobe lights flash. These can be overwhelming sensations. Although IEPs and 504 plans detail the accommodations students need to access education, they do not always include a clear plan for accommodating the student and ensuring their safety during drills or emergencies.

When students do not understand the expectations or rationale of an emergency drill, it can be scary and confusing—and have a negative impact on their sense of safety and belonging in school. Therefore, to reduce the risk of negative mental health impacts, educators should consider accessibility needs in advance of drills. Educators may find that some students benefit from direct instruction and practice opportunities for drill procedures, check-ins during the drill, a peer or buddy partner, the use of headphones or other tools to limit sensory impact, and debriefing opportunities after the drill (Center on PBIS, 2025).

STOP AND REFLECT

1. Consider a student who has recently moved to the United States and speaks very little English. How might you proactively plan to make a lockdown drill more inclusive and accessible for this student?
2. Consider a student with a seizure disorder induced by flashing lights. How might you proactively plan to make a fire drill more inclusive and accessible for this student?

Even if students can participate in a drill without accommodations, these exercises may be distressing because they surface community members' fear regarding potential emergencies. Everytown for Gun Safety (2024), a nonprofit focused on addressing gun violence in schools, provides recommendations for reducing this risk. Schools should provide advanced notice of drills to families, so that family caregivers can have developmentally appropriate conversations with their children about school-based emergencies. In addition, educators should watch for signs of enduring distress during and after a drill, so that they can identify impacted students and connect them with the appropriate resources (see Chapter 11 for support recognizing signs of trauma).

Strategies for Responding to Individual Crises: Threat Assessment and De-Escalation

In the previous section, we discussed educators' roles in becoming knowledgeable about schoolwide emergency plans and supporting inclusive drill procedures. In this section, we describe strategies that educators can use when individual students are experiencing crises. When individual students display concerning or unsafe behaviors, it is important for educators to have strategies to assess and respond to these behaviors in ways that address the cause without creating harm for the student, educator, or others involved. Educators' knowledge of threat assessment procedures and de-escalation strategies can play an important role in reducing the use of responses that have a higher risk of traumatic effects (for both students and educators), such as restraint, seclusion, or interaction with external first responders. Educators are supporting student mental health when they are able to prevent the use of these practices.

Understanding the Threat Assessment Process

Throughout development, students may push boundaries of what is considered safe and acceptable behavior and threaten to engage in behaviors that risk their own well-being or that of others. Understanding how to respond to such threats can be complicated. For example, educators may feel unsure of how to respond if they overhear a student say "I'm going to kill myself" or notice that a student has created graphic artwork depicting a violent act. Educators need to be able to assess whether these threats are likely to be actualized and intervene accordingly so that the student can be connected with the appropriate resources and support. Understanding how to respond to threats of self-harm or suicide is particularly relevant for educators. In 2023, 20% of U.S. adolescents reported seriously considering suicide and almost 10% attempted suicide (Verlenden et al., 2024). Therefore, should educators have concerns about the mental health or suicidal ideation of a student, it is crucial that they share this information with an administrator or school mental health professional.

Cornell (2020) defines threat assessment as "a form of risk assessment that is conducted when someone threatens to commit a violent act or engages in threatening behavior" (p. 241). Threat assessment aims to neutralize the situation by helping individuals to resolve the problem or conflict that led to the threat (Cornell, 2020). Threat assessment may be used in cases of threatened harm toward others as well as cases of threatened harm toward oneself. A common threat assessment framework, CSTAG: Comprehensive School Threat Assessment Guidelines, was created in 2006 and updated in 2018. Based on its guidance, schools should have a threat assessment team that includes administrators, school mental health professionals, and law enforcement.

If a student communicates something that an educator perceives as potentially threatening to the student or others in the school community, educators should inform a member of the threat assessment team as soon as possible. Some schools have formal referral processes; in others, these conversations happen more informally. When in doubt, we encourage educators to err on the side of referral, in part because we encourage them not to carry these types of decisions alone. In addition to educator referral, the threat assessment process may also be initiated by the universal screening procedures described in Chapter 6 (e.g., a student endorsing suicidality on a screening measure or peer referral).

After a referral has been made, the threat assessment team (or a member of the team) will begin evaluating the threat. They will often begin by talking with the student. They will then decide if the threat is transient or substantive and develop a plan for responding and supporting the student. For substantive threats, the team will conduct a safety evaluation and create a safety plan to reintegrate the student into their classes and community. By providing the threat assessment team with timely information, educators play an important role in supporting individual students experiencing crisis.

STOP AND REFLECT

1. Who in your setting would you consult if you had concerns about student safety (e.g., threatened violence against self or others)?
2. Does your setting have a threat assessment team? Who is on this team?

Understanding the Cycle of Escalation and De-Escalation

Another way that educators can support individual students who are experiencing a potential crisis is by understanding the cycle of escalation and de-escalation. De-escalation refers to efforts that reduce the intensity of negative emotions present in a conflict situation (Spielfogel & McMillen, 2017). De-escalation is a crucial emergency response strategy because it helps educators to proactively support students' emotional regulation and safely respond when students become dysregulated. By understanding the cycle of escalation, educators can work to identify where in the cycle their students are and intervene before dysregulation becomes severe. Understanding the cycle of escalation can reduce more intense behavioral needs as well as the need for external intervention (such as contacting law enforcement), which can be distressing for both students and educators. We provide an overview of the cycle here, and more information is available in the IRIS modules created by the Vanderbilt University (IRIS Center, 2026a, 2026b). The IRIS modules offer specific and tailored content for elementary (2026a) and secondary (2026b) educators. Educators should note that this process is not always linear and students may oscillate between phases. Having knowledge of each phase enables educators to respond more effectively as certain strategies are most useful in each phase.

Calm Phase

In the calm phase, students participate in classroom activities in an emotionally regulated state. Educators can increase students' likelihood of remaining emotionally regulated using a variety of proactive strategies, such as providing direct instruction in classroom expectations and reviewing them before and during classroom transitions. Engaging lessons that incorporate student choice and agency can also help students to remain emotionally regulated. Educators can further support emotional regulation by providing students with noncontingent attention and behavior specific praise, in addition to corrective feedback. When students and educators have positive relationships, each is more likely to remain in the calm phase.

Trigger Phase

During the trigger phase, something happens that causes the student to experience emotions that are difficult for them to navigate. Triggers of emotional dysregulation can include negative social interactions, changes in schedule, failure, confusion, hunger, sleep, medical issues, stressors inside or outside of school, and personal conflicts. Students may become emotionally dysregulated for a variety of reasons, including sensory overwhelm or high task demand. Emotional dysregulation may also occur during what Kennedy and Junker (2024) describe as "loaded moments" between students and educators, or "points in time when two or more parties realize that their needs differ and that they must confront that difference" (p. 660). During a "loaded moment," the educator's response can either de-escalate or escalate the situation. Calm, neutral responses that redirect student behavior can be useful in these moments.

Agitation and Acceleration Phase

In this phase, the student displays signs of emotional dysregulation, which may present as either *hyper-* or *hypo*arousal. Students experiencing hyper-arousal often appear agitated, fidgety in their seats, or pace around the classroom. They may quickly shift their attention and energy between tasks, rapidly starting and stopping activities. For other students, emotional dysregulation may take a very different, more subtle form: putting their heads down, staring into space, or withdrawing from activities and social interactions (hypo-arousal). Often, dysregulation rapidly accelerates, resulting in either verbal conflict or adamant refusal to verbally communicate. As the student's emotional dysregulation escalates, educators can help students use emotional regulation strategies, such as practicing breathing exercises, using grounding techniques, and reducing perceived threats. While doing so, it is important to minimize the number of people interacting with the dysregulated student to reduce sensory input.

In both this and the next stage, it is important to avoid using language that initiates power struggles. Students in these stages are unable to respond productively to threats of punishment. Although educators should not validate harmful behaviors, it can be helpful for them to validate student feelings (e.g., "I see that you are frustrated."). As also described in Chapter 11, escalated behavior is a form of communication, which may communicate that the student is overwhelmed by intense emotions and unable to regulate them in a healthy way.

Peak Phase

In the peak phase of emotional dysregulation, external displays of emotional dysregulation reach their height. During this stage, the student is experiencing an emotional crisis: they are unable to navigate the intense emotions they are experiencing, and their attempts to do so are futile and often harmful. They may attempt to destroy property, escape the room or building, physically harm themselves or others, and verbalize demeaning thoughts about themselves or others. Safety is the top priority during this stage. Students cannot process large amounts of language or respond productively to threats of punishment. Therefore, any redirection should be stated neutrally and concisely.

De-Escalation and Recovery Phases

Once the student has found a way to regulate their emotions, they experience de-escalation and recovery phases. In these phases, emotional distress begins to wane, and the student begins to return to the calm phase.

Students may appear confused or disoriented. They may withdraw, deny responsibility or involvement, blame others, or refuse to address the incident. They may also reconcile or comply. They may remain guarded, wish to work alone, or avoid talking. It is important to give students time in these phases to avoid re-escalation. Reintegrating into classroom activities will be slower for some students than for others.

STOP AND REFLECT

1. Consider a student in the trigger phase. What actions can you take to support the student to de-escalate?
2. Consider a student in the de-escalation and recovery phases. How can you help the student reintegrate into classroom activities?

Strategies for Responding to Community-Wide Emergencies

In the previous sections we described educators' roles in emergency preparation and responding to individual students in crisis. Here, we describe strategies and frameworks that educators can use to navigate their roles in responding to schoolwide emergencies. As demonstrated in the opening vignette, even when a community has engaged in emergency preparation efforts, a schoolwide emergency or crisis may still occur.

Frameworks for Immediate Emergency Response

There are two key formal crisis response models that can help educators to navigate their roles in the immediate aftermath of an emergency: Psychological First Aid for Schools (PFA-S), developed by the National Child Traumatic Stress Network (Brymer et al., 2012), and the PREPaRE model, developed by the National Association of School Psychologists (Brock et al., 2016). Each of these crisis response models includes tiered levels of mental health support and mechanisms for identifying community members' support needs.

Psychological First Aid for Schools

Since at least the mid-1900s, scholars and practitioners across many disciplines have used the term *psychological first aid* to describe a wide range of interventions delivered in response to an emergency or crisis (Schultz & Forbes, 2013). In 2012, the National Child Traumatic Stress Network (NCTSN) published the first field operations guide designed specifically for implementing psychological first aid in schools, known as *Psychological First Aid for Schools* (PFA-S; Brymer et al., 2012). The field operations guide—as well as many accompanying resources for implementing PFA-S—are freely available on NCTSN's website (*nctsn.org*). Although we summarize PFA-S in this section, we encourage readers to explore NCTSN's materials in greater depth.

After an emergency, the distress of the experience can interfere with school community members' ability to cope, and this distress can evolve into serious mental health conditions (Brymer et al., 2012). PFA-S is designed to be a short-term, systematic response that school community members can use in response to a variety of emergencies, including natural disasters, death, violence, or terrorism, to cope with the distress of an emergency—both immediately afterward and in the longer term (Brymer et al., 2012).

PFA-S can be implemented by educators in the school community as well as by external partners, such as the American Red Cross. Brymer and colleagues (2012) write, "In many ways, teachers and staff are the 'first and last responders' for children in an emergency" (p. 4). PFA-S is not psychotherapy and does not need to be delivered by a mental health professional. Its goal is to establish positive connections, increase safety and comfort, help students and community members gain access to the information and resources they need, and empower community members to draw upon existing coping skills. Next, we describe the eight core actions of PFA-S.

1. **Establish contact and engagement.** The first step is to respond to potentially impacted community members in a nonintrusive and compassionate way. Immediately after a crisis, educators should monitor changes in student behavior and consult mental health professionals regarding extreme distress or concerning changes. Educators should remember that the "contact" does not have to be verbal: students may benefit from being in the same space as a trusted adult even if they are not talking. In addition, it is important for educators to recognize that community members may communicate their desire for contact or difficulties reengaging in a wide variety of ways—often shaped by culture, disability identity, and linguistic background.

2. **Promote safety and comfort.** After establishing contact, educators should seek ways to enhance their students' immediate and ongoing safety and provide physical and emotional comfort. Educators might engage students and colleagues in active, practical, and familiar activities as a means to soothe immediate discomfort. When safely possible, educators should allow students and colleagues to be around people they know and trust. It is important to monitor and quickly report any safety concerns or rumors at this stage.

3. **Support stabilization.** Next, educators can help calm and orient students and adults who are emotionally overwhelmed or disoriented. For example, educators might offer grounding and breathing activities to distressed students or provide emotional validation without discussing the more disturbing details of the event. Educators can support stabilization by providing direct and transparent information about available resources and how to access accurate informational updates.

4. **Gather information on current needs and concerns.** Educators can help to identify immediate needs and concerns following the crisis. It is important not to assume how students and colleagues are impacted, but to directly ask what they need. Sometimes it can be helpful to ask students if they know of classmates who need support, as peers may be able to identify needs more easily than educators.

5. **Provide practical assistance.** Using information gathered, educators can offer practical help to students and colleagues to address immediate concerns. Without trying to meet all the needs themselves, educators can play an important role by collecting information about the material or social needs of students and their families. Educators can then connect with colleagues (e.g., administrators, school mental health professionals) to facilitate student and family connections to associated resources.

6. **Connect community members with social supports.** Next, educators can help establish contact with community members' support networks, such as family, friends, educators, or other trusted adults in the community. Educators can help students reconnect with their loved ones and receive the support they need. Educators should also connect with their own support networks and loved ones.

7. **Offer information on coping.** Educators can provide opportunities to learn about coping strategies and promoting functioning post-crisis. Educators can also help students by modeling their own emotional regulation and coping strategies.

8. **Link community members with collaborative services.** Finally, educators can help community members access additional services to help with longer-term recovery. For example, educators can provide families with information about other services in the community that they might access as they continue to process their experiences.

STOP AND REFLECT

1. Which of these eight actions do you feel most comfortable taking? Why?
2. Which of these might you want to learn more about? Consider reviewing PFA-S resources on *nctsn.org* to learn more.

The PREPaRE Model

Another crisis response model is the PREPaRE model, designed by the National Association of School Psychologists (see Brock et al., 2011). The trainings and framework itself have been updated multiple times with the most recent handbook published in 2019. PREPaRE is an acronym for the following crisis response steps:

- Prevent/Prepare for crisis (psychological trauma)
- Reaffirm physical health and welfare, and perceptions of safety and security
- Evaluate psychological trauma risk
- Provide interventions
- [and]
- Respond to mental health needs
- Examine the effectiveness of crisis preparedness

These steps overlap with many of the core actions of PFA-S previously described. The developers of the PREPaRE model have a variety of resources and training opportunities available on their website. To view these resources, please visit *www.nasponline.org/professional-development/prepare-training-curriculum/about-prepare.*

Long-Term Crisis Response Considerations

Both the PFA-S and PREPaRE models are designed as short-term, immediate responses in the first few days or weeks following a crisis. Both models assume the involvement of mental health professionals and first responders who are not members of the school community. At some point, however, the school community must develop processes for continued and sustained recovery within itself. One of the longer-term challenges to mental health after a crisis is finding the balance between a "return to normalcy" and allowing for differentiated and flexible recovery pathways.

Effective, long-term emergency response includes recognizing that school community members' mental health needs and trajectories will vary, and flexible accommodations will be needed (Crepeau-Hobson et al., 2012). One of the most important things for educators to remember during long-term crisis response is that emergencies impact each member of the school community differently. As described in Chapter 11, trauma is not the event itself, but one's response to it. In other words, experiencing the same event may result in different levels of mental health challenges for different members of the school community. Crisis response should include tiered levels of support (like those described in Chapter 7). For example, consider what Principal Kim could do to offer tiered levels of support to educators after the death of Mr. Williams.

> Ms. Marino, the art teacher, was particularly close with Mr. Williams. Principal Kim has provided approval for Ms. Marino to leave school half an hour early once a week to go to therapy, since she has a prep period at the end of the day. In addition, some of the school staff have developed a rotating schedule to continue to host the informal "music jam" that Mr. Williams used to host once a week after school. Students and educators who were close to Mr. Williams have found this space to be a helpful, informal way to process their grief. Principal Kim has set aside a small amount of funds to pay for snacks at these weekly gatherings to reduce the burden on educators taking on this role. In addition, Principal Kim has established weekly check-ins with the long-term substitute teacher who replaced Mr. Williams in his role. During these check-ins, she helps the long-term substitute to access any resources she needs. She also asks about any students who are having a particularly difficult time in music class, knowing that students may communicate difficulty processing the loss through emotions or behavior. Finally, Principal Kim partners with the school psychologist and school social worker to gather the names of any students who seem to be having difficulty processing the loss. They reach out to all staff and families once a month to ask for this information and invite referrals at any time between these communications. The school social worker and school psychologist set up individual and group sessions with these students to help them process the loss. They also collaborate with the classroom teachers of these students to identify appropriate accommodations or supports to help the students succeed in the classroom while they cope with this tremendous loss.

Conclusion

Preparing for emergencies, and responding to them when they happen, can be a daunting process. In this chapter, we have discussed how educators can familiarize themselves with emergency operations plans and help facilitate inclusive drills for their students. We also described threat assessment and de-escalation as two strategies educators can use to respond to individual crises. Finally, we discussed available frameworks for responding to community crises. Whether responding to an individual or schoolwide emergency, educators play an important role with significant implications for school mental health.

RELATED RESOURCES

National Center for School Safety
www.nc2s.org
Offers resources for improving school safety.

Readiness and Emergency Management for Schools Technical Assistance Center
https://rems.ed.gov
Provides guidance for developing and implementing emergency operations plans.

SAMHSA Creating Safe Scenes Training Course
www.samhsa.gov/technical-assistance/dtac/training/safe-scenes
A free 1.5-hour course on de-escalation in crisis.

APPENDIX

Action Planning Reflection Questions

As described in Chapter 1, educators cannot take on all the recommendations offered in this book at once. It is wise to select one to three action steps at a time. This allows the time needed to learn, implement, and evaluate change. Here, we offer guidance on how to narrow the recommendations down to one to three areas of focus. Once these areas of focus become second nature, educators might revisit this process to identify a new set of action steps, continually strengthening their practices over time.

Prioritizing Areas of Focus

1. What practices or recommendations suggested in this book resonated most with you?
2. To maximize potential for success, consider the goodness-of-fit (see Chapter 1) of each idea. Consider:
    a. **Work:** Is this a priority for our setting? Is there data indicating need?
    b. **People:** Are there sufficient personnel to implement this initiative? Do personnel have the necessary knowledge and skills to implement, or is professional learning needed?
    c. **Structure:** Are the resources necessary for implementation available? Is the initiative aligned with school or district priorities?
    d. **Culture:** Is the initiative aligned with community values? Are there positive attitudes about the initiative?
3. Reflecting on your answers above, make a plan. Will you *pursue this idea, pursue the idea with some modifications*, or *set it aside?*

4. Repeat 2 and 3 from this list for each idea you might pursue to determine which are most feasible.
5. Choose one to three goal areas that are the most feasible in your setting at this time.

Action Plan for Success

Goal area: By ______________________________, I will
(date)

____.
(ambitious but achievable goal)

1. How will this practice improve mental health in your setting? *Documenting your "why" can help you to persist when things get tough!*
2. Is this practice replacing something else? *Consider what practices you need to unlearn or remove from your practice. How can you build this new practice as a habit?*
3. What steps do you need to take to implement this practice?
4. Who might you tell about your goal to increase personal accountability and support?
5. On what timeline can you feasibly implement this? What smaller steps do you need to take along the way for successful implementation?
6. What implementation challenges might you encounter? How might you overcome them?
7. When will you check in to see how it is going? *Consider setting a calendar reminder to assess your progress toward each goal.*

References

Abrams, Z. (2023, September 1). Teaching social–emotional learning is under attack. *Monitor on Psychology, 54*(6), 28. *www.apa.org/monitor/2023/09/social-emotional-learning-under-fire*

Acharya, B., Basnet, M., Rimal, P., Citrin, D., Hirschman, S., Swar, S., . . . Kohrt, B. (2017). Translating mental health diagnostic and symptom terminology to train health workers and engage patients in cross-cultural, non-English speaking populations. *International Journal of Mental Health Systems, 11*(62), 1–6.

Achenbach, T. (1978). The Child Behavior Profile: I. Boys aged 6–11. *Journal of Consulting and Clinical Psychology, 46*(3), 478–488.

Acton, R., & Glasgow, P. (2015). Teacher wellbeing in neoliberal contexts: A review of the literature. *Australian Journal of Teacher Education, 40*(8), 99–114.

Agyapong, B., Bobi-Donkor, G., Burback, L., & Wei, Y. (2022). Stress, burnout, anxiety and depression among teachers: A scoping review. *International Journal of Environmental Research and Public Health, 19*(17), 10706.

Aldridge, J. M., & McChesney, K. (2018). The relationships between school climate and adolescent mental health and wellbeing: A systematic literature review. *International Journal of Educational Research, 88*, 121–145.

Alexander, J. (2019). *Building trauma-sensitive schools: Your guide to creating safe, supportive learning environments for all students.* Brookes.

Allegretto, S., García, E., & Weiss, E. (2022, July 12). *Public education funding in the U.S. needs an overhaul: How a larger federal role would boost equity and shield children from disinvestment during downturns.* Economic Policy Institute. *www.epi.org/publication/public-education-funding-in-the-us-needs-an-overhaul*

Allwood, M., Ghafoori, B., Salgado, C., Slobodin, O., Kreither, J., Waelde, L. C., . . . Ramos, N. (2022). Identity-based hate and violence as trauma: Current research, clinical implications, and advocacy in a globally connected world. *Journal of Traumatic Stress, 35*(2), 349–361.

American Academy of Pediatrics. (2014). *Adverse childhood experiences and the lifelong consequences of trauma. https://downloads.aap.org/AAP/PDF/ttb_aces_consequences.pdf*

American Civil Liberties Union. (2017, April 12). *Bullies in blue: The origins and consequences of school policing. www.aclu.org/publications/bullies-blue-origins-and-consequences-school-policing*

American Civil Liberties Union. (2025). *Mapping attacks on LGBTQ rights in U.S. state legislatures in 2025. www.aclu.org/legislative-attacks-on-lgbtq-rights-2025*

American Psychiatric Association. (2022). *Diagnostic and statistical manual of mental disorders* (5th ed., text rev.). Author.

American Psychological Association. (2017). Multicultural guidelines: An ecological approach to context, identity, and intersectionality. *www.apa.org/about/policy/multicultural-guidelines.pdf*

American Psychological Association. (2018a, April 19). *APA dictionary of psychology: Anxiety. https://dictionary.apa.org/anxiety*

American Psychological Association. (2018b, April 19). *APA dictionary of psychology: Reframing. https://dictionary.apa.org/reframing*

American Psychological Association. (2023, November 15). *APA dictionary of psychology: Self-talk. https://dictionary.apa.org/self-talk*

American School Counseling Association (2025). *School counselor roles and ratios. www.schoolcounselor.org/about-school-counseling/school-counselor-roles-ratios*

Arain, M., Haque, M., Johal, L., Mathur, P., Nel, W., Rais, A., . . . Sharma, S. (2013). Maturation of the adolescent brain. *Neuropsychiatric Disease and Treatment, 9*, 449–461.

Arnold, L. E., Hodgkins, P., Kahle, J., Madhoo, M., & Kewley, G. (2020). Long-term outcomes of ADHD: Academic achievement and performance. *Journal of Attention Disorders, 24*(1), 73–85.

Arseneault, L., Bowes, L., & Shakoor, S. (2010). Bullying victimization in youths and mental health problems: "Much ado about nothing?" *Psychological Medicine, 40*(5), 717–729.

Aspiranti, K. B., McCleary, D. F., Ebner, S., Blake, J., Biggs, L. E., & Rios, R. N. (2024). Examining school crisis plan components using the Comprehensive Crisis Plan Checklist—Second edition. *Psychology in the Schools, 61*(11), 4189–4202.

August, G. J., Piehler, T. F., & Miller, F. G. (2018). Getting "SMART" about implementing multi-tiered systems of support to promote school mental health. *Journal of School Psychology, 66*, 85–96.

Baglieri, S., & Lalvani, P. (2019). *Undoing ableism: Teaching about disability in K–12 classrooms*. Routledge.

Bailey, Z. D., Feldman, J. M., & Bassett, M. T. (2021). How structural racism works—Racist policies as a root cause of U.S. racial health inequities. *New England Journal of Medicine, 384*(8), 768–773.

Baker, C. N., Peele, H., Daniels, M., Saybe, M., Whalen, K., Overstreet, S., & The New Orleans Trauma-Informed Schools Learning Collaborative. (2021). The experience of COVID-19 and its impact on teachers' mental health, coping, and teaching. *School Psychology Review, 50*(4), 491–504.

Bakker, A. B., & Demerouti, E. (2007). The job demands-resources model: State of the art. *Journal of Managerial Psychology, 22*(3), 309–328.

Banks, T., & Obiakor, F. E. (2015). Culturally responsive positive behavior supports: Considerations for practice. *Journal of Education and Training Studies, 3*(2), 83–90.

Barrett, S., Eber, L., McIntosh, K., Perales, K., & Romer, N. (2018). *Teaching social–emotional competencies within a PBIS framework*. Center on PBIS. *www.pbis.org/resource/teaching-social-emotional-competencies-within-a-pbis-framework*

Barry, C. T., Sidoti, C. L., Briggs, S. M., Reiter, S. R., & Lindsey, R. A. (2017). Adolescent social media use and mental health from adolescent and parent perspectives. *Journal of Adolescence, 61*, 1–11.

Belfield, C., Bowden, B., Klapp, A., Levin, H., Shand, R., & Zander, S. (2015). The economic value of social and emotional learning. *Journal of Benefit–Cost Analysis, 6*(03), 508–544.

Berg, J., Osher, D., Same, M. R., Nolan, E., Benson, D., & Jacobs, N. (2017). *Identifying, defining, and measuring social and emotional competencies: Final report*. American Institutes for Research. *www.air.org/sites/default/files/downloads/report/Identifying-Defining-and-Measuring-Social-and-Emotional-Competencies-December-2017-rev.pdf*

Berkeley, S., Scanlon, D., Bailey, T. R., Sutton, J. C., & Sacco, D. M. (2020). A snapshot of RTI implementation a decade later: New picture, same story. *Journal of Learning Disabilities, 53*(5), 332–342.

Berking, M., & Wupperman, P. (2012). Emotion regulation and mental health: Recent findings, current challenges, and future directions. *Current Opinion in Psychiatry, 25*(2), 128–134.

Bernard, D. L., Calhoun, C. D., Banks, D. E., Halliday, C. A., Hughes-Halbert, C., & Danielson, C. K. (2020). Making the "C-ACE" for a culturally-informed adverse childhood experiences framework to understand the pervasive mental health impact of racism on Black youth. *Journal of Child & Adolescent Trauma, 14*(2), 233–247.

Bettini, E., Gilmour, A. F., Williams, T. O., & Billingsley, B. (2020). Predicting special and general educators' intent to continue teaching using conservation of resources theory. *Exceptional Children, 86*(3), 310–329.

Bettini, E., Jones, N., Brownell, M., Conroy, M., Park, Y., Leite, W., . . . Benedict, A. (2017). Workload manageability among novice special and general educators: Relationships with emotional exhaustion and career intentions. *Remedial and Special Education, 38*(4), 246–256.

Bieg, S., Grassinger, R., & Dresel, M. (2019). Teacher humor: Longitudinal effects on students' emotions. *European Journal of Psychology of Education, 34*(3), 517–534.

Bitsko, R. H., Claussen, A. H., Lichstein, J., Black, L. I., Jones, S. E., Danielson, M.

L., . . . Ghandour, R. M. (2022). Mental health surveillance among children—United States, 2013–2019. *Morbidity and Mortality Weekly Report Supplements, 71*(2), 1–42.

Blanchette, I., & Richards, A. (2010). The influence of affect on higher level cognition: A review of research on interpretation, judgement, decision making and reasoning. *Cognition & Emotion, 24*(4), 561–595.

Bohanon, H., & Wu, M. J. (2011). Can prevention programs work together? An example of school-based mental health with prevention initiatives. *Advances in School Mental Health Promotion, 4*(4), 35–46.

Brackett, M. A., Reyes, M. R., Rivers, S. E., Elbertson, N. A., & Salovey, P. (2011). Assessing teachers' beliefs about social and emotional learning. *Journal of Psychoeducational Assessment, 30*(3), 219–236.

Bradshaw, C. P., Waasdorp, T. E., & Leaf, P. J. (2012). Effects of school-wide positive behavioral interventions and supports on child behavior problems. *Pediatrics, 130*(5), e1136–e1145.

Bridgeland, J., Bruce, M., & Hariharan, A. (2013, January 1). *The missing piece: A national teacher survey on how social and emotional learning can empower children and transform schools.* Civic Enterprises. *https://casel.org/the-missing-piece*

Briesch, A. M., Chafouleas, S. M., Dineen, J. N., McCoach, D. B., & Donaldson, A. (2022). School building administrator reports of screening practices across academic, behavioral, and health domains. *Journal of Positive Behavior Interventions, 24*(4), 266–277.

Brock, S. E., Nickerson, A. B., Louvar Reeves, M. A., Conolly, C. N., Jimerson, S. R., Pesce, R. C., & Lazzaro, B. R. (2016). *School crisis prevention and intervention: The PREPaRE model* (2nd ed.). National Association of School Psychologists.

Brock, S. E., Nickerson, A. B., Reeves, M. A., Savage, T. A., & Woitaszewski, S. A. (2011). Development, evaluation, and future directions of the PREPaRE school crisis prevention and intervention training curriculum. *Journal of School Violence, 10*(1), 34–52.

Bronfenbrenner, U. (1979). *The ecology of human development: Experiments by nature and design.* Harvard University Press.

Brown, C., & Applegate, B. (2012). Holistic wellness assessment for young adults: Psychometric analysis. *Journal of Holistic Nursing, 30*(4), 235–243.

Brown, C., Maggin, D. M., & Buren, M. (2018). Systematic review of cultural adaptations of school-based social, emotional, and behavioral interventions for students of color. *Education and Treatment of Children, 41*(4), 431–456.

Brown-Chidsey, R., & Bickford, R. (2016). *Practical handbook of multi-tiered systems of support: Building academic and behavioral success in schools.* Guilford.

Bruhn, A. L., Woods-Groves, S., & Huddle, S. (2014). A preliminary investigation of emotional and behavioral screening practices in K–12 schools. *Education and Treatment of Children, 37*(4), 611–634.

Bryk, A. S. (2002). *Trust in schools: A core resource for improvement.* Russell Sage Foundation.

Brymer, M., Taylor, M., Escudero, P., Jacobs, A., Kronenberg, M., Macy, R., . . .

Vogel, J. (2012). *Psychological first aid for schools: Field operations guide* (2nd ed.). National Child Traumatic Stress Network. *www.nctsn.org/sites/default/files/resources//pfa_schools.pdf*

Burdick, L. S., & Corr, C. (2021). Helping teachers understand and mitigate trauma in their classrooms. *TEACHING Exceptional Children, 56*(6), 502–509.

Burgess, L. G., Riddell, P. M., Fancourt, A., & Murayama, K. (2018). The influence of social contagion within education: A motivational perspective. *Mind, Brain, and Education, 12*(4), 164–174.

Burić, I., & Frenzel, A. C. (2023). Teacher emotions are linked with teaching quality: Cross-sectional and longitudinal evidence from two field studies. *Learning and Instruction, 88*, 101822.

Burns, D. D. (1999). *The feeling good handbook*. Plume.

Burns, J. R., & Rapee, R. M. (2021). Barriers to universal mental health screening in schools: The perspective of school psychologists. *Journal of Applied School Psychology, 38*(3), 223–240.

Cain, K. S., Meyer, S. C., Cummer, E., Patel, K. K., Casacchia, N. J., Montez, K., . . . Brown, C. L. (2022). Association of food insecurity with mental health outcomes in parents and children. *Academic Pediatrics, 22*(7), 1105–1114.

Campbell, A., & Anderson, C. (2013). Check-in/check-out: A systematic evaluation and component analysis. *Journal of Applied Behavior Analysis, 44*(2), 315–326.

Cann, R., Sinnema, C., Rodway, J., & Daly, A. J. (2024). What do we know about interventions to improve educator wellbeing? A systematic literature review. *Journal of Educational Change, 25*(2), 231–270.

Cantor, P., Osher, D., Berg, J., Steyer, L., & Rose, T. (2019). Malleability, plasticity, and individuality: How children learn and develop in context. *Applied Developmental Science, 23*(4), 307–337.

Caplan, S. (2019). Intersection of cultural and religious beliefs about mental health: Latinos in the faith-based setting. *Hispanic Health Care International, 17*(1), 4–10.

Caringi, J. C., Stanick, C., Trautman, A., Crosby, L., Devlin, M., & Adams, S. (2015). Secondary traumatic stress in public school teachers: Contributing and mitigating factors. *Advances in School Mental Health Promotion, 8*(4), 244–256.

Cave, L., Cooper, M. N., Zubrick, S. R., & Shepherd, C. C. J. (2020). Racial discrimination and child and adolescent health in longitudinal studies: A systematic review. *Social Science & Medicine, 250*, 112864.

Center on PBIS. (2025, January 16). *Supporting students who need additional assistance during safety drills. www.pbis.org/resource/supporting-students-who-need-additional-assistance-during-safety-drills*

Centers for Disease Control and Prevention. (2024a). *Youth Risk Behavior Survey (YRBS) explorer. http://yrbs-explorer.services.cdc.gov*

Centers for Disease Control and Prevention. (2024b, October 28). *Prepping for a school emergency. www.cdc.gov/children-and-school-preparedness/php/preparation.html?CDC_AAref_Val=https://www.cdc.gov/orr/school-preparedness/emergency_preparedness.html*

Centers for Disease Control and Prevention. (2024c, August 6). *Youth Risk*

Behavior Survey data summary & trends report: 2013–2023. www.cdc.gov/yrbs/dstr/index.html

Chafouleas, S. M. (2020, August 20). 4 questions to ask now in preparing your child for school: Strategies to support your kids' social, emotional, and behavioral learning. *Psychology Today. www.psychologytoday.com/us/blog/promoting-student-well-being/202008/4-questions-to-ask-now-in-preparing-your-child-for-school*

Chafouleas, S. M., & Iovino, E. A. (2021). Engaging a whole child, school, and community lens in positive education to advance equity in schools. *Frontiers in Psychology, 12*, 758788.

Chafouleas, S. M., Kilgus, S. P., & Wallach, N. (2010). Ethical dilemmas in school-based behavioral screening. *Assessment for Effective Intervention, 35*(4), 245–252.

Chafouleas, S. M., Koriakin, T. A., Roundfield, K. D., & Overstreet, S. (2019). Addressing childhood trauma in school settings: A framework for evidence-based practice. *School Mental Health, 11*(1), 40–53.

Chafouleas, S. M., & Koslouski, J. B. (2026). *WSCC Practice Blueprint: A school planning guide for whole child initiatives.* UConn Collaboratory on School and Child Health. *https://csch.uconn.edu/wscc-practice-blueprint*

Chan, D. W. (2010). Gratitude, gratitude intervention and subjective well-being among Chinese school teachers in Hong Kong. *Educational Psychology, 30*(2), 139–153.

Chang, M. L. (2009). An appraisal perspective of teacher burnout: Examining the emotional work of teachers. *Educational Psychology Review, 21*(3), 193–218.

Cheung, A. H., Zuckerbrot, R. A., Jensen, P. S., Laraque, D., Stein, R. E. K., GLAD-PC Steering Group, . . . Sarvet, B. (2018). Guidelines for adolescent depression in primary care (GLAD-PC): Part II. Treatment and ongoing management. *Pediatrics, 141*(3), e20174082.

Chiang, H. L., Chuang, Y. F., Chen, Y. A., Hsu, C. T., Ho, C. C., Hsu, H. T., . . . Liang, L. L. (2024). Physical fitness and risk of mental disorders in children and adolescents. *JAMA Pediatrics, 178*(6), 595–607.

Child and Adolescent Health Measurement Initiative. (2023). *2022–2023 National Survey of Children's Health (NSCH) data query.* Data Resource Center for Child and Adolescent Health supported by the U.S. Department of Health and Human Services, Health Resources and Services Administration (HRSA), Maternal and Child Health Bureau (MCHB). *www.childhealthdata.org/browse/survey/results?q=11968&r=1*

Cicchetti, D., & Doyle, C. (2016). Child maltreatment, attachment and psychopathology: Mediating relations. *World Psychiatry, 15*(2), 89–90.

Cipriano, C., Ha, C., Wood, M., Sehgal, K., Ahmad, E., & McCarthy, M. F. (2024). A systematic review and meta-analysis of the effects of universal school-based SEL programs in the United States: Considerations for marginalized students. *Social and Emotional Learning: Research, Practice, and Policy, 3*, 100029.

Cipriano, C., Strambler, M., Naples, L., Ha, C., Kirk, M., Wood, M., . . . Durlak, J. (2023). The state of evidence for social and emotional learning: A contemporary meta-analysis of universal school-based SEL interventions. *Child Development, 94*(5), 1181–1204.

Coccaro, E. F., & McCloskey, M. S. (2019). Phenomenology of impulsive aggression and intermittent explosive disorder. In E. F. Coccaro & M. S. McCloskey (Eds.), *Intermittent explosive disorder* (pp. 37–65). Academic Press.

Cohen, J. A., & Mannarino, A. P. (2015). Trauma-focused cognitive behavior therapy for traumatized children and families. *Child and Adolescent Psychiatric Clinics of North America, 24*(3), 557–570.

Cole, S. F., Eisner, A., Gregory, M., & Ristuccia, J. (2013). *Helping traumatized children learn: Creating and advocating for trauma-sensitive schools* (Vol. 2). Massachusetts Advocates for Children.

Cole, S. F., O'Brien, J. G., Gadd, M. G., Ristuccia, J., Wallace, D. L., & Gregory, M. (2005). *Helping traumatized children learn* (Vol. 1). Massachusetts Advocates for Children.

Collaborative for Academic, Social, and Emotional Learning. (n.d.). What is the CASEL framework? *https://casel.org/fundamentals-of-sel/what-is-the-casel-framework*

Collie, R. J., Shapka, J. D., & Perry, N. E. (2012). School climate and social–emotional learning: Predicting teacher stress, job satisfaction, and teaching efficacy. *Journal of Educational Psychology, 104*(4), 1189.

Colvin, S., Egan, J. E., & Coulter, R. W. (2019). School climate & sexual and gender minority adolescent mental health. *Journal of Youth and Adolescence, 48*(10), 1938–1951.

Comer, J. P. (2020). Commentary: Relationships, developmental contexts, and the school development program. *Applied Developmental Science, 24*(1), 43–47.

Comer, J. P., Joyner, E. T., & Ben-Avie, M. (Eds.). (2004). *Six pathways to healthy child development and academic success: The field guide to Comer Schools in action.* Corwin.

Compton, M. T., & Shim, R. S. (2015). The social determinants of mental health. *Focus, 13*(4), 419–425.

Conijn, J. M., Smits, N., & Hartman, E. E. (2020). Determining at what age children provide sound self-reports: An illustration of the validity-index approach. *Assessment, 27*(7), 1604–1618.

Connolly, S., Govoni, T. D., Jiang, X., Terranella, A., Guy Jr., G. P., Green, J. L., & Mikosz, C. (2024). Characteristics of alcohol, marijuana, and other drug use among persons aged 13–18 years being assessed for substance use disorder treatment—United States, 2014–2022. *Morbidity and Mortality Weekly Report, 73*, 93–98.

Coomer, M. N. (2019). *Centering equity in social emotional learning.* Great Lakes Equity Center. *https://greatlakesequity.org/sites/default/files/201926081967_equity_tool.pdf*

Cornell, D. G. (2020). Threat assessment as a school violence prevention strategy. *Criminology & Public Policy, 19*(1), 235–252.

Craig, S. (2016). *Trauma-sensitive schools: Learning communities transforming children's lives, K–5.* Teachers College Press.

Craske, M. G., Stein, M. B., Eley, T. C., Milad, M. R., Holmes, A., Rapee, R. M., & Wittchen, H. U. (2017). Anxiety disorders. *Nature Reviews Disease Primers, 3*(1), 17024.

Crepeau-Hobson, F., Sievering, K. S., Armstrong, C., & Stonis, J. (2012). A coordinated mental health crisis response: Lessons learned from three Colorado school shootings. *Journal of School Violence, 11*(3), 207–225.

Crespo, M., & Fernández-Lansac, V. (2016). Memory and narrative of traumatic events: A literature review. *Psychological Trauma: Theory, Research, Practice, and Policy, 8*(2), 149–156.

Cribb Fabersunne, C., Lee, S. Y., McBride, D., Zahir, A., Gallegos-Castillo, A., LeWinn, K. Z., & Morris, M. D. (2023). Exclusionary school discipline and school achievement for middle and high school students, by race and ethnicity. *JAMA Network Open, 6*(10), e2338989–e2338989.

Cross, D., Fani, N., Powers, A., & Bradley, B. (2017). Neurobiological development in the context of childhood trauma. *Clinical Psychology, 24*(2), 111–124.

Darling-Hammond, L. & Cook-Harvey, C. M. (2018, September 7). *Educating the whole child: Improving school climate to support student success.* Learning Policy Institute. *https://learningpolicyinstitute.org/product/educating-whole-child-report*

Darling-Hammond, L., & DePaoli, J. (2020). Why school climate matters and what can be done to improve it. *State Education Standard, 20*(2), 7–11.

Datnow, A. (2018). Time for change? The emotions of teacher collaboration and reform. *Journal of Professional Capital and Community, 3*(3), 157–172.

Davis, A. S., Moss, L. E., Nogin, M. M., & Webb, N. E. (2015). Neuropsychology of child maltreatment and implications for school psychologists. *Psychology in the Schools, 52*(1), 77–91.

de Boer, H., Donker, A. S., Kostons, D. D. N. M., & van der Werf, G. P. C. (2018). Long-term effects of metacognitive strategy instruction on student academic performance: A meta-analysis. *Educational Research Review, 24*(4), 98–115.

DeBoer, J. L., Allouche, S. F., Vasquez, J. I., & Rhodes, J. (2022). Equitable practices in school mental health. *Psychology in the Schools, 59*(6), 1222–1238.

DeMatthews, D. (2020). Addressing racism and ableism in schools: A discrit leadership framework for principals. *The Clearing House: A Journal of Educational Strategies, Issues and Ideas, 93*(1), 27–34.

Denham, S. A. (2018). *Keeping SEL developmental: The importance of a developmental lens for fostering and assessing SEL competencies.* Establishing Practical Social-Emotional Competence Assessments Work Group. *https://casel.org/casel-resources-keeping-sel-developmental*

DeNike, M., & Ohlson, B. (2013). *Elev8 Oakland community school costs and benefits: Making dollars and cents of the research.* Brightstar Research Group. *www.brightresearchgroup.com/wp-content/uploads/2015/10/Elev8-Oakland-Community-Schools-Cost-Benefit-Analysis.pdf*

Diamond, A. (2010). The evidence base for improving school outcomes by addressing the whole child and by addressing skills and attitudes, not just content. *Early Education and Development, 21*(5), 780–793.

Doan, S., Steiner, E. D., & Pandey, R. (2024, June 18). *Teacher well-being and intentions to leave in 2024: Findings from the 2024 State of the American Teacher Survey.* RAND. *www.rand.org/pubs/research_reports/RRA1108-12.html*

Doan, S., Steiner, E. D., Pandey, R., & Woo, A. (2023, June 21). *Teacher well-being and intentions to leave: Findings from the 2023 State of the American*

Teacher Survey. RAND. *www.rand.org/pubs/research_reports/RRA1108-8.html*

Dorado, J. S., Martinez, M., McArthur, L. E., & Leibovitz, T. (2016). Healthy environments and response to trauma in schools (HEARTS): A whole-school, multi-level, prevention and intervention program for creating trauma-informed, safe and supportive schools. *School Mental Health, 8*(1), 163–176.

Dougy Center. (2023). *Developmental responses to grief. www.dougy.org/assets/uploads/Developmental-Responses-to-Grief-ages-2-18.pdf*

Dow, S. J., & Kelly, J. F. (2013). Listening to youth: Adolescents' reasons for substance use as a unique predictor of treatment response and outcome. *Psychology of Addictive Behaviors, 27*(4), 1122–1131.

Dowdy, E., Doane, K., Eklund, K., & Dever, B. V. (2013). A comparison of teacher nomination and screening to identify behavioral and emotional risk within a sample of underrepresented students. *Journal of Emotional and Behavioral Disorders, 21*(2), 127–137.

Dreer, B. (2023). On the outcomes of teacher wellbeing: A systematic review of research. *Frontiers in Psychology, 14*, 1205179.

Drummond, T. (1994). *The Student Risk Screening Scale (SRSS)*. Josephine County Mental Health Program.

Dunn, M. B. (2021). Teaching literature following loss: Teachers' adherence to emotional rules. *English Teaching: Practice & Critique, 20*(3), 354–367.

Duong, M. T., Bruns, E. J., Lee, K., Cox, S., Coifman, J., Mayworm, A., & Lyon, A. R. (2021). Rates of mental health service utilization by children and adolescents in schools and other common service settings: A systematic review and meta-analysis. *Administration and Policy in Mental Health and Mental Health Services Research, 48*(3), 420–439.

Duong, M. T., Pullmann, M. D., Buntain-Ricklefs, J., Lee, K., Benjamin, K. S., Nguyen, L., & Cook, C. R. (2019). Brief teacher training improves student behavior and student-teacher relationships in middle school. *School Psychology, 34*(2), 212–221.

Durlak, J. A., Weissberg, R. P., Dymnicki, A. B., Taylor, R. D., & Schellinger, K. B. (2011). The impact of enhancing students' social and emotional learning: A meta-analysis of school-based universal interventions. *Child Development, 82*(1), 405–432.

Dweck, C. S. (2008). *Mindset: The new psychology of success*. Ballantine.

Dymond, S. (2019). Overcoming avoidance in anxiety disorders: The contributions of Pavlovian and operant avoidance extinction methods. *Neuroscience & Biobehavioral Reviews, 98*, 61–70.

Economic Modeling Specialists Inc. (2012). *The economic impact of communities in schools*. Communities In Schools. *www.communitiesinschools.org/media/uploads/attachments/CIS_2.pdf*

Education Week Research Center. (2024). *Technology and student well-being: 10 charts. www.edweek.org/research-center/reports/technology-and-student-well-being-10-charts*

Educators for Excellence. (2023). *Voices from the classroom 2023: A survey of America's educators. https://e4e.org/sites/default/files/voices_from_the_classroom_2023.pdf*

Eiraldi, R., McCurdy, B., Schwartz, B., Wolk, C. B., Abraham, M., Jawad, A. F., . . . Mautone, J. A. (2019). Pilot study for the fidelity, acceptability, and effectiveness of a PBIS program plus mental health supports in under-resourced urban schools. *Psychology in the Schools, 56*(8), 1230–1245.

Emerson, L. M., Leyland, A., Hudson, K., Rowse, G., Hanley, P., & Hugh-Jones, S. (2017). Teaching mindfulness to teachers: A systematic review and narrative synthesis. *Mindfulness, 8*(5), 1136–1149.

English, D., Lambert, S. F., Tynes, B. M., Bowleg, L., Zea, M. C., & Howard, L. C. (2020). Daily multidimensional racial discrimination among Black U.S. American adolescents. *Journal of Applied Developmental Psychology, 66*, 101068.

Every Student Succeeds Act, 20 U.S.C. § 6301 (2015).

Everytown for Gun Safety. (2023). *Talking to children about gun violence. https://everytownsupportfund.org/report/talking-to-children-about-gun-violence*

Everytown for Gun Safety. (2024). *The impact of active shooter drills in schools. https://everytownresearch.org/report/the-impact-of-active-shooter-drills-in-schools*

Evidence for Learning. (2020). *Insights into de-implementation. https://evidenceforlearning.org.au/support-for-implementation/school-planning-and-recovery/de-implementation*

Eysenck, M. W., Derakshan, N., Santos, R., & Calvo, M. G. (2007). Anxiety and cognitive performance: Attentional control theory. *Emotion, 7*(2), 336.

Fahle, E. M., Kane, T. J., Patterson, T., Reardon, S. F., Staiger, D. O., & Stuart, E. A. (2023). *School district and community factors associated with learning loss during the COVID-19 pandemic.* Center for Education Policy Research, Harvard University.

Fairchild, G., Hawes, D. J., Frick, P. J., Copeland, W. E., Odgers, C. L., Franke, B., . . . Brito, S. A. (2019). Conduct disorder. *Nature Reviews Disease Primers, 5*(1), 43.

Fallon, L. M., Veiga, M., & Sugai, G. (2023). Strengthening MTSS for behavior (MTSS-B) to promote racial equity. *School Psychology Review, 52*(5), 518–533.

Family Educational Rights and Privacy Act. (FERPA). (1974). 20 U.S.C. § 1232g; 34 C.F.R. Part 99.

Faraone, S. V., Bellgrove, M. A., Brikell, I., Cortese, S., Hartman, C. A., Hollis, C., . . . Buitelaar, J. K. (2024). Attention-deficit/hyperactivity disorder. *Nature Reviews Disease Primers, 10*(1), 11.

Faulstich, M. E., Carey, M. P., Ruggiero, L., Enyart, P., & Gresham, F. (1986). Assessment of depression in childhood and adolescence: An evaluation of the Center for Epidemiological Studies Depression Scale for Children (CES-DC). *The American Journal of Psychiatry, 143*(8), 1024–1027.

Felitti, V. J., Anda, R. F., Nordenberg, D., Williamson, D. F., Spitz, A. M., Edwards, V., . . . Marks, J. S. (1998). Relationship of childhood abuse and household dysfunction to many of the leading causes of death in adults: The Adverse Childhood Experiences (ACE) study. *American Journal of Preventive Medicine, 14*(4), 245–258.

Figley, C. R. (1995). Compassion fatigue as secondary traumatic stress disorder: An overview. In C. R. Figley (Ed.), *Compassion fatigue: Coping with secondary traumatic stress disorder in those who treat the traumatized* (pp. 1–20). Brunner/Mazel.

Figley, C. R. (2002). *Treating compassion fatigue.* Brunner-Routledge.

Fiorilli, C., Benevene, P., De Stasio, S., Buonomo, I., Romano, L., Pepe, A., & Addimando, L. (2019). Teachers' burnout: The role of trait emotional intelligence and social support. *Frontiers in Psychology, 10*, 2743.

First, M. B., Yousif, L. H., Clarke, D. E., Wang, P. S., Gogtay, N., & Appelbaum, P. S. (2022). DSM-5-TR: Overview of what's new and what's changed. *World Psychiatry, 21*(2), 218–219.

Flaherty, L. T., & Osher, D. (2003). History of school-based mental health services in the United States. In M. D. Weist, S. W. Evans, & N. A. Lever (Eds.), *Handbook of school mental health: Advancing practice and research* (pp. 11–22). Kluwer Academic/Plenum.

Fortuna, L. R., Tolou-Shams, M., Robles-Ramamurthy, B., & Porche, M. V. (2020). Inequity and the disproportionate impact of COVID-19 on communities of color in the United States: The need for a trauma-informed social justice response. *Psychological Trauma: Theory, Research, Practice, and Policy, 12*(5), 443–445.

Francis, G. L., Blue-Banning, M., Haines, S. J., Turnbull, A. P., & Gross, J. M. S. (2016). Building "our school": Parental perspectives for building trusting family-professional partnerships. *Preventing School Failure, 60*(4), 329–336.

Franco, K., Baumler, E., Torres, E. D., Lu, Y., Wood, L., & Temple, J. R. (2023). The link between school climate and mental health among an ethnically diverse sample of middle school youth. *Current Psychology, 42*(22), 18488–18498.

Fredrickson, B. L. (2013). Positive emotions broaden and build. *Advances in Experimental Social Psychology, 47*, 1–53.

Freeman, R., Miller, D., & Newcomer, L. (2015). Integration of academic and behavioral MTSS at the district level using implementation science. *Learning Disabilities: A Contemporary Journal, 13*(1), 59–72.

Frenzel, A. C., Becker-Kurz, B., Pekrun, R., Goetz, T., & Lüdtke, O. (2018). Emotion transmission in the classroom revisited: A reciprocal effects model of teacher and student enjoyment. *Journal of Educational Psychology, 110*(5), 628.

Frenzel, A. C., Daniels, L., & Buri?, I. (2021). Teacher emotions in the classroom and their implications for students. *Educational Psychologist, 56*(4), 250–264.

Frey, A. J., Mitchell, B. D., Kelly, M. S., McNally, S., & Tillett, K. (2022). School-based mental health practitioners: A resource guide for educational leaders. *School Mental Health, 14*(4), 789–801.

Friedman, J., Godvin, M., Shover, C. L., Gone, J. P., Hansen, H., & Schriger, D. L. (2022). Trends in drug overdose deaths among US adolescents, January 2010 to June 2021. *JAMA, 327*(14), 1398–1400.

Galanti, R. (2024). *Parenting anxious kids: Understanding anxiety in children by age and stage.* Sourcebooks.

García, E., & Weiss, E. (2016). *Making the whole-child education the norm. (Policy Brief).* Economic Policy Institute. *https://files.epi.org/pdf/107051.pdf*

Garner, A., Yogman, M., & The Committee on Psychosocial Aspects of Child and Family Health, Section on Developmental and Behavioral Pediatrics, Council on Early Childhood. (2021). Preventing childhood toxic stress: Partnering with families and communities to promote relational health. *Pediatrics, 148*(2), 1–24.

Garwood, J. D. (2023). Special educator burnout and fidelity in implementing behavior support plans: A call to action. *Journal of Emotional and Behavioral Disorders, 31*(2), 84–96.

Gearhart, C. A., Blaydes, M., & McCarthy, C. J. (2022). Barriers to and facilitators for teachers' wellbeing. *Frontiers in Psychology, 13*, 867433.

Gimbert, B. G., Miller, D., Herman, E., Breedlove, M., & Molina, C. E. (2023). Social emotional learning in schools: The importance of educator competence. *Journal of Research on Leadership Education, 18*(1), 3–39.

Goetz, T., Bieleke, M., Gogol, K., van Tartwijk, J., Mainhard, T., Lipnevich, A. A., & Pekrun, R. (2021). Getting along and feeling good: Reciprocal associations between student-teacher relationship quality and students' emotions. *Learning and Instruction, 71*, 101349.

Goetz, T., Lüdtke, O., Nett, U. E., Keller, M. M., & Lipnevich, A. A. (2013). Characteristics of teaching and students' emotions in the classroom: Investigating differences across domains. *Contemporary Educational Psychology, 38*(4), 383–394.

Goldman, B. (2021, October 29). *Addictive potential of social media, explained.* Stanford Medicine News Center. *https://med.stanford.edu/news/insights/2021/10/addictive-potential-of-social-media-explained.html*

Goodman-Scott, E., Betters-Bubon, J., & Pianta, R. (2022). MTSS for suicide prevention and intervention: Considerations for school counseling preparation. *Teaching and Supervision in Counseling, 4*(2), 10.

Gottlieb, L. M., Hessler, D., Long, D., Laves, E., Burns, A. R., Amaya, A., . . . Adler, N. E. (2016). Effects of social needs screening and in-person service navigation on child health: A randomized clinical trial. *JAMA Pediatrics, 170*(11), e162521–e162521.

Granziera, H., Martin, A. J. & Collie, R. J. (2023). Teacher well-being and student achievement: A multilevel analysis. *Social Psychology of Education, 26*, 279–291.

Gray, C., Wilcox, G., & Nordstokke, D. (2017). Teacher mental health, school climate, inclusive education and student learning: A review. *Canadian Psychology/Psychologie Canadienne, 58*(3), 203–210.

Grayson, J. L., & Alvarez, H. K. (2008). School climate factors relating to teacher burnout: A mediator model. *Teaching and Teacher Education, 24*(5), 1349–1363.

Green, J. G., Oblath, R., & Holt, M. (2022). Teacher and school characteristics associated with the identification and referral of adolescent depression and oppositional defiant disorders by U.S. teachers. *School Mental Health, 14*(3), 498–513.

Hadland, S. E., Bagley, S. M., Gai, M. J., Earlywine, J. J., Schoenberger, S. F., Morgan, J. R., & Barocas, J. A. (2021). Opioid use disorder and overdose among youth following an initial opioid prescription. *Addiction, 116*(10), 2790–2800.

Hallam, P. R., Smith, H. R., Hite, J. M., Hite, S. J., & Wilcox, B. R. (2015). Trust and collaboration in PLC teams: Teacher relationships, principal support, and collaborative benefits. *NASSP Bulletin, 99*(3), 193–216.

Haltigan, J. D., Pringsheim, T. M., & Rajkumar, G. (2023). Social media as an incubator of personality and behavioral psychopathology: Symptom and disorder authenticity or psychosomatic social contagion? *Comprehensive Psychiatry, 121*, 152362.

Hambrick, E. P., Brawner, T. W., Perry, B. D., Brandt, K., Hofmeister, C., & Collins, J. O. (2019). Beyond the ACE score: Examining relationships between timing of developmental adversity, relational health and developmental outcomes in children. *Archives of Psychiatric Nursing, 33*(3), 238–247.

Happy Teacher Revolution. (2025). *Happy Teacher Revolution. www.happyteacherrevolution.com*

Harpin, V., Mazzone, L., Raynaud, J. P., Kahle, J., & Hodgkins, P. (2016). Long-term outcomes of ADHD: A systematic review of self-esteem and social function. *Journal of Attention Disorders, 20*(4), 295–305.

Harter, S. (1998). The effects of child abuse on the self-system. *Journal of Aggression, Maltreatment & Trauma, 2*(1), 147–169.

Harvey, M. (1996). An ecological view of psychological trauma and trauma recovery. *Journal of Traumatic Stress, 9*(1), 3–23.

Hawes, D. J., Gardner, F., Dadds, M. R., Frick, P. J., Kimonis, E. R., Burke, J. D., & Fairchild, G. (2023). Oppositional defiant disorder. *Nature Reviews Disease Primers, 9*(1), 1–17.

Hays, P. A. (2022). *Addressing cultural complexities in counseling and clinical practice: An intersectional approach* (4th ed.). American Psychological Association.

Henrikson, N. B., Blasi, P. R., Dorsey, C. N., Mettert, K. D., Nguyen, M. B., Walsh-Bailey, C., . . . Lewis, C. C. (2019). Psychometric and pragmatic properties of social risk screening tools: A systematic review. *American Journal of Preventative Medicine, 57*(6, Suppl. 1), s13–s24.

Herbener, A. B., & Damholdt, M. F. (2025). Are lonely youngsters turning to chatbots for companionship? The relationship between chatbot usage and social connectedness in Danish high-school students. *International Journal of Human–Computer Studies, 196*, 103409

Herman, J. L. (1997). *Trauma and recovery*. Basic Books.

Hickey, B. A., Chalmers, T., Newton, P., Lin, C. T., Sibbritt, D., McLachlan, C. S., . . . Lal, S. (2021). Smart devices and wearable technologies to detect and monitor mental health conditions and stress: A systematic review. *Sensors, 21*(10), 3461

Hill, C., Waite, P., & Creswell, C. (2016). Anxiety disorders in children and adolescents. *Paediatrics and Child Health, 26*(12), 548–553.

Hobbiss, M., Sims, S. and Allen, R. (2021). Habit formation limits growth in teacher effectiveness: A review of converging evidence from neuroscience and social science. *Review of Educational Research, 9*, 3–23.

Hodes, M., Gau, S. S. & De Vries, P. J. (Eds.). (2018). *Understanding uniqueness and diversity in child and adolescent mental health.* Academic Press.

Holt-Lunstad, J., Smith, T. B., & Layton, J. B. (2010). Social relationships and mortality risk: A meta-analytic review. *PLOS Medicine, 7*(7), e1000316.

Holzberger, D., Philipp, A., & Kunter, M. (2013). How teachers' self-efficacy is related to instructional quality: A longitudinal analysis. *Journal of Educational Psychology, 105*(3), 774–786.

Hon, D., Suave, J., Mahfouz, J., & Schonert-Reichl, K. (2023). Cultivating SEL-ready teachers: Social and emotional learning in teacher preparation. In S. Rimm-Kaufman, M. Strambler, & K. Schonert-Reichel (Eds.), *Social and emotional learning in action: Creating systemic change in schools* (pp. 115–137). Guilford.

Hong, J., Cross Francis, D., Haskins, C., Chong, K., Habib, K., Ataide Pinheiro, W., . . . Dickinson, J. (2024). Wellbeing under threat: Multiply marginalized and underrepresented teachers' intersecting identities. *Teachers and Teaching, 30*(6), 762–782.

Hong, J. S., Kim, D. H., Colpin, H., Llorent, V. J., Voisin, D. R., & Johns, S. (2024). Do caring teachers protect African American youth with adverse adolescent experiences from risky behaviors? *Clinical Child Psychology and Psychiatry, 29*(4), 1318–1332.

Horner, R. H., Sugai, G., & Lewis, T. (2020). *Is school-wide positive behavioral interventions and supports (PBIS) an evidence-based practice?* Center on Positive Behavioral Intentions and Supports. *https://wvpbis.org/wp-content/uploads/PBIS-Research-Evidence-Based.pdf*

Howells, K. (2015). *Gratitude in education: A radical view.* SensePublishers.

Hua, L. L., Lee, J., Rahmandar, M. H., Sigel, E. J., Committee on Adolescence & Committee on Injury, Violence, and Poison Prevention. (2023). Suicide and suicide risk in adolescents. *Pediatrics, 153*(1), e2023064800.

Huang, F. L., & Cornell, D. G. (2021). Teacher support for zero tolerance is associated with higher suspension rates and lower feelings of safety. *School Psychology Review, 50*(2–3), 388–405.

Huebner, E. S. (1991). Initial development of the Student's Life Satisfaction Scale. *School Psychology International, 12*(3), 231–240.

Hughes, C. A., Morris, J. R., Therrien, W. J., & Benson, S. K. (2017). Explicit instruction: Historical and contemporary contexts. *Learning Disabilities Research & Practice, 32*(3), 140–148.

Hughes, J. N., & Im, M. H. (2016). Teacher-student relationship and peer disliking and liking across grades 1–4. *Child Development, 87*(2), 593–611.

Hughes, K., Bellis, M. A., Hardcastle, K. A., Sethi, D., Butchart, A., Mikton, C., . . . Dunne, M. P. (2017). The effect of multiple adverse childhood experiences on health: A systematic review and meta-analysis. *Lancet Public Health, 2*(8), e356–e366.

Humble, J. J., Summers, N. L., Villarreal, V., Styck, K. M., Sullivan, J. R., Hechler, J. M., & Warren, B. S. (2018). Child-centered play therapy for youths who have experienced trauma: A systematic literature review. *Journal of Child & Adolescent Trauma, 12*(3), 365–375.

Husky, M. M., Sheridan, M., McGuire, L., & Olfson, M. (2011). Mental health screening and follow-up care in public high schools. *Journal of American Academy of Child & Adolescent Psychiatry, 50*(9), 881–891.

Hwang, Y. S., Bartlett, B., Greben, M., & Hand, K. (2017). A systematic review of mindfulness interventions for in-service teachers: A tool to enhance teacher wellbeing and performance. *Teaching and Teacher Education, 64*, 26–42.

Hydon, S., Wong, M., Langley, A. K., Stein, B. D., & Kataoka, S. H. (2015). Preventing secondary traumatic stress in educators. *Child and Adolescent Psychiatric Clinics of North America, 24*(2), 319–333.

Idsoe, T., Dyregrov, A., & Idsoe, E. C. (2012). Bullying and PTSD symptoms. *Journal of Abnormal Child Psychology, 40*(6), 901–911.

Individuals with Disabilities Education Act, 20 U.S.C. § 1400 (2004).

IRIS Center. (2025). *Intensive intervention (Part 2): Collecting and analyzing data for data-based individualization. https://iris.peabody.vanderbilt.edu/module/dbi2/cresource/q2/p03*

IRIS Center. (2026a). *Addressing challenging behaviors (part 1, elementary): Understanding the acting-out cycle.* Vanderbilt University. *https://iris.peabody.vanderbilt.edu/module/bi1-elem*

IRIS Center. (2026b). *Addressing challenging behaviors (part 1, secondary): Understanding the acting-out cycle.* Vanderbilt University. *https://iris.peabody.vanderbilt.edu/module/bi1-sec*

Jackson, K. M., Janssen, T., & Gabrielli, J. (2018). Media/marketing influences on adolescent and young adult substance abuse. *Current Addiction Reports, 5*(2), 146–157.

Jacobsson, C., Åkerlund, M., Graci, E., Cedstrand, E., & Archer, T. (2016). Teacher team effectiveness and teachers well-being. *Clinical and Experimental Psychology, 2*(2), 1–5.

Jagers, R. J., Rivas-Drake, D., & Borowski, T. (2018). *Equity & social and emotional learning: A cultural analysis [Frameworks Briefs: Special Issues Series].* Establishing Practical Social-Emotional Competence Assessments Work Group. *https://measuringsel.casel.org/wp-content/uploads/2018/11/Frameworks-Equity.pdf*

Jagers, R. J., Rivas-Drake, D., & Williams, B. (2019). Transformative social and emotional learning (SEL): Toward SEL in service of educational equity and excellence. *Educational Psychologist, 54*(3), 162–184.

James, A. C., Reardon, T., Soler, A., James, G., & Creswell C. (2020). Cognitive behavioural therapy for anxiety disorders in children and adolescents. *Cochrane Database of Systematic Reviews, 11*, CD013162.

Jensen, E. J., & Mendenhall, T. (2018). Call to action: Family therapy and rural mental health. *Contemporary Family Therapy, 40*(4), 309–317.

Johnson, J. A., Sanghvi, P., & Mehrotra, S. (2022). Technology-based interventions to improve help-seeking for mental health concerns: A systematic review. *Indian Journal of Psychological Medicine, 44*(4), 332–340.

Jones, D. J., Forehand, R., Cuellar, J., Kincaid, C., Parent, J., Fenton, N., & Goodrum, N. (2013). Harnessing innovative technologies to advance children's mental health: Behavioral parent training as an example. *Clinical Psychology Review, 33*(2), 241–252.

Jones, S., Bailey, R., Brush, K., & Nelson, B. (2019). *Introduction to the*

Taxonomy Project: Tools for selecting & aligning SEL frameworks. Establishing Practical Social-Emotional Competence Assessments Work Group. *https://measuringsel.casel.org/wp-content/uploads/2019/02/Frameworks-C.1.pdf*

Jones, S. M., Brush, K. E., Ramirez, T., Mao, Z. X., Marenus, M., Wettje, S., . . . Bailey, R. (2021). *Navigating SEL from the inside out: Looking inside and across 33 leading SEL programs—A practical resource for schools and OST providers: Preschool and elementary focus.* The EASEL Lab, Harvard University. *www.wallacefoundation.org/knowledge-center/Documents/navigating-social-and-emotional-learning-from-the-inside-out-2ed.pdf*

Jones, S. M., Brush, K. E., Wettje, S., Ramirez, T., Poddar, A., Kannar, A., . . . Chng, E. (2022). *Navigating SEL from the inside out: Looking inside and across leading SEL programs—A practical resource for schools and OST providers: Middle and high school focus.* The EASEL Lab, Harvard University. *https://wallacefoundation.org/sites/default/files/2024-10/navigating-social-and-emotional-learning-from-the-inside-out-middle-high-school.doi_.10.59656%252FYD-OS7616.001.pdf*

Jones, S. M. & Kahn, J. (2017). *The evidence base for how we learn: Supporting students' social, emotional, and academic development.* National Commission on Social, Emotional, and Academic Development Aspen Institute. *www.aspeninstitute.org/wp-content/uploads/2017/09/SEAD-Research-Brief-9.12_updated-web.pdf*

Jorm, A. F. (2000). Mental health literacy: Public knowledge and beliefs about mental disorders. *The British Journal of Psychiatry, 177*(5), 396–401.

Kabat-Zinn, J. (2003). Mindfulness-based interventions in context: Past, present, and future. *Clinical Psychology: Science and Practice, 10*, 144–156.

Kalyanpur, M. & Harry, B. (2012). *Cultural reciprocity in special education: Building family-professional relationships.* Paul H. Brooks.

Kazdin, A. E., & Weisz, J. R. (1998). Identifying and developing empirically supported child and adolescent treatments: Empirically supported psychological therapies. *Journal of Consulting and Clinical Psychology, 66*(1), 19–36.

Keles, B., McCrae, N., & Grealish, A. (2020). A systematic review: The influence of social media on depression, anxiety and psychological distress in adolescents. *International Journal of Adolescence and Youth, 25*(1), 79–93.

Kelly, J. F., Brown, S. A., Abrantes, A., Kahler, C. W. and Myers, M. (2008). Social recovery model: An 8-year investigation of adolescent 12-step group involvement following inpatient treatment. *Alcohol: Clinical and Experimental Research, 32*, 1468–1478.

Kelly, J. F. & Urbanoski, K. (2012). Youth recovery contexts: The incremental effects of 12-step attendance and involvement on adolescent outpatient outcomes. *Alcohol: Clinical and Experimental Research, 36*, 1219–1229.

Kelm, J. L., & McIntosh, K. (2012). Effects of school-wide positive behavior support on teacher self-efficacy. *Psychology in the Schools, 49*(2), 137–147.

Kennedy, B. L., & Junker, R. (2024). The evolution of "loaded moments" toward escalation or de-escalation in student–teacher interactions. *Review of Educational Research, 94*(5), 660–698.

Kilgus, S. P., Reinke, W. M., & Jimerson, S. R. (2015). Understanding mental health intervention and assessment within a multi-tiered framework: Contemporary science, practice, and policy. *School Psychology Quarterly, 30*(2), 159.

Kim, E. K., & Choe, D. (2022). Universal social, emotional, and behavioral strength and risk screening: Relative predictive validity for students' subjective well-being in schools. *School Psychology Review, 51*(1), 40–54.

Kim, L. E., Oxley, L., & Asbury, K. (2022). "My brain feels like a browser with 100 tabs open": A longitudinal study of teachers' mental health and well-being during the COVID-19 pandemic. *British Journal of Educational Psychology, 92*(1), 299–318.

Kim, Y., Lee, H., & Park, A. (2022). Patterns of adverse childhood experiences and depressive symptoms: Self-esteem as a mediating mechanism. *Social Psychiatry and Psychiatric Epidemiology, 57*(2), 331–341.

Klein, A. (2024, March 25). *Kids turn to TikTok for mental health diagnoses. What should schools know?* EducationWeek. *www.edweek.org/technology/kids-turn-to-tiktok-for-mental-health-diagnoses-what-should-schools-know/2024/03*

Knight, J. R. (2020). *CRAFFT 2.1 self-administered questionnaire.* Center for Adolescent Behavioral Health Research (CABHRe), Boston Children's Hospital. *https://crafft.org/wp-content/uploads/2021/07/CRAFFT_2.1_Self-administered_2021-07-03.pdf*

Kohoulat, N., Dehghani, M. R., & Kohoulat, N. (2015). Perceived school climate and students' mental health. *International Journal of School Health, 2*(4), 12–17.

Kolassa, I. T., & Elbert, T. (2007). Structural and functional neuroplasticity in relation to traumatic stress. *Current Directions in Psychological Science, 16*(6), 321–325.

Komase, Y., Watanabe, K., Hori, D., Nozawa, K., Hidaka, Y., Iida, M., . . . Kawakami, N. (2021). Effects of gratitude intervention on mental health and well-being among workers: A systematic review. *Journal of Occupational Health, 63*(1), e12290.

Koriakin, T. A., McKee, S. L., Schwartz, M. B., & Chafouleas, S. M. (2020). Development of a comprehensive tool for school health policy evaluation: The WellSAT WSCC. *Journal of School Health, 90*(12), 923–939.

Koslouski, J. B., Chafouleas, S. M., Briesch, A. M., Caemmerer, J. M., Perry, H. Y., Oas, J., . . . Charamut, N. R. (2024). School-based screening of social determinants of health: A scoping review. *School Mental Health, 16*(1), 1–14.

Koslouski, J. B., Stark, K, & Chafouleas, S. M. (2023). Understanding and responding to the effects of trauma in the classroom: A primer for educators. *Social and Emotional Learning: Research, Practice, and Policy, 1*, 100004.

Koydemir, S., & Essau, C. A. (2018). Anxiety and anxiety disorders in young people: A cross-cultural perspective. In M. Hodes, S. S. Gau, & P. J. De Vries (Eds.), *Understanding uniqueness and diversity in child and adolescent mental health* (pp. 115–134). Academic Press.

Kroenke, K., Spitzer, R. L., & Williams, J. B. (2003). The Patient Health Questionnaire–2: Validity of a two-item depression screener. *Medical Care, 41*, 1284–1292.

Kübler-Ross, E. (1969). *On death and dying.* Macmillan.

Kushner J. D. (2016). Attention-deficit/hyperactivity disorder. In B. Flamez & C.

J. Sheperis (Eds.), *Diagnosing and treating children and adolescents: A guide for mental health professionals* (pp. 128–147). Wiley.

Kuypers, L. (2011). *The zones of regulation*. Social Thinking.

La Salle, T. P., Rocha-Neves, J., Jimerson, S., Di Sano, S., Martinsone, B., Majercakova Albertova, S., . . . Zvyagintsev, R. (2021). A multinational study exploring adolescent perception of school climate and mental health. *School Psychology, 36*(3), 155–160.

Lagattuta, K. H., Sayfan, L., & Bamford, C. (2012). Do you know how I feel? Parents underestimate worry and overestimate optimism compared to child self-report. *Journal of Experimental Child Psychology, 113*(2), 211–232.

Latino, F., Cataldi, S., & Fischetti, F. (2021). Effects of an 8-week yoga-based physical exercise intervention on teachers' burnout. *Sustainability, 13*(4), 2104.

Lawson, H. A., Caringi, J. C., Gottfried, R., Bride, B. E., & Hydon, S. P. (2019). Educators' secondary traumatic stress, children's trauma, and the need for trauma literacy. *Harvard Educational Review, 89*(3), 421–447.

Lazarus R. S., & Folkman S. (1984). *Stress, appraisal and coping*. Springer.

Leadbeater, B. J., Sukhawathanakul, P., Thompson, K., & Holfeld, B. (2015). Parent, child, and teacher reports of school climate as predictors of peer victimization, internalizing and externalizing in elementary school. *School Mental Health, 7*(4), 261–272.

Learning Policy Institute. (2024). *2024 update: What's the cost of teacher turnover? [Interactive tool]. https://learningpolicyinstitute.org/product/2024-whats-cost-teacher-turnover*

LeBlanc, V. R., McConnell, M. M., & Monteiro, S. D. (2015). Predictable chaos: A review of the effects of emotions on attention, memory and decision making. *Advances in Health Sciences Education, 20*(1), 265–282.

Lee, J., Shapiro, V. B., & Kim, B. K. E. (2023). Universal school-based social and emotional learning (SEL) for diverse student subgroups: Implications for enhancing equity through SEL. *Prevention Science, 24*(5), 1011–1022.

Lee, S. J., & Thomas, S. (2024). Protect Black women teachers: Influencing sustainability through mental health literacy. *Urban Education, 59*(5), 1523–1551.

Leger, D., Ferini-Strambi, L., Han, F., Poyares, D., Uchiyama, M., & Zee, P. C. (2024). Novel perspective of 'poor sleep' in public health: A narrative review. *BMJ Public Health, 2*, e000952.

Lei, X., & MacKenzie, C. (2023). Quantifying the risk of mass shootings at specific locations. *Risk Analysis, 44*(4), 868–882.

Lenz, A. S., & Lancaster, C. (2016). Disruptive, impulse-control, and conduct disorders. In B. Flamez & C. J. Sheperis (Eds.), *Diagnosing and treating children and adolescents: A guide for mental health professionals* (pp. 386–412). Wiley.

Lever, N., Mathis, E., & Mayworm, A. (2017). School mental health is not just for students: Why teacher and school staff wellness matters. *Report on Emotional & Behavioral Disorders in Youth, 17*(1), 6–12.

Levitt, G., & Grubaugh, S. (2024). Misinformation: The greatest threat to democracy-empowering K–12 teachers to build critical media literacy skills in students. *Technium Social Sciences Journal, 66*, 104–111.

Levy, J. J. & Spurgeon, S. L. (2016). Addressing client diversity throughout the diagnostic process. In B. Flamez & C. J. Sheperis (Eds.), *Diagnosing and treating children and adolescents: A guide for mental health professionals* (pp. 81–100). Wiley.

Lewallen, T. C., Hunt, H., Potts-Datema, W., Zaza, S., & Giles, W. (2015). The Whole School, Whole Community, Whole Child model: A new approach for improving educational attainment and healthy development for students. *Journal of School Health, 85*(11), 729–739.

Lin, L., Parker, K., & Horowitz, J. (2024). *What's it like to be a teacher in America today?* Pew Research Center. *www.pewresearch.org/social-trends/2024/04/04/whats-it-like-to-be-a-teacher-in-america-today*

Liu, J., Chen, X., & Lewis, G. (2011). Childhood internalizing behaviour: Analysis and implications. *Journal of Psychiatric and Mental Health Nursing, 18*(10), 884–894.

Liu, J., Ji, X., Pitt, S., Wang, G., Rovit, E., Lipman, T., & Jiang, F. (2024). Childhood sleep: Physical, cognitive, and behavioral consequences and implications. *World Journal of Pediatrics, 20*(2), 122–132.

Liu, S., Tan, Q., Han, S., Li, W., Wang, X., Gan, Y., . . . Xhang, L. (2019). The language context effect in facial expressions processing and its mandatory characteristic. *Scientific Reports*, 9, 11045.

Loades, M. E. & Mastroyannopoulou, K. (2010). Teachers' recognition of children's mental health problems. *Child and Adolescent Mental Health, 15*, 150–156.

Locher, C., Koechlin, H., Zion, S. R., Werner, C., Pine, D. S., Kirsch, I., . . . Kossowsky, J. (2017). Efficacy and safety of selective serotonin reuptake inhibitors, serotonin–norepinephrine reuptake inhibitors, and placebo for common psychiatric disorders among children and adolescents: A systematic review and meta-analysis. *JAMA Psychiatry, 74*(10), 1011–1020.

Long, M. W., Albright, G., McMillan, J., Shockley, K. M., & Price, O. A. (2018). Enhancing educator engagement in school mental health care through digital simulation professional development. *Journal of School Health, 88*(9), 651–659.

Lubell, E. (2021). *Building community schools: A guide for action. www.nccs.org/wp-content/uploads/2021/10/NCCS_BuildingCommunitySchools.pdf*

Lunenburg, F. C. (2011). The Comer School Development program: Improving education for low-income students. *National Forum of Multicultural Issues, 8*(1), 1–14.

Lyon, A. R. (2017). *Implementation science and practice in the education sector. University of Washington. https://education.uw.edu/sites/default/files/Implementation%20Science%20Issue%20Brief%20072617.pdf*

Lyon, A. R., Whitaker, K., French, W. P., Richardson, L. P., Wasse, J. K., & McCauley, E. (2016). Collaborative care in schools: Enhancing integration and impact in youth mental health. *Advances in School Mental Health Promotion, 9*(3–4), 148–168.

Magalhães E. (2024). Dual-factor models of mental health: A systematic review of empirical evidence. *Psychosocial Intervention, 33*(2), 89–102.

Maier, A., Daniel, J., Oakes, J., & Lam, L. (2017). *Community schools as an effective school improvement strategy: A review of the evidence.* Learning Policy Institute.

Makol, B. A., & Polo, A. J. (2018). Parent-child endorsement discrepancies among youth at chronic-risk for depression. *Journal of Abnormal Child Psychology, 46*(5), 1077–1088.

Malone, C. M., Wycoff, K., & Turner, E. A. (2022). Applying a MTSS framework to address racism and promote mental health for racial/ethnic minoritized youth. *Psychology in the Schools, 59*(12), 2438–2452.

Mapping Collective Wellbeing Project. (2023). *About wellbeing. https://mappingcollectivewellbeing.org/*

Mawhinney, L. (2008). Laugh so you don't cry: Teachers combating isolation in schools through humour and social support. *Ethnography and Education, 3*(2), 195–209.

Mawhinney, L., Baker-Doyle, K. J., & Rosen, S. M. (2024). "In it together": Activist teachers of color networks combating isolation. *Race Ethnicity and Education, 27*(5), 737–755.

McCabe, S. E., Schulenberg, J. E., Schepis, T. S., McCabe, V. V., & Veliz, P. T. (2022). Longitudinal analysis of substance use disorder symptom severity at age 18 years and substance use disorder in adulthood. *JAMA Network Open, 5*(4), e225324–e225324.

McCann, L., & Pearlman, L. A. (1990). Vicarious traumatization: A framework for understanding the psychological effects of working with victims. *Journal of Traumatic Stress, 3*(1), 131–147.

McGhee, H. (2021). *The sum of us: What racism costs everyone and how we can prosper together.* One World.

McGlynn-Wright, T., & Briner, L. (2021, March). Integrative trauma and healing framework. In the Works. *https://intheworksllc.squarespace.com/inflections/2021/3/30/integrative-trauma-and-healing-framework*

McKay, V. R., Morshed, A. B., Brownson, R. C., Proctor, E. K., & Prusaczyk, B. (2018). Letting go: Conceptualizing intervention de-implementation in public health and social service settings. *American Journal of Community Psychology, 62*(1–2), 189–202.

McKibben (2014, July 1). *The two-minute relationship builder.* ACSD. *www.ascd.org/el/articles/the-two-minute-relationship-builder*

McKinnon, I. I., Krause, K. H., Suarez, N. A, Jones, T. M., Verlenden, J. V., Cavalier, Y., . . . Mpofu, J. J. (2024). Experiences of racism in school and associations with mental health, suicide risk, and substance use among high school students—Youth Risk Behavior Survey, United States, 2023. *Morbidity and Mortality Weekly Report Supplement, 73*(Supp l–4), 31–38.

McLean, L., & Connor, C. M. (2018). Relations between third grade teachers' depressive symptoms and their feedback to students, with implications for student mathematics achievement. *School Psychology Quarterly, 33*(2), 272–282.

McLeskey, J., Barringer, M-D., Billingsley, B., Brownell, M., Jackson, D., Kennedy, M., . . . Ziegler, D. (2017). *High-leverage practices in special education.* Council for Exceptional Children & CEEDAR Center.

Merikangas, K., He, J. P., Burstein, M., Swanson, S. A., Avenevoli, S., Cui, L., . . . Swendsen, J. (2010). Lifetime prevalence of mental disorders in the U.S. Adolescent Comorbidity Survey Replication—Adolescent Supplement (NCS-A). *Journal of the American Academy of Child and Adolescent Psychiatry, 49*, 980–988.

Merrick, M. T., Ford, D. C., Ports, K. A., Guinn, A. S., Chen, J., Klevens, J., . . . Mercy, J. A. (2019). Vital signs: Estimated proportion of adult health problems attributable to adverse childhood experiences and implications for prevention—25 states, 2015–2017. *Morbidity and Mortality Weekly Report, 68*, 999–1005. *https://doi.org/10.15585/mmwr.mm6844e1*

Mesquita, B. (2022). *Between us: How cultures create emotions.* Norton.

Meyerson, D. A., Grant, K. E., Carter, J. S., & Kilmer, R. P. (2011). Posttraumatic growth among children and adolescents: A systematic review. *Clinical Psychology Review, 31*(6), 949–964.

Miech, R. A., Johnston, L. D., Patrick, M. E., O'Malley, P. M., & Bachman, J. G. (2023). *Monitoring the Future national survey results on drug use, 1975–2023: Secondary school students.* Monitoring the Future Monograph Series. Institute for Social Research, University of Michigan.

Mikami, A. Y., Griggs, M. S., Lerner, M. D., Emeh, C. C., Reuland, M. M., Jack, A., & Anthony, M. R. (2013). A randomized trial of a classroom intervention to increase peers' social inclusion of children with attention-deficit/hyperactivity disorder. *Journal of Consulting and Clinical Psychology, 81*(1), 100–112.

Miliauskas, C. R., Faus, D. P., da Cruz, V. L., do Nascimento Vallaperde, J. G. R., Junger, W., & Lopes, C. S. (2022). Community violence and internalizing mental health symptoms in adolescents: A systematic review. *BMC Psychiatry, 22*, 253.

Miller, S. J. (2019). The impact and role of emotions in schools for teachers and students with complex gender identities. *Teachers College Record, 121*(13), 1–16.

Minahan, J. (2014). *The behavior code companion: Strategies, tools, and interventions for supporting students with anxiety-related or oppositional behaviors.* Harvard Education Press.

Minahan, J. & Rappaport, N. (2012). *The behavior code: A practical guide to understanding and teaching the most challenging students.* Harvard Education Press.

Mohammad, E. T., Shapiro, E. R., Wainwright, L. D., & Carter, A. S. (2015). Impacts of family and community violence exposure on child coping and mental health. *Journal of Abnormal Child Psychology, 43*(2), 203–215.

Moore, K. A., & Ramirez, A. N. (2016). Adverse childhood experience and adolescent well-being: Do protective factors matter? *Child Indicators Research, 9*(2), 299–316.

Moore, S., Long, A. C. J., Coyle, S., Cooper, J. M., Mayworm, A. M., Amirazizi, S., . . . Dowdy, E. (2023). A roadmap to equitable school mental health screening. *Journal of School Psychology, 96*, 57–74.

Morin, C. M., Bjorvatn, B., Chung, F., Holzinger, B., Partinen, M., Penzel, T., . . . Espie, C. A. (2021). Insomnia, anxiety, and depression during the COVID-19 pandemic: An international collaborative study. *Sleep Medicine, 87*, 38–45.

Morone, J. (2017). An integrative review of social determinants of health assessment and screening tools used in pediatrics. *Journal of Pediatric Nursing, 37*, 22–28.

Morris, E. (2016). Children: Extremism and online radicalization. *Journal of Children and Media, 10*(4), 508–514.

Mufson, L., Dorta, K. P., Wickramaratne, P., Nomura, Y., Olfson, M., & Weissman, M. M. (2004). A randomized effectiveness trial of interpersonal psychotherapy for depressed adolescents. *Archives of General Psychiatry, 61*(6), 577–584.

Mullen, S. (2018). Major depressive disorder in children and adolescents. *Mental Health Clinician, 8*(6), 275–283.

Murphey, D., & Sacks, V. (2019). Supporting students with adverse childhood experiences: How educators and schools can help. *American Educator, 43*(2), 8–11.

Nadler, D. A., & Tushman, M. L. (1980). A model for diagnosing organizational behavior. *Organizational Dynamics, 9*(2), 35–51.

Nagaoka, J., Farrington, C. A., Ehrlich, S. B., & Heath, R. D. (2015). *Foundations for young adult success: A developmental framework*. The University of Chicago Consortium on Chicago School Research. *https://consortium.uchicago.edu/publications/foundations-young-adult-success-developmental-framework*

Naslund, J. A., Aschbrenner, K. A., Marsch, L. A., & Bartels, S. J. (2016). The future of mental health care: Peer-to-peer support and social media. *Epidemiology and Psychiatric Sciences, 25*(2), 113–122.

National Academies of Sciences, Engineering, and Medicine. (2016). *Preventing bullying through science, policy, and practice.* National Academies Press.

National Academies of Sciences, Engineering, and Medicine. (2019a). *Fostering healthy mental, emotional, and behavioral development in children and youth: A national agenda.* National Academies Press.

National Academies of Sciences, Engineering, and Medicine. (2019b). *The promise of adolescence: Realizing opportunity for all youth.* National Academies Press.

National Academies of Sciences, Engineering, and Medicine. (2022). *Ontologies in the behavioral sciences: Accelerating research and the spread of knowledge.* National Academies Press.

National Association of School Psychologists. (2025). *Student to school psychologist ratio 2023–2024. www.nasponline.org/Documents/Research%20and%20Policy/Reseach%20Center/24-25_ratio_chart.pdf*

National Center for Education Statistics. (2022). *U.S. education in the time of covid. https://nces.ed.gov/surveys/annualreports/topical-studies/covid/*

National Center for Education Statistics. (2023). *Most public schools face challenges in hiring teachers and other personnel entering the 2023–24 academic year. https://nces.ed.gov/learn/press-release/most-u-s-public-elementary-and-secondary-schools-faced-hiring-challenges-start-2024-25-academic-year*

National Center for Education Statistics. (2024a). *English learners in public schools. Condition of Education.* U.S. Department of Education, Institute of Education Sciences. *https://nces.ed.gov/programs/coe/indicator/cgf/english-learners-in-public-schools*

National Center for Education Statistics. (2024b, July). *Prevalence of mental health services provided by public schools and limitations in schools' efforts to provide mental health services.* Condition of Education. U.S. Department of Education, Institute of Education Sciences. *https://nces.ed.gov/programs/coe/indicator/a23*

National Center for Education Statistics. (2024c, July). *Safety and security practices at public schools.* Condition of Education. U.S. Department of Education, Institute of Education Sciences. *https://nces.ed.gov/programs/coe/indicator/a19/school-reported-safety-practices*

National Center for Education Statistics. (2024d, July). *Student bullying.* The Condition of Education. U.S. Department of Education. *https://nces.ed.gov/programs/coe/indicator/a10*

National Center for Education Statistics. (2024e, May). Students with disabilities. Condition of Education. U.S. Department of Education, Institute of Education Sciences. *https://nces.ed.gov/programs/coe/indicator/cgg*

National Center for Education Statistics. (2025, February 19). *More than half of public school leaders say cell phones hurt academic performance.* Institute of Education Sciences, U.S. Department of Education. *https://nces.ed.gov/whatsnew/press_releases/2_19_2025.asp*

National Center for School Mental Health (2023). *School mental health quality guide: Screening.* University of Maryland School of Medicine. *www.schoolmentalhealth.org/media/som/microsites/ncsmh/documents/quality-guides/Screening.pdf*

National Center for School Mental Health. (n.d.). *Foundations of school mental health. www.schoolmentalhealth.org/resources/foundations-of-school-mental-health*

National Institute on Drug Abuse. (2023, December 13). *Unintentional drug overdose death rates among US youth aged 15-19. https://nida.nih.gov/research-topics/trends-statistics/infographics/unintentional-drug-overdose-death-rates-among-us-youth-aged-15-19*

Noltemeyer, A., Shaw, K., & Palmer, K. (2016). *School-wide universal screening for behavioral and mental health issues: Implementation guidance.* Project AWARE Ohio. *https://resources.oberlinkconsulting.com/uploads/compendiums/Screening_Guidance_Document.pdf*

Nowinski, C. J., DeWalt, D. A., Carter, A. S., Chacko, A., Gross, H. E., Perrin, E. M., . . . Gershon, R. C. (2021). Recommendations for assessment of social, emotional, and behavioral health for the National Children's Study. *Frontiers in Pediatrics, 9*, 1–18.

O'Brien, K. M., Brunsting, N. C., Bettini, E., Cumming, M. M., Ragunathan, M., & Sutton, R. (2019). Special educators' working conditions in self-contained settings for students with emotional or behavioral disorders: A descriptive analysis. *Exceptional Children, 86*(1), 40–57.

O'Neil, A., Quirk, S. E., Housden, S., Brennan, S. L., Williams, L. J., Pasco, . . .

Jacka, F. N. (2014). Relationship between diet and mental health in children and adolescents: A systematic review. *American Journal of Public Health, 104*(10), e31–e42.

Osher, D., Cantor, P., Berg, J., Steyer, L., & Rose, T. (2020). Drivers of human development: How relationships and context shape learning and development. *Applied Developmental Science, 24*(1), 6–36.

PACER Center. (2020). *Bullying statistics*. National Bullying Prevention Center. *www.pacer.org/bullying/info/stats*

Palmer, C., Kane, J., Patterson, P., & Tuomainen, H. (2025). Universal mental health screening in schools: How acceptable is this to key stakeholders? A systematic review. *Journal of Child and Family Studies, 34*, 366–380.

Paruthi, S., Brooks, L. J., D'Ambrosio, C., Hall, W. A., Kotagal, S., Lloyd, R. M., . . . Wise, M. S. (2016). Recommended amount of sleep for pediatric populations: A consensus statement of the American Academy of Sleep Medicine. *Journal of Clinical Sleep Medicine, 12*(6), 785–786.

Passey, D., Ntebutse, J. G., Ahmad, M. Y. A., Cochrane, J., Collin, S., Ganayem, A., . . . Somasi, S. (2024). Populations digitally excluded from education: Issues, factors, contributions and actions for policy, practice and research in a post-pandemic era. *Technology, Knowledge and Learning, 29*, 1733–1755.

Paulus, F. W., Ohmann, S., Möhler, E., Plener, P., & Popow, C. (2021). Emotional dysregulation in children and adolescents with psychiatric disorders: A narrative review. *Frontiers in Psychiatry, 12*.

Payne, L., Pynoos, R., & Vogel, J. (2012). *Psychological first aid for schools: Field operations guide* (2nd ed.). National Child Traumatic Stress Network. *www.nctsn.org/sites/default/files/resources//pfa_schools.pdf*

Pearson, H., & Wilbiks, J. (2021). Effects of audiovisual memory cues on working memory recall. *Vision, 5*(1), 14.

Peetz, C. (2024, February 23). A mental health screening saved students' lives in this district. *Education Week*. *www.edweek.org/leadership/a-mental-health-screening-saved-students-lives-in-this-district/2024/02*

Perfect, M. M., Turley, M. R., Carlson, J. S., Yohanna, J., & Saint Gilles, M. P. (2016). School-related outcomes of traumatic event exposure and traumatic stress symptoms in students: A systematic review of research from 1990 to 2015. *School Mental Health, 8*(1), 7–43.

Perry, B. D. (2008). Child maltreatment: A neurodevelopmental perspective on the role of trauma and neglect in psychopathology. In T. Beauchaine & S. P. Hinshaw (Eds.), *Child and adolescent psychopathology* (pp. 93–129). Wiley.

Perry, B. D. (2009). Examining child maltreatment through a neurodevelopmental lens: Clinical applications of the Neurosequential Model of Therapeutics. *Journal of Loss and Trauma, 14*, 240–255.

Perry, B. D. (2020). The neurosequential model. In J. Mitchell, J. Tucci, & E. Tronick (Eds.), *The handbook of therapeutic care for children: Evidence-informed approaches to working with traumatized children and adolescents in foster, kinship, and adoptive care* (pp. 137–155). Jessica Kingsley.

Perry, B. D., & Pollard, R. (1998). Homeostasis, stress, trauma, and adaptation: A neurodevelopmental view of childhood trauma. *Child and Adolescent Psychiatric Clinics of North America, 7*(1), 33–51.

Perry, B. D., Pollard, R., Blakley, T. L., Baker, W. L., & Vigilante, D. (1995). Childhood trauma, the neurobiology of adaptation, and "use-dependent" brain development of the brain: How "states" become "traits." *Infant Mental Health Journal, 16*(4), 271–291.

Petito, A., Pop, T. L., Namazova-Baranova, L., Mestrovic, J., Nigri, L., Vural, M., . . . Pettoello-Mantovani, M. (2020). The burden of depression in adolescents and the importance of early recognition. *The Journal of Pediatrics, 218*, 265–267.

Pickens, I. B., & Tschopp, N. (2017). *Trauma-informed classrooms*. National Council on Juvenile and Family Courts. *www.ncjfcj.org/wp-content/uploads/2025/12/NCJFCJ_SJP_Trauma_Informed_Classrooms_Final.pdf*

Planey, A. M., Smith, S. M., Moore, S., & Walker, T. D. (2019). Barriers and facilitators to mental health help-seeking among African American youth and their families: A systematic review study. *Children and Youth Services Review, 101*, 190–200.

Plass, J. L., & Kalyuga, S. (2019). Four ways of considering emotion in cognitive load theory. *Educational Psychology Review, 31*, 339–359.

Posamentier, J., Seibel, K., & DyTang, N. (2022). Preventing youth suicide: A review of school-based practices and how social–emotional learning fits into comprehensive efforts. *Trauma, Violence, & Abuse, 24*(2), 746–759.

Posner, K., Brown, G. K., Stanley, B., Brent, D. A., Yershova, K. V., Oquendo, M. A., . . . Mann, J. J. (2011). The Columbia-Suicide Severity Rating Scale: Initial validity and internal consistency findings from three multisite studies with adolescents and adults. *The American Journal of Psychiatry, 168*(12), 1266–1277.

Pretorius, C., McCashin, D., & Coyle, D. (2022). Mental health professionals as influencers on TikTok and Instagram: What role do they play in mental health literacy and help-seeking? *Internet Interventions, 30*, 100591.

Priest, N., Paradies, Y., Trenerry, B., Truong, M., Karlsen, S., & Kelly, Y. (2013). A systematic review of studies examining the relationship between reported racism and health and wellbeing for children and young people. *Social Science & Medicine, 95*, 115–127.

Prothero, A. (2024, January 31). School district lawsuits against social media companies are piling up. *Education Week*. *www.edweek.org/policy-politics/school-district-lawsuits-against-social-media-companies-are-piling-up/2024/01*

Prothero, A., Langreo, L., & Klein, A. (2026, June 2). Which states ban or restrict cellphones in schools? *Education Week*. *www.edweek.org/technology/which-states-ban-or-restrict-cellphones-in-schools/2024/06*

Radez, J., Reardon, T., Creswell, C., Orchard, F., & Waite, P. (2021). Adolescents' perceived barriers and facilitators to seeking and accessing professional help for anxiety and depressive disorders: A qualitative interview study. *European Child & Adolescent Psychiatry, 31*(6), 891–907.

Ramirez, T., Brush, K., Raisch, N., Bailey, R., & Jones, S. M. (2021). Equity in social emotional learning programs: A content analysis of equitable practices in PreK–5 SEL programs. *Frontiers in Education, 6*, 1–14.

Rappolt-Schlichtmann, G., Cipriano, C., Robinson, K. H., & Boucher, A. (2023).

Universal design for social and emotional learning. In T. E. Hall, K. H. Robinson, & D. Gordon (Eds.), *Universal design for learning in the classroom: Practical applications for K–12 and beyond* (2nd ed., pp. 113–135). Guilford.

Ray, D. C., Stulmaker, H. L., & Bratton, S. C. (2016). Anxiety disorders. In B. Flamez & C. J. Sheperis (Eds.), *Diagnosing and treating children and adolescents: A guide for mental health professionals* (pp. 235–258). Wiley.

Readiness and Emergency Management for Schools Technical Assistance Center. (2022). *Building blocks to school safety. https://safesupportivelearning.ed.gov/resources/building-blocks-school-safety-toolkit-schools-and-districts-developing-high-quality*

Rideout, V., Peebles, A., Mann, S., & Robb, M. B. (2022). *Common sense census: Media use by tweens and teens, 2021.* Common Sense. *www.commonsensemedia.org/sites/default/files/research/report/8-18-census-integrated-report-final-web_0.pdf*

Riggs, S. A. (2010) Childhood emotional abuse and the attachment system across the life cycle: What theory and research tell us. *Journal of Aggression, Maltreatment & Trauma, 19*(1), 5–51.

Robertson, R., & Microys, G. (2001). *Life balance assessment and action planning guide. https://settingup.weebly.com/uploads/4/2/6/6/42663717/balance_wheel.pdf*

Roffey, S. (2012). Pupil wellbeing—Teacher wellbeing: Two sides of the same coin? *Educational and Child Psychology, 29*(4), 8–17.

Romer, N., von der Embse, N., Eklund, K., Kilgus, S., Perales, K., Splett, J. W., . . . Wheeler, D. (2020). *Best practices in social, emotional, and behavioral screening: An implementation guide. Version 2.0. smhcollaborative.org/universalscreening*

Romero, V. E., Robertson, R., & Warner, A. N. (2019). *Building resilience in students impacted by adverse childhood experiences: A whole-staff approach.* Corwin.

Ronfeldt, M., Farmer, S. O., McQueen, K., & Grissom, J. A. (2015). Teacher collaboration in instructional teams and student achievement. *American Educational Research Journal, 52*(3), 475–514.

Rooney, L. E., Videto, D. M., & Birch, D. A. (2015). Using the whole school, whole community, whole child model: Implications for practice. *The Journal of School Health, 85*(11), 817–823.

Roscoe, L. J. (2009). Wellness: A review of theory and measurement for counselors. *Journal of Counseling & Development, 87*, 216–226.

Rothwell, J. (2023). *Teens spend average of 4.8 hours on social media per day.* Gallup. *https://news.gallup.com/poll/512576/teens-spend-average-hours-social-media-per-day.aspx*

Şahin, F., & Tabak, H. (2020). Investigation of school administrators' humour styles and school climate according to teacher perceptions. *Acta Educationis Generalis, 10*(3), 34–49.

Salter, M., Brand, B. L., Robinson, M., Loewenstein, R., Silberg, J., & Korzekwa, M. (2025). Self-diagnosed cases of dissociative identity disorder on social media: Conceptualization, assessment, and treatment. *Harvard Review of Psychiatry, 33*(1), 41–48.

Sanetti, L. M., & Collier-Meek, M. A. (2019). *Supporting successful interventions in schools: Tools to plan, evaluate, and sustain effective implementation.* Guilford.

Sannon, S., Young, J., Shusas, E., & Forte, A. (2023, April). Disability activism on social media: Sociotechnical challenges in the pursuit of visibility. In *Proceedings of the 2023 CHI Conference on Human Factors in Computing Systems* (pp. 1–15).

Savina, E., & Wan, K. P. (2017). Cultural pathways to socio-emotional development and learning. *Journal of Relationships Research, 8*, e19.

Schaffer, G. (2022). *Multi-tiered systems of support: A practical guide to preventative practice.* Sage.

Schonert-Reichl, K. A., Kitil, M. J., & Hanson-Peterson, J. (2017). *To reach the students, teach the teachers: A national scan of teacher preparation and social and emotional learning.* A report prepared for the Collaborative for Academic, Social, and Emotional Learning (CASEL). University of British Columbia.

School Social Work Association of America. (2025). *The national census: The status of school social work. www.sswaa.org/national-census*

Schroeder, A. R., Dehghan, M., Newman, T. B., Bentley, J. P., & Park, K. T. (2019). Association of opioid prescriptions from dental clinicians for U.S. adolescents and young adults with subsequent opioid use and abuse. *JAMA Internal Medicine, 179*(2), 145–152.

Schudel, C., & Adler, N. E. (2016). Effects of social needs screening and in-person service navigation on child health: A randomized clinical trial. *JAMA Pediatrics, 170*(11), e162521–e162521.

Schultz, M. J., & Forbes, D. (2013). Psychological first aid: Rapid proliferation and search for evidence. *Disaster Health, 1*(2), 1–10.

Sciaraffa, M. A., Zeanah, P. D., & Zeanah, C. H. (2018). Understanding and promoting resilience in the context of adverse childhood experiences. *Early Childhood Education Journal, 46*(3), 343–353.

Seabrook, E. M., Kern, M. L., & Rickard, N. S. (2016). Social networking sites, depression, and anxiety: A systematic review. *JMIR Mental Health, 3*(4), e5842.

Seligman, L. D., & Ollendick, T. H. (2011). Cognitive-behavioral therapy for anxiety disorders in youth. *Child and Adolescent Psychiatric Clinics of North America, 20*(2), 217–238.

Seligman, M. E. (2019). Positive psychology: A personal history. *Annual Review of Clinical Psychology, 15*(1), 1–23.

SHAPE America. (2018). *Physical education/SEL Crosswalk: Aligning SHAPE American national standards and grade-level outcomes for K–12 physical education with CASEL social and emotional learning competencies.* Retrieved February 29, 2024, from *www.shapeamerica.org/Common/Uploaded%20files/document_manager/standards/guidelines/PE-SEL-Crosswalk.pdf*

Sheridan, S. M., Smith, T. E., Moorman Kim, E., Beretvas, S. N., & Park, S. (2019). A meta-analysis of family–school interventions and children's social-emotional functioning: Moderators and components of efficacy. *Review of Educational Research, 89*(2), 296–332.

Sherin, J. E., & Nemeroff, C. B. (2011). Post-traumatic stress disorder: The neurobiological impact of psychological trauma. *Dialogues in Clinical Neuroscience, 13*(3), 263–278.

Shonkoff, J. P., Garner, A. S., & The Committee on Psychosocial Aspects of Child and Family Health, Committee on Early Childhood, Adoption, and Dependent Care, & Section on Developmental and Behavioral Pediatrics. (2012). The lifelong effects of early childhood adversity and toxic stress. *Pediatrics, 129*(1), e232–e246.

Short, M. A., Bartel, K., & Carskadon, M. A. (2019). Sleep and mental health in children and adolescents. In M. A. Grandner (Ed.), *Sleep and health* (pp. 435–445). Academic Press.

Siegel, D. J. (1999). *The developing mind: Toward a neurobiology of interpersonal experience.* Guilford.

Siegel, D. J., & Bryson, T. P. (2012). *The whole-brain child.* Bantam.

Simmons, D. (2019). Why we can't afford whitewashed social–emotional learning. *Education Update, 61*(4). *www.ascd.org/el/articles/why-we-cant-afford-whitewashed-social-emotional-learning*

Simonsen, B., Robbie, K., Meyer, K., Freeman, J., Everett, S., & Feinberg, A. (2021). *Multi-tiered system of supports (MTSS) in the classroom.* Center on Positive Behavioral Interventions and Supports. *https://assets-global.website-files.com/5d3725188825e071f1670246/618172fb89f9b52f694a5c8c_Multi-Tiered%20System%20of%20Supports%20(MTSS)%20in%20the%20Classroom.pdf*

Smith, T. E., Sheridan, S. M., Kim, E. M., Park, S., & Beretvas, S. N. (2020). The effects of family-school partnership interventions on academic and social–emotional functioning: A meta-analysis exploring what works for whom. *Educational Psychology Review, 32*, 511–544.

Snyder, C. R., Hoza, B., Pelham, W. E., Rapoff, M., Ware, L., Danovsky, M., . . . Stahl, K. J. (1997). The development and validation of the Children's Hope Scale. *Journal of Pediatric Psychology, 22*(3), 399–421.

Sokol, R., Austin, A., Chandler, C., Byrum, E., Bousquette, J., Lancaster, C., . . . Shanahan, M. (2019). Screening children for social determinants of health: A systematic review. *Pediatrics, 144*(4), e20191622.

Spector, C. (2024, February 14). *How technology is reinventing education.* Stanford Report. *https://news.stanford.edu/stories/2024/02/technology-in-education*

Spencer, N. (2018). The social determinants of child health. *Paediatrics and Child Health, 28*(3), 138–143.

Spielfogel, J. E., & McMillen, J. C. (2017). Current use of de-escalation strategies: Similarities and differences in de-escalation across professions. *Social Work in Mental Health, 15*(3), 232–248.

Spilt, J. L., Koomen, H. M., & Thijs, J. T. (2011). Teacher wellbeing: The importance of teacher–student relationships. *Educational Psychology Review, 23*, 457–477.

Spitzer, R. L., Kroenke, K., Williams, J. B, Löwe, B. (2006). A brief measure for assessing generalized anxiety disorder: The GAD-7. *Archives of Internal Medicine, 166*, 1092–1097.

Splett, J. W., Trainor, K. M., Raborn, A., Halliday-Boykins, C. A., Garzona, M. E., Dongo, M. D., & Weist, M. D. (2018). Comparison of universal mental health screening to students already receiving intervention in a multitiered system of support. *Behavioral Disorders, 43*(3), 344–356.

Stamm, B. H. (2002). Measuring compassion satisfaction as well as fatigue: Developmental history of the compassion satisfaction and fatigue test. In C. R. Figley (Ed.), *Treating compassion fatigue* (pp. 107–119). Routledge.

Standford, L., & Meisner, C. (2023, July 27). Social–emotional learning persists despite political backlash. *Education Week. www.edweek.org/leadership/social-emotional-learning-persists-despite-political-backlash/2023/07*

Stanford, L. (2023, May 5). Despite their promise, school mental health screenings face resistance. *Education Week. www.edweek.org/leadership/despite-their-promise-school-mental-health-screenings-face-resistance/2023/05*

Stark, K., & Bettini, E. (2021). Teachers' perceptions of emotional display rules in schools: A systematic review. *Teaching and Teacher Education, 104*, 103388.

Stark, K., Bettini, E., Cumming, M., O'Brien, K., Brunsting, N., Huggins-Manley, A., . . . Shaheen, T. (2022). Measuring special educators' working conditions: A systematic review. *Remedial and Special Education, 44*, 074193252210790.

Stark, K., Jones, N., Camburn, E., & Kaler, L. (2023). Measuring teachers' momentary affect: An exploratory experience sampling study. *Contemporary Educational Psychology, 74, 3*, 100043.

Stark, K., Koslouski, J. B., Vadhan, J., & Wallace, M. (2024). The future is inclusive: Social emotional learning and special education. *Social and Emotional Learning: Research, Practice, and Policy, 100043.*

Starvaggi, I., Dierckman, C., & Lorenzo-Luaces, L. (2024). Mental health misinformation on social media: Review and future directions. *Current Opinion in Psychology, 56*, 101738.

Steiner, E. D., Levine, P. R., Doan, S., & Woo, A. (2025). *Teacher well-being, pay, and intentions to leave in 2025: Findings from the state of the American Teacher Survey. www.rand.org/pubs/research_reports/RRA1108-16.html*

Steiner, T. G., Levy, K. N., Brandenburg, J. C., & Adams, R. B. (2021). In the mind of the beholder: Narcissism relates to a distorted and enhanced self-image. *Personality and Individual Differences, 173*, 110608.

Substance Abuse and Mental Health Services Administration. (2014a). *SAMHSA's concept of trauma and guidance for a trauma-informed approach* (HHS Publication No. [SMA] 14-4884). *www.nctsn.org/sites/default/files/resources/resource-guide/samhsa_trauma.pdf*

Substance Abuse and Mental Health Services Administration. (2014b). *Trauma-informed care in behavioral health services. Treatment Improvement Protocol (TIP) Series 57* (HHS Publication No. [SMA] 13-4801).

Substance Abuse and Mental Health Services Administration. (2019a). *Ready, set, go, review: Screening for behavioral health risk in schools*. Office of the Chief Medical Officer, Substance Abuse and Mental Health Services Administration.

Substance Abuse and Mental Health Services Administration. (2019b). *Student assistance: A guide for school administrators* (SAMHSA Publication No. PEP19-03-01-001). *https://store.samhsa.gov/sites/default/files/tthy-student-assistance-guide-pep19-03-01-001.pdf*

Substance Abuse and Mental Health Services Administration. (2022a). *2022 National Survey on Drug Use and Health. Table 2.44B—Alcohol use in lifetime, past year, and past month and binge alcohol and heavy alcohol use in past month: among people aged 12 to 20; by demographic characteristics, percentages, 2021 and 2022. www.samhsa.gov/data/sites/default/files/reports/rpt42728/NSDUHDetailedTabs2022/NSDUHDetailedTabs2022/NSDUHDetTabs2-44and2-45pe2022.pdf*

Substance Abuse and Mental Health Services Administration. (2022b). *School & educator resources. www.samhsa.gov/talk-they-hear-you/materials-school*

Sugai, G., & Horner, R. H. (2009). Responsiveness-to-intervention and school-wide positive behavior supports: Integration of multi-tiered system approaches. *Exceptionality, 17*(4), 223–237.

Suldo, S. M., & Shaffer, E. J. (2008). Looking beyond psychopathology: The dual-factor model of mental health in youth. *School Psychology Review, 37*(1), 52–68.

Suldo, S. M., Thalji-Raitano, A., Kiefer, S. M., & Ferron, J. M. (2016). Conceptualizing high school students' mental health through a dual-factor model. *School Psychology Review, 45*(4), 434–457.

Sullivan, E. T. (2022, September 30). Demystifying social-emotional learning and the controversy surrounding it. *EdSurge. www.edsurge.com/news/2022-09-30-demystifying-social-emotional-learning-and-the-controversy-surrounding-it*

Sutton, R. E., & Harper, E. (2009). Teachers' emotion regulation. In L. J. Saha & A. G. Dworkin (Eds.), *International handbook of research on teachers and teaching* (pp. 389–401). Springer.

Swedo, E. A., Pampati, S., Anderson, K. N., Thorne, E., McKinnon, I. I., Brener, N. D., . . . Niolon, P. H. (2024). Adverse childhood experiences and health conditions and risk behaviors among high school students—Youth Risk Behavior Survey, United States, 2023. *MMWR Suppl, 73*(Suppl-4), 39–49.

Taylor, R. D., Oberle, E., Durlak, J. A., & Weissberg, R. P. (2017). Promoting positive youth development through school-based social and emotional learning interventions: A meta-analysis of follow-up effects. *Child Development, 88*(4), 1156–1171.

Tedeschi, R. G., & Calhoun, L. G. (1995). *Trauma & transformation: Growing in the aftermath of suffering*. SAGE.

Tedeschi, R. G., Shakespeare-Finch, J., & Taku, K. (2018). *Posttraumatic growth: Theory, research, and applications*. Routledge.

Thapa, A., Cohen, J., Guffey, S., & Higgins-D'Alessandro, A. (2013). A review of school climate research. *Review of Educational Research, 83*(3), 357–385.

Thomas, E. R., Lembke, E. S., & Gandhi, A. G. (2023). Universal design for learning within an integrated multitiered system of support. *Learning Disabilities Research & Practice, 38*(1), 57–69.

Tianqi, X., & Jinhao, J. (2024). Intimacy and trust in interpersonal relationships: A sociological perspective. *Journal of Sociology and Ethnology, 6*(3), 38–42.

Toffolo, M. B., Smeets, M. A., & van den Hout, M. A. (2012). Proust revisited: Odours as triggers of aversive memories. *Cognition and Emotion, 26*(1), 83–92.

Tomlinson, C. A. (2014). *The differentiated classroom. Responding to the needs of all learners* (2nd ed.). ASCD.

Tomlinson, C. A., Brighton, C., Hertberg, H., Callahan, C. M., Moon, T. R., Brimijoin, K., . . . Reynolds, T. (2003). Differentiating instruction in response to student readiness, interest and learning profile in academically diverse classrooms: A review of literature. *Journal for the Education of the Gifted, 27*, 119–145.

Trickett, P. K., Negriff, S., Ji, J., & Peckins, M. (2011). Child maltreatment and adolescent development. *Journal of Research on Adolescence, 21*(1), 3–20.

Tschannen-Moran, M. (2020). Organizational trust in schools. In *Oxford Research Encyclopedia of Education. https://oxfordre.com/education/display/10.1093/acrefore/9780190264093.001.0001/acrefore-97801902644093-e-681*

Turner, K., & Theilking, M. (2019). Teacher wellbeing: Its effects on teaching practice and student learning. *Issues in Educational Research, 29*(3), 938–960.

Turner, K., Thielking, M., & Prochazka, N. (2022). Teacher wellbeing and social support: A phenomenological study. *Educational Research, 64*(1), 77–94.

Tyner, A. (2021). How to sell SEL: Parents and the politics of social-emotional learning. Thomas B. Fordham Institute. *http://fordhaminstitute.org/how-to-sell-sel*

U.S. Department of Education. (2019). Protecting student privacy. *https://studentprivacy.ed.gov/resources/joint-guidance-application-ferpa-and-hipaa-student-health-records*

U.S. Department of Education, Institute of Education Sciences, National Center for Education Statistics. (2022, April 12–25). School Pulse Panel. *https://ies.ed.gov/schoolsurvey/spp/*

U.S. Department of Health and Human Services. (n.d.). *Healthy People 2030: Social determinants of health. https://odphp.health.gov/healthypeople/priority-areas/social-determinants-health*

U.S. Department of Health and Human Services (2025). *What is cyberbullying. www.stopbullying.gov/cyberbullying/what-is-it*

U.S. Department of Justice. (2019). *Operation prevention. www.operationprevention.com/about*

U.S. Department of Justice. (2023). *Community oriented policing services: Fact sheet. https://cops.usdoj.gov/pdf/2025ProgramDocs/ctas/SRO_MOU.pdf*

U.S. Preventive Services Task Force. (2022). Screening for depression and suicide risk in children and adolescents: U.S. Preventive Services Task Force recommendation statement. *JAMA, 328*(15), 1534–1542.

Van Mechelen, M., Smith, R. C., Schaper, M. M., Tamashiro, M., Bilstrup, K. E., Lunding, M., . . . Iversen, O. S. (2023). Emerging technologies in K–12 education: A future HCI research agenda. *ACM Transactions on Computer–Human Interaction, 30*(3), 1–40.

van Woerkom, M. (2021). Building positive organizations: A typology of positive psychology interventions. *Frontiers in Psychology, 12*, 769782.

VanBronkhorst, S. B., Abraham, E., Dambreville, R., Ramos-Olazagasti, M. A., Wall, M., Saunders, D. C., . . . Duarte, C. S. (2024). Sociocultural risk and resilience in the context of adverse childhood experiences. *JAMA Psychiatry, 81*(4), 406–413.

Verlenden, J. V., Fodeman, A., Wilkins, N., Jones, T. M., Moore, S., Cornett, K., . . . Brener, N. D. (2024). Mental health and suicide risk among high school students and protective factors—Youth Risk Behavior Survey, United States, 2023. *Morbidity and Mortality Weekly Report Supplement, 73*(Suppl. 4), 79–86.

Vetter, J. B., Fuxman, S., & Dong, Y. E. (2024). A statewide multi-tiered system of support (MTSS) approach to social and emotional learning (SEL) and mental health. *Social and Emotional Learning: Research, Practice, and Policy, 3*, 100046.

Victoria Department of Health. (2022). *Wellbeing. www.betterhealth.vic.gov.au/health/healthyliving/wellbeing*

Voight, A., Hanson, T., O'Malley, M., & Adekanye, L. (2015). The racial school climate gap: Within-school disparities in students' experiences of safety, support, and connectedness. *American Journal of Community Psychology, 56*(3–4), 252–267.

Volkow, N. D., & Blanco, C. (2023). Substance use disorders: A comprehensive update of classification, epidemiology, neurobiology, clinical aspects, treatment, and prevention. *World Psychiatry, 22*(2), 203–229.

Vuorre, M., Orben, A., & Przybylski, A. K. (2021). There is no evidence that associations between adolescents' digital technology engagement and mental health problems have increased. *Clinical Psychological Science, 9*(5), 823–835.

Wagner, L. (2025, March 20). *Remote learning was supposed to make snow days obsolete. But did it really?* The 74. *www.the74million.org/article/remote-learning-was-supposed-to-make-snow-days-obsolete-but-did-it-really*

Walker, H. M., Horner, R. H., Sugai, G., Bullis, M., Sprague, J. R., Bricker, D., & Kaufman, M. J. (1996). Integrated approaches to preventing antisocial behavior patterns among school-age children and youth. *Journal of Emotional and Behavioral Disorders, 4*(4), 194–209.

Walker, T. (2024, October 3). *Take cellphones out of classrooms, educators say.* neaToday. *www.nea.org/nea-today/all-news-articles/take-cellphones-out-classroom-educators-say*

Walter, H. J., Bukstein, O. G., Abright, A. R., Keable, H., Ramtekkar, U., Ripperger-Suhler, J., & Rockhill, C. (2020). Clinical practice guideline for the assessment and treatment of children and adolescents with anxiety disorders. *Journal of the American Academy of Child and Adolescent Psychiatry, 59*(10), 1107–1124.

Wang, C., Do, K. A., Frese, K., & Zheng, L. (2019). Asian immigrant parents' perception of barriers preventing adolescents from seeking school-based mental health services. *School Mental Health, 11*, 364–377.

Wang, M. T., & Degol, J. L. (2016). School climate: A review of the construct, measurement, and impact on student outcomes. *Educational Psychology Review, 28*(2), 315–352.

Wang, M. T., & Sheikh-Khalil, S. (2014). Does parental involvement matter for student achievement and mental health in high school? *Child Development, 85*(2), 610–625.

Wang, Z., Whiteside, S. P. H., Sim, L., Farah, W., Morrow, A. S., Alsawas, M., . . . Murad, M. H. (2017). Comparative effectiveness and safety of cognitive behavioral therapy and pharmacotherapy for childhood anxiety disorders: A systematic review and meta-analysis. *JAMA Pediatrics, 171*(11).

Watkins, E. R. (2008). Constructive and unconstructive repetitive thought. *Psychological Bulletin, 134*(2), 163–206.

Watkins, E. R., & Roberts, H. (2020). Reflecting on rumination: Consequences, causes, mechanisms and treatment of rumination. *Behaviour Research and Therapy, 127*, 103573.

Watts, L. L., Hamza, E. A., Bedewy, D. A., & Moustafa, A. A. (2024). A meta-analysis study on peer influence and adolescent substance use. *Current Psychology, 43*, 3866–3881.

Weist, M. D., Eber, L., Horner, R., Splett, J., Putnam, R., Barrett, S., . . . Hoover, S. (2018). Improving multitiered systems of support for students with "internalizing" emotional/behavioral problems. *Journal of Positive Behavior Interventions, 20*(3), 172–184.

Weist, M. D., Flaherty, L., Lever, N., Stephan, S., Van Eck, K., & Bode, A. (2017). The history and future of school mental health. In J. R. Harrison, B. K., Schultz, & S. W. Evans (Eds.), *School mental health services for adolescents* (pp. 3–23). Oxford University Press.

Weist, M. D., Lever, N. A., Bradshaw, C. P., & Owens, J. S. (Eds.). (2014). *Handbook of school mental health: Research, training, practice, and policy.* Springer.

Weist, M. D., Splett, J. W., Halliday, C. A., Gage, N. A., Seaman, M. A., Perkins, K. A., . . . DiStefano, C. (2022). A randomized controlled trial on the interconnected systems framework for school mental health and PBIS: Focus on proximal variables and school discipline. *Journal of School Psychology, 94*, 49–65.

Whitcomb, S. A. (2017). *Behavioral, social, and emotional assessment of children and adolescents* (5th ed.). Routledge.

Whitebread, D. (2017). Free play and children's mental health. *The Lancet Child & Adolescent Health, 1*(3), 167–169.

Wigelsworth, M., Verity, L., Mason, C., Qualter, P., & Humphrey, N. (2022). Social and emotional learning in primary schools: A review of the current state of evidence. *British Journal of Educational Psychology, 92*(3), 898–924.

Wolf, K. C., & Kupchik, A. (2016). School suspensions and adverse experiences in adulthood. *Justice Quarterly, 34*(3), 407–430.

Wong, V. W., Ruble, L. A., Yu, Y., & McGrew, J. H. (2017). Too stressed to teach? Teaching quality, student engagement, and IEP outcomes. *Exceptional Children, 83*(4), 412–427.

Wood, B. J., & Ellis, F. (2022). Universal mental health screening practices in midwestern schools: A window of opportunity for school psychologist leadership and role expansion? *Contemporary School Psychology, 28*, 186–196.

World Health Organization. (2020, January 28). Adverse Childhood Experiences International Questionnaire (ACE-IQ). *www.who.int/publications/m/item/adverse-childhood-experiences-international-questionnaire-(ace-iq)*

World Health Organization. (2025, October 8). *Mental health. www.who.int/news-room/fact-sheets/detail/mental-health-strengthening-our-response*

Xiao, Y., Mann, J. J., Chow, J. C.-C., Brown, T. T., Snowden, L. R., Yip, P. S.-F., . . . Su, C. (2023). Patterns of social determinants of health and child mental health, cognition, and physical health. *JAMA Pediatrics, 177*(12), 1294–1305.

Yale Child Study Center. (2024). SDP theory of change. *https://medicine.yale.edu/childstudy/services/community-and-schools-programs/comer/theory/*

Yosso, T. J. (2005). Whose culture has capital? A critical race theory discussion of community cultural wealth. *Race Ethnicity and Education, 8*(1), 69–91.

Youth Wellness Hubs Ontario. (2022). *Substance use and school: What youth want educators to know. https://smho-smso.ca/wp-content/uploads/2023/06/YWHO-substance-use-and-school-what-you-want-educators-to-know.pdf*

Zablotsky, B., Ng, A. E., Black, L. I., Bose, J., Jones, J. R., Maitland, A. K., & Blumberg, S. J. (2024). Perceived social and emotional support among teenagers: United States, July 2021–December 2022. *National Health Statistics Reports* (206). *www.ncbi.nlm.nih.gov/books/NBK606852*

Zalaquett, C. P., & Chatters-Smith, S. (2016). Depressive disorders. In B. Flamez & C. J. Sheperis (Eds.), *Diagnosing and treating children and adolescents: A guide for mental health professionals* (pp. 203–234). Wiley.

Index

Note. f or *t* following a page number indicates a figure or a table.